Sexual Citizenship and Social Change

SEXUALITY, IDENTITY, AND SOCIETY SERIES

Series Editor
Philip L. Hammack

BOOKS IN THE SERIES
The Monogamy Gap:
Men, Love, and the Reality of Cheating
Eric Anderson

Modernizing Sexuality:
U.S. HIV Prevention in Sub-Saharan Africa
Anne W. Esacove

Technologies of Sexiness:
Sex, Identity, and Consumer Culture
Adrienne Evans and Sarah Riley

The Story of Sexual Identity:
Narrative Perspectives on the Gay and Lesbian Life Course
Philip L. Hammack and Bertram J. Cohler

The Declining Significance of Homophobia:
How Teenage Boys Are Redefining Masculinity and Heterosexuality
Mark McCormack

Queering Families:
The Postmodern Partnerships of Cisgender Women and Transgender Men
Carla A. Pfeffer

Kinky in the Digital Age:
Gay Men's Subcultures and Social Identities
Liam Wignall

The Power of BDSM:
Play, Communities, and Consent in the 21st Century
Edited by Brandy L. Simula, Robin Bauer, and Liam Wignall

Sexual Citizenship and Social Change:
A Dialectical Approach to Narratives of Tradition and Critique
Darren Langdridge

Sexual Citizenship and Social Change

A Dialectical Approach to Narratives of Tradition and Critique

DARREN LANGDRIDGE

OXFORD
UNIVERSITY PRESS

Oxford University Press is a department of the University of Oxford. It furthers
the University's objective of excellence in research, scholarship, and education
by publishing worldwide. Oxford is a registered trade mark of Oxford University
Press in the UK and certain other countries.

Published in the United States of America by Oxford University Press
198 Madison Avenue, New York, NY 10016, United States of America.

© Oxford University Press 2024

All rights reserved. No part of this publication may be reproduced, stored in
a retrieval system, or transmitted, in any form or by any means, without the
prior permission in writing of Oxford University Press, or as expressly permitted
by law, by license, or under terms agreed with the appropriate reproduction
rights organization. Inquiries concerning reproduction outside the scope of the
above should be sent to the Rights Department, Oxford University Press, at the
address above.

You must not circulate this work in any other form
and you must impose this same condition on any acquirer.

CIP data is on file at the Library of Congress

ISBN 978–0–19–992631–2

DOI: 10.1093/oso/9780199926312.001.0001

Printed by Integrated Books International, United States of America

Series Editor Foreword

The Oxford Series on Sexuality, Identity, and Society emerged at a time of considerable social change in the meaning and expression of sexual identities across the globe. When the late Bert Cohler and I conceived the Series in the first decade of the century, a discourse was emerging that a new generation might be eschewing sexual identity labels, both to challenge the limitations of the inherited taxonomy and to 'normalize' sexual attraction beyond a heteronormative compulsion. We wrote and studied this phenomenon, referring to a new narrative of 'emancipation' from traditional sexual identity labels. And yet we simultaneously saw the endurance of a narrative of struggle in the development and social acceptance of sexual identities beyond the heteronormative. Indeed, the story of the 21st century has been the story of competing narratives of the legitimacy of sexual diversity and its recognition in cultural discourse, law, and social policy. Simply put, we develop our own sexual stories at a time of simultaneous critique of what came before us (e.g., 20th-century binaries) and a recognition of its value (e.g., the ability to embody our sexual desires more authentically thanks to the work of 20th-century social movements).

Darren Langdridge's book arrives at a key historical moment in contested narratives of sexuality within societies. He offers a compelling and provocative treatise on the nature of 'critique' within sexuality scholarship, applying and expanding upon notions of sexual citizenship beyond the authority of the state. The book will be of interest for those who appreciate the value of linking social theory (e.g., narrative, citizenship) with conceptions of psychological experience (e.g., subjectivity). As a narrative psychologist inspired by the philosophy of Paul Ricoeur, I value Langdridge's application of Ricoeur's conception of both the ideological and utopian in narratives. At the same time, the book engages with more contemporary sexuality theory and research, including both canonical and contemporary perspectives in queer theory and social science.

The text is by design polemic: Langdridge has been a key intellectual architect this century in pushing the psychology of sexuality to engage more closely with critical social theory and notions of citizenship. Hence he offers a meditation on the production of knowledge within sexuality studies, as well as the very meaning of being a sexual subject in our time—our own personal narratives being the product of a dynamic engagement with both critique and reverence for prior narratives of sexual subjectivity. I especially appreciate Langdridge's commitment to challenge the critique/tradition binary in the development of his position, which is fundamentally 'dialectic' in its recognition of the complexity of human lives. As a scholar with great reverence for the social theorist and philosopher Mikhail Bakhtin, I appreciated the 'multivocality' Langdridge recognizes in the narrative terrains we navigate as we formulate, embody, and disseminate our own sexual stories—as both subjects to a particular 'regime' of sexual normativity and authors of ever-expanding narrative possibilities. It is precisely this position of dynamic complexity that will likely both compel and repel the reader—reactions that Langdridge both anticipates and invites. Either way, the text will stand as a testament of this cultural moment—a time of both emancipation and continued contestation in the way we experience, practice, and name our sexual desire.

At a time in my own development as a scholar in which I am increasingly focused on the documentation of new (or newly visible) forms of sexual diversity, the opportunity to step back and engage more critically with social and political theories of sexualities is most welcome. As scholars produce discourse about sexuality, we run the risk of creating our own narrow paradigms that see the world only through the lens of critique. Langdridge provokes us to think more deeply about our paradigms and to consider the extent to which they capture the dynamic complexities and tensions of sexual citizenship in our time.

As our century unfolds, so too does our recognition that the sexual stories that circulate embody both inherited frameworks and radical disruptions that challenge prior understandings. This book contributes to this recognition by highlighting the simultaneous value of critique and tradition, interrupting the allure of a binary narrative of utopian progress in sexual citizenship.

Phillip L. Hammack
Santa Cruz, California
November 2023

Contents

SECTION 1

1. Introduction	3
2. On sexual citizenship	30
3. The narrative nature of sexual life	58

SECTION 2

4. Sexual citizenship and a clash of rights	83
5. Conservative claims for citizenship	109
6. Spectacular critique and abject citizenship	132

SECTION 3

7. Towards a politics of hospitality	157
Appendix: A dialectic of ideology and utopia	175
References	181
Index	199

SECTION 1

1

Introduction

The time has come to think about sex. To some, sexuality may seem to be an unimportant topic, a frivolous diversion from the more critical problems of poverty, war, disease, racism, famine, or nuclear annihilation. But it is precisely at times such as these, when we live with the possibility of unthinkable destruction, that people are likely to become dangerously crazy about sexuality. Contemporary conflicts over sexual values and erotic conduct have much in common with the religious disputes of earlier centuries. They acquire immense symbolic weight. Disputes over sexual behaviour often become vehicles for displacing social anxieties, and discharging their attendant emotional intensity. Consequently, sexuality should be treated with special respect in times of great social stress.

—Rubin (1984/1993: 3–4)

We are living in a time of great social stress that appears to grow more acute every year. At the time of writing, we are witness to a horrific war in Europe, something most of us thought would never be seen again on this continent. This of course comes immediately after a deadly global pandemic that few ever imagined. It really does feel as if much of the security and certainty that many, though by no means all, people have experienced in the liberal West since the last world war is gradually being eroded as new risks appear with alarming frequency. Threats of disease, social unrest, and terror are myriad and continually mutating to form a social cloud of anxiety that may overwhelm us at any point: the end of history appears a very long way off (Fukuyama, 1992). Rubin might have been writing in 1984, but she was undoubtedly correct that people can become 'dangerously crazy' about sex at times like these, with it assuming 'immense symbolic weight'.

As I walked my dog in Clapham, London, during the time I was writing this book, I saw the bench dedicated to the memory of Jodi Dubrowski, a

Sexual Citizenship and Social Change. Darren Langdridge, Oxford University Press. © Oxford University Press 2024.
DOI: 10.1093/oso/9780199926312.003.0001

4 SEXUAL CITIZENSHIP AND SOCIAL CHANGE

24-year-old bar manager who was brutally murdered by two men in a homophobic attack in 2005. It is now almost 20 years later, so surely this terrible incident is now a matter of history. Things have apparently moved on and queer folk apparently no longer suffer such abuse. And yet over the last 20 years or so there have been multiple murders of LGBTQ people in London alone, one of the most cosmopolitan and socially progressive cities on the planet. Furthermore, only a relatively few years ago in 2016 we witnessed the deadliest act of violence against LGBTQ people ever recorded in the West, when 49 people were killed in a shooting at the Pulse nightclub in Orlando in the United States. Have things really progressed as much as we imagine?

But I hear you say: 'surely things have improved for sexual liberation since the early 1980s when Rubin was writing?' We have LGBTQ characters in popular television and music, 'out' sportspeople, publication of bestselling books like *Fifty Shades of Grey*, and legislative change in the form of same-sex marriage. We talk about sex of all kinds much more openly now, do we not? I think the answer to whether things have improved is very definitely one of 'yes' and 'no'. While out walking my dog on the same day I paused at the memorial bench, I saw a same-sex couple walking hand in hand by the road on the receiving end of homophobic abuse from random car drivers. The young men shouted back defiantly, 'Yes, we're gay, so what!' and I cheered them on but felt my heart sink. Much has changed for the better, without a doubt, and yet this prosaic tale reveals that things are not quite as good for sexually diverse folk as we might imagine. There remains much still to do if we are to achieve true equality. This is not my focus in this book, however. The reader interested in such debates is advised to look elsewhere (e.g., Duberman, 2018; Mowlabocus, 2021; Signorile, 2016; Walters, 2014; Yoshino, 2007). My focus in this book is instead on a more pernicious contemporary problem, the use and abuse of critique in ostensibly progressive sexuality scholarship.

I will argue that a new danger for contemporary sexual life emerges from an excess of critique. This is a particular form of critique that is detached and unfettered, set loose from the usual anchor of tradition. What is most dangerous of all with this excess of unfettered critique is that it emerges from within minority sexual communities (and their allies), not from the usual conservative opposition to progressive change. I will argue that even the most ostensibly well-meaning critic—and associated critique—can become problematic when their arguments are detached from tradition. To this end, I intend to show that critique can provoke unnecessary conflict within communities, result in the internalization of pathology, become conservative within the context of an ersatz performative radicalism, inadvertently repathologize sexual subjects, and result in dangerous consequences when using the language of progressive sexual citizenship with that which is abject. The list is long and the danger to contemporary culture great: this is a treatise that seeks to speak directly to the culture wars (Hunter, 1991), no matter how difficult that conversation. I think it really is time for us to think about sex, again. And this time, the conversation is arguably going to be even more difficult.

The changing nature of sexual stories

There has, of course, been enormous change in social and state acceptance regarding sex and sexualities over the last 30 years or so in the West, much of which is positive, with an apparent new acceptance and openness towards diverse sexual practices, sexualities, and other aspects of our intimate lives (see, e.g., Curtice et al., 2019; Mowlabocus, 2021; Seidman, 2002; Weeks, 2007). Whilst progressive social change concerning sex and sexuality is apparent and seemingly unstoppable, battles continue to wage between traditionalists wanting a return to the certainties of the past and reformists wanting and willing to embrace uncertainty and contingency through a new radical sexual politics. There are also others, however, who do not see such a march of progress so positively, fearing an assimilationist or otherwise politically troubling move with much of the apparent progress concerning sex, sexualities, and intimacies (see, e.g., Bell & Binnie, 2000; Duberman, 2018; Mowlabocus, 2021; Walters, 2014). And we might also stress here that everyday life has not necessarily improved as much as has been claimed for large numbers of people. Progress remains highly conditional on sex, gender, class, poverty, race/ethnicity, and more, even where it has occurred.

In academic circles things have been changing too, of course. Since the work of McIntosh (1968), Foucault (1976), and Weeks (1977), studies of human sex and sexuality have gradually moved away from being the sole province of biology, medicine, and psychology. That is, these theorists, along with the many others that followed them, have provided a serious challenge to sexual essentialism and the notion that sex must be understood solely as a natural (biological) force outwith the social world. Michel Foucault's (1977–1978) *The History of Sexuality* has been particularly influential in transforming the field of sex research, with his compelling theoretical argument about sex having a

6 SEXUAL CITIZENSHIP AND SOCIAL CHANGE

history opening new avenues for social scientific research. What now might appear to be a rather simple—even mundane, and also arguably not completely original—argument for those of us working in the social sciences, that sexual practices have had different meanings in different historical periods and places, was a radical intervention in the 1970s. Indeed, it remains remarkably challenging even today for some people working on sex within very traditional versions of the biomedical sciences. Furthermore, his modern historical argument that sexuality, as we know it now, was actually an invention of the late 18th and 19th centuries was—and remains—a fundamentally radical notion for sex research. This work has—for better and worse—helped produce a methodological shift away from behaviours as the object of study and towards an analysis of the discourses that describe (or rather 'construct') them. This has, in some instances, gone too far and resulted in a rather unfortunate eschewal of the material world, and most notably the loss of the body that is surely central to understanding the meaning of sex (Butt & Langdridge, 2003; Plummer, 2019). Additionally, some of this work—particularly within the humanities—has become overly reliant on postmodern theory, with almost no critical interrogation of the empirical basis of these theoretical arguments about sexuality and human nature (see Paglia, 1991). Regardless, this work has inspired many others, most notably Judith Butler (1990, 1993) and Eve Kosofsky Sedgwick (1990, 1992), whose work provides the foundation for contemporary 'queer theory' (see Fuss, 1991, and Seidman, 1996, for a good account of this theoretical emergence).

Most immediately relevant for this book, Gayle Rubin (1984/1993) built on the ideas of Foucault and Weeks to advance a radical theory of sex in her highly significant article 'Thinking Sex'. At the heart of this work was recognition of the way that culture shapes the meaning of modern sexual practice and, in particular, how this leads to an ideological hierarchy of sexual practices and identities. Rubin describes five 'ideological formations', in addition to sexual essentialism, which shape contemporary sexual thought. These include sex negativity, the fallacy of misplaced scale, the hierarchical valuation of sex acts, the domino theory of sexual peril, and the lack of a concept of benign sexual variation. Rubin considered sex negativity to be the most important of these ideological formations for the way that it underpins the notion within the West that sex is dangerous and destructive. As she describes it, in post-Pauline Christian societies: 'Sex is presumed guilty until proven innocent. Virtually all erotic behaviour is considered bad unless a specific reason to exempt it has been established. The most acceptable excuses are marriage, reproduction,

INTRODUCTION 7

and love' (Rubin, 1984/1993: 11). The fallacy of misplaced scale is related to sex negativity and pertains to the way that sex appears to be burdened (within Western societies at least) with disproportionate significance. This is particularly apparent in the way that sexual practices that fall outside the boundaries of acceptability are harshly punished. Rubin pays particular attention to the next ideological formation concerned with the way that modern Western societies operate a strict hierarchy of sexual value. The value system when Rubin was writing in the 1980s has changed somewhat, but the central thrust of her thesis remains correct. Rubin argues that the top of the hierarchy involves marital, heterosexual, reproductive sexuality, whilst at the bottom are transsexuals, transvestites, fetishists, sadomasochists, and sex workers, with the lowliest of all those whose sexuality involves the transgression of generational boundaries. Sexual practices and identities at the top (or near the top) are rewarded with 'certified mental health, respectability, legality, social and physical mobility, institutional support, and material benefits' (p. 12). In essence, sex that is 'good', 'normal', and 'natural' should ideally be heterosexual, marital (or at least coupled), monogamous, reproductive, within the same generation, and noncommercial and should happen at home. Sex that involves pornography, fetish objects or sex toys, roles other than traditionally male or female, same-sex activity, or promiscuity; that is public or casual; or that crosses generational lines is 'bad', 'abnormal', and 'unnatural'. And whilst we may argue about the position of individual sexual practices/identities within the hierarchy and whether some practices might be appropriately illegitimate, the point that there is an imaginary line drawn (and policed) between 'good' and 'bad' sex stands.

The final two ideological formations are the domino theory of sexual peril and the lack of a concept of benign sexual variation. The former is key to understanding the way that the line between good and bad sex is drawn and why this is policed so strongly. The domino theory is the expression of the fear that if anything is allowed to cross this line of demarcation, then there is a risk of chaos and the destruction of society as we know it. The last ideological formation at work in upholding the hierarchy of sexual practice concerns the lack of a notion of benign sexual variation and the pernicious idea that there is only one acceptable way to have sex:

Most people find it difficult to grasp that whatever they like to do sexually will be thoroughly repulsive to someone else, and whatever repels them sexually will be the most treasured delight of someone, somewhere. One

8 SEXUAL CITIZENSHIP AND SOCIAL CHANGE

need not like or perform a particular sex act in order to recognize that someone else will, and that this difference does not indicate a lack of good taste, mental health, or intelligence in either party. Most people mistake their sexual preferences for a universal system that will or should work for everyone. (Rubin, 1984/1993: 15)

The attempt to challenge this hierarchy of sex has resulted in a proliferation of new sexual stories (Plummer, 1995) competing to be heard over the last 30 to 40 years, with different and conflicting claims for rights, acknowledgement, and acceptance (Weeks, 2007). That is, many of the new sexual stories that have emerged in recent years are narrated in the language of citizenship, invoking claims for rights (Richardson, 2018). Whilst there are some who view an opening up of citizenship as a welcome progressive move (Weeks, 2007), offering new opportunities for rights and responsibilities amongst sexual minorities, others see dangers of increasing assimilation or accommodation to hegemonic notions of sex and sexualities, and a failure to provide the necessary critique to an inherently normative concept (see, e.g., Bell & Binnie, 2000; Brandzel, 2005; Lee, 2016; Richardson, 2004; Sabsay, 2016; Spade, 2015). That said, some critics—while recognizing potential limitations—still seek to conceptually engage with citizenship as a productive 'momentum concept' (Lister, 2008), albeit in an expanded form (see, e.g., Lee, 2016), as I will also do herein.

In the light of concerns about the perceived progress regarding contemporary sexual life, it seems like a good time to step back and evaluate what progress looks like for sexual citizenship and, indeed, what we even mean by progress (see Richardson, 2004). Things have changed so much over the last 30 years or so that we are increasingly seeing people proclaiming societies in the West as 'postgay', where sexual orientation no longer matters (e.g., Anderson, 2009; Anderson & McCormac, 2016; Ghaziani, 2014; Savin-Williams, 2005, 2011; but see also criticism and discussion from, e.g., Cohler & Hammack, 2007; de Boise, 2015; Ingram & Waller, 2014; Li et al., 2014; Meyer, 2010; O'Neill, 2014). That said, a recent national social attitudes survey in the United Kingdom showed that the number of people holding negative attitudes towards people who are LGBTQ has now bottomed out, staying consistent at around the mid-30% level for the last 3 years (Curtice et al., 2019: 19):

> The proportion stating that sexual relations between two adults of the same sex are 'not wrong at all' has now remained at around two-thirds (64%, 68%

and 66%) for the past three years, indicating that while social norms have changed, there is a significant minority of the population who remain uncomfortable with same-sex relationships, and as such we may have reached a point of plateau.

This 'stubborn rump' of a group appears to consist mostly of men, older people and/or those with strongly held religious convictions. (Curtice et al., 2019: 130)

Like some authors (e.g., Mowlabocus, 2021), I believe strongly that much progress is real, offering tangible benefits for a good variety of sexual minority folk, but the emergent story that we are at an end point for sexual emancipation is of course a myth. This is not an original insight, of course, as a variety of authors have made this point, in various forms. For instance, writing from a legal perspective, Yoshino (2007) discusses how 'covering', a term originating from Goffman (1963) concerning the way that we may hide aspects of our identity to avoid violating the norms of the group, continues to operate with regard to sexuality (and race). Walters (2014) stresses the difference between tolerance and acceptance, and how tolerance is a trap that leads to a pernicious state in which true equality is never achieved. Through the trope of 'victory blindness', Signorile (2016) covers near-identical territory to Walters (2014) and Yoshino (2007), arguing that tolerance is not sufficient for true equality. Adopting a longer historical perspective, Duberman (2018) also questions the sidelining of early radical goals originating from organizations such as the Gay Liberation Front. He argues, in a similar vein to some other contemporary authors of sexual and gender politics (see, e.g., Faye, 2021), that LGBTQ equality needs to be part of a broader left-wing political agenda. And, most recently, Mowlabocus (2021) offers another critique of contemporary sexual politics, this time through a critique of homonormativity (see also Richardson, 2004).

Many similar concerns were raised even earlier by authors including, notably, Califia (1994) and Warner (1993, 2000), but also by theorists such as Fuss (1991) and Bell and Binnie (2000). This was framed through discussions about the dangers of repression, censorship, normality—or more properly, *normativity*—political accommodation, and/or assimilation. To a large extent, these lines of critique reflect the political ambition of the author and whether their utopian vision for sexual citizenship has been met or not. That is the nature of all critical social theory of course, it being founded upon a teleologically driven Marxism.

10 SEXUAL CITIZENSHIP AND SOCIAL CHANGE

The argument of Mowlabocus (2021) provides us with a good contemporary segue to the question of what progress looks like today. Mowlabocus (2021) argues that much contemporary gay sexuality is highly individualized and homonormative. While not denying the progress that has unfolded and is enjoyed by many, Mowlabocus argues that this is a highly conditional progress, and one that results in considerable remaining injustice. Duberman (2018) is similarly sceptical about the nature of this progress, as are other authors such as Sabsay (2016) and Lee (2016), with them all arguing that change with respect to sexual (and gender) diversity is not only exclusive (of, e.g., people from the Global South, people of colour [POC], immigrants, and the working class/poor) and highly individualized but also the proximal result of capitalism, in the form of neoliberalism. I think much of this criticism is valid, even if I am somewhat more sceptical than other writers of the deployment of—at times rather simplistic—versions of the relatively ill-defined concept of 'neoliberalism'. I will explain this latter point a little more below when discussing the theoretical framework for this text. Regardless, in the main, I agree with these critics that while there has been—often quite remarkable—progress with respect to sexual citizenship, this is not unconditional or completely unproblematic.

That said, as mentioned above, I have a different and additional worry, one that moves the discussion regarding progress and how it is manifest today in a very different direction indeed and forms the basis of this book. None of these other writers have raised the spectre that critique itself may become problematic, as I will do here. This is where I deviate considerably—and controversially—from these authors, and the field of sexuality studies more generally. While I agree there is undoubted and proven value in critique, I also think it has limits and that we are currently witness to some sensible limits being breached, such that critique is becoming detached from its necessary opposite—tradition—or being otherwise dangerously distorted or deployed in ill-informed ways. While other authors focus their critical efforts on resistance to change and the limitations of tradition, I take on critique itself.

The focus of this book

In the following chapters, I engage with contemporary critical citizenship theory that has addressed these issues with respect to sexual practice. To

INTRODUCTION   11

further develop an understanding of sexual citizenship, I draw on a number of theoretical resources beyond that currently usually employed within sexual citizenship studies, notably the philosophy of Paul Ricoeur. Previously, I have suggested that the political philosophy of Ricoeur, particularly his attempt to work with both ideological and utopian narratives, provides a way of illuminating the social positioning of people, practices, and identities within the social imaginary of stories into which we are all thrown, as well as offering at least one possible way out of the inevitable conflict between different ideological positions (Langdridge, 2006, 2013, 2022). That is, Ricoeur's philosophy offers up a radical but inherently generous alternative to many existing theoretical resources for the way in which it offers dialectical solutions to entrenched ideological positions. This analytic focus forms one of the key moves in this text that, I argue, requires us to engage politically with both tradition and critique in a spirit of openness and generosity. Ricoeur's ideas also enable us to recognize an embodied psychological subject that we may seek to understand through narrative (Langdridge, 2003, 2008). This psychosocial framework provides for a more psychologically fleshed-out political analysis, in which the inherent interrelatedness of individual and society is acknowledged.

Further to this, I move beyond (predominantly legal) state-centric models of citizenship and the state as primary interlocutor. To this end, I work with an expanded notion of citizenship, informed by the work of Shane Phelan (2001) and Engin Isin (2009), in which wider social acknowledgement, performativity, and the construction of new subjectivities is as important as state recognition, status, and the law. This strategy to explore critical challenges to traditional notions of citizenship ultimately calls the dominance of the state into question with regard to the writing of narratives of sex and sexualities and highlights the role of individual subjects in opening up new spaces for radical acts of (sexual) citizenship (cf. Lee, 2016; Sabsay, 2016). Citizenship, in these terms, becomes a much more dynamic concept, in which legal recognition plays a part but only within the much wider context of the political and sociocultural.

The first chapters in this book present the theoretical background of sexual citizenship and the role of narrative. Then, in Chapters 4, 5, and 6, I explore the challenges and dangers of unfettered critique through discussion of a variety of topics concerned with sexual citizenship. My aim is to show how critique can itself become problematic, especially when detached from tradition. The claim that I intend to illustrate through a variety of substantive

12 SEXUAL CITIZENSHIP AND SOCIAL CHANGE

examples related to sex and sexuality is that critique—and associated social change—carries risks regarding social justice, just like tradition. My primary argument is one about the need for openness and balance, in this instance between tradition and critique, such that the two poles of this binary serve to inform and correct each other. Critique can go awry in a variety of ways:

- It can become completely detached from tradition (Chapter 4).
- It can become distorted such that it effectively becomes a form of internalized tradition (Chapter 5).
- It can be deployed to spectacular effect but with little or no care for the people and communities in question and extended so far as to lose sight of important limits (Chapter 6).

In more substantive terms, the problem of critique detached from tradition can be seen in the conflict between and within communities, for example, between some religious communities and diversity educators and with the current fight between some gender critical and trans folk (and their allies). Claims to be engaged in progressive critical scholarship and activism appear distorted when minority communities internalize the tools of the oppressor, as we see with the ready embrace of a therapy narrative within bondage and discipline, dominance and submission, and sadomasochism (BDSM). Critique is twisted even further when it becomes a shallow conservatism within the context of an ersatz performative radicalism, as can be observed with some stories of polyamory (and other sexual identities, such as asexuality). Ostensibly radical community members and allies may also deploy critique in ways that (inadvertently) harm the very communities they represent or seek to support. This can be seen, for instance, with the spectacular reinvention of an older pathologizing tradition in the promotion of a racist bisexual bridge theory and queer misappropriation of barebacking among HIV/AIDS scholars. And finally, and arguably most disturbing, is the attempt to extend hard-fought-for progressive sexual citizenship to the most abject sexual noncitizen: the child sexual abuser or now so-called minority-attracted person. With this move, tradition and critique come full circle, with early arguments about gay equality being a 'slippery slope'—Rubin's domino effect—being unhelpfully realized, as critical thinkers deploy ostensibly progressive concepts of citizenship with those engaged in violence and abuse.

So, unlike much work on contemporary political theory, and notably within queer theory, this project seeks to recognize the importance of tradition as a necessary corrective for critique by looking critically at critique itself, while not eschewing the importance or value of critique. This will undoubtedly be controversial and likely be met with a claim it is conservative, old-fashioned, or otherwise out of touch with the latest thinking in political theory and activism. I am choosing not to follow the trend towards the ready embrace of the latest critical theory while believing strongly that the case I am making remains in the spirit of early queer activism, even if not so closely aligned with contemporary versions. I see value in many contemporary theoretical positions—whether queer, feminist, or postcolonial—of course, but recognize them as utopian critique in the stories we tell about sexual life, especially within academia in the West, and it is utopian critique—when detached from tradition—that I seek to problematize in this text. That is, whilst these contemporary theoretical developments may be normative within certain strands of the academy and some activism, I will not be framing my analysis primarily through any one or more of these critical theoretical lenses.

Some will find this position untenable, convinced as they are of the intellectual and moral truth of their own theoretical position, and how all contemporary life must be read through a particular critical lens or be part of the problem of systemic injustice itself. This latter claim is one that I find particularly pernicious, with worrying echoes of totalitarian rather than genuinely critical thinking. My interest in both tradition and critique results in a need to steer a steady course between the two, such that I attend as much to ideology (and tradition) as utopian imaginings, believing as I do that bringing both together in a dialectic is the necessary precondition for effecting long-lasting social change. I do not intend this to be another book in the growing canon of 'critical' books, especially among those concerned with sexuality and gender, that present their case through an almost hegemonic theoretical ground of Anglophone contemporary critical theory and cultural critique. To be more specific, this will not be a book that frames its content exclusively through a critique of neoliberalism or through the lens of intersectional feminist, queer, or postcolonial theory, even though these positions have become increasingly normative within this field.

I will explain this position further below by drawing on arguments made by Lisa Downing (2019) concerning her worries about intersectional feminism, which apply equally to queer theory, and then seek to extend this thinking to postcolonial theory and the critique of neoliberalism. To that end, I will also engage, albeit necessarily briefly, with recent critical thinking from philosophy and political theory about these theoretical perspectives. Common to

14 SEXUAL CITIZENSHIP AND SOCIAL CHANGE

intersectional feminism, postcolonial theory/critical race theory, and even, paradoxically, contemporary queer theory is a tendency to resort to dividing practices. That is, this body of contemporary scholarship, while often raising important questions about systemic inequality and injustice that I often agree with strongly, has become increasingly productive of binary categories and atomized but reified notions of identity, which were themselves the subject of considerable critique within early queer theory (e.g., Fuss, 1991; see also Hall, 2009) and yet now perversely reappear normatively within much—though thankfully not all—contemporary critical scholarship and activism.

Intersectionality

So, while I see conceptual value in intersectionality (Crenshaw, 1989; see also hooks, 1981) and will draw upon this theoretical lens in this text, I agree with Downing (2019) that contemporary intersectional feminism has moved considerably from the original position espoused by Kimberlé Crenshaw. Crenshaw (1989), and those that immediately engaged with her argument, rightly highlighted the need to attend to the way that sex and race intersect—in her instance, in the form of Black women's experience—to render particular subjects invisible or otherwise subject to discriminatory practice. This is undoubtedly true and has proven to be a valuable corrective to the neglect of Black experience among the feminism of the time, with the concept later extended to other identity categories—for example, LGBTQ folk—to good effect. For Downing (2019: 139), 21st-century intersectionality has, however, become

> a particular version of individuality, so that each person needs to think of themselves in terms of the particular multiple oppressions to which they are subject and the particular privileges from which they benefit—that then become the sum of their situated political identity. This both sidelines class-based analysis or strategic consensus building, such as that on which much second-wave feminism rested, *and* silences the possibility of eccentric individual dissent.

Through the example of a dispute involving the writer Chimamanda Ngozi Adichie and (some) trans activists and their allies, Downing (2019) raises an important point about the focus of intersectional feminism and the question

INTRODUCTION 15

of whom it 'centres'. In an equivalent manner to the tension regarding J. K. Rowling and trans activists, Adichie, who has a similar record of supporting LGBTQ rights to Rowling, questioned whether trans women's experience is the same as that of cis women who have been raised within a culture that privileges men. As Downing (2019) observes, this statement by Adichie was met with a barrage of criticism, with Adichie, like Rowling, refusing to apologize but instead arguing that contemporary social justice activism is operating a 'language orthodoxy', where the words a person uses are prioritized over their political history or intention, and in a manner that is fundamentally hostile and coercive. This version of intersectional feminism results in a collective policing that, as Downing (2019) notes, resonates more closely with very conservative cultures rather than those seeking to liberate individuals from unjust societal constraints.

> The way intersectional feminism is currently practiced—especially in the heated echo chambers of online fora—thus pits members of one marginalized 'identity group' against another. In this case, a woman of colour activist was pitted against trans women in a competition over which had the greatest claim to oppression. Rather than allowing for and respecting difference, intersectionality, in its current iteration, divides. It is, in fact, much more like the 'neoliberal model of competition' that the left purports to despise than either straightforward individualism or straightforward collectivism. (Downing, 2019: 141)

I couldn't agree more. The need for much contemporary intersectional politics to enforce a rigid narrative of acceptable and permissible thought and language, within a pernicious zero-sum game, is particularly troubling.

Additionally, Downing (2019: 141–142) notes how third-wave feminism is presented as 'the ethical corrective to earlier feminism—and as a superior mode'. As she rightly points out, the imposition of the values of the present onto the past results in an overly simplified and thoroughly unforgiving enlightenment model of historical progress. And, as she notes, it is particularly ironic to perceive the present moment—one in which 'calling-out, no-platforming, and purity-testing' are central—as a superior mode of political engagement. This is the 'presentism' that historian Lynn Hunt (2002) rightly critiques as a pernicious phenomenon that risks reducing history to just another branch of contemporary identity politics. In these terms, paradoxically, history becomes focussed on the valorization of sameness rather

16 SEXUAL CITIZENSHIP AND SOCIAL CHANGE

than difference, imbued with a self-congratulatory moral complacency. All this said, I will, of course, seek to ensure I attend to Crenshaw's (1989) original vision regarding the intersection of identity categories, and how they might structurally manifest in fundamentally prejudiced ways, in this text. Her early critique regarding the erasure of Black women is important and not something I intend to forget or neglect, regardless of how this may now be deployed by contemporary theorists and activists.

Postcolonial theory

Postcolonial theory is a form of intersectional analysis that is currently ascending within the arts and social sciences. This theoretical development, that emerged within literary and cultural studies, is difficult to define, being identified primarily on the basis of a general allegiance to the ideas of a small set of original thinkers including Frantz Fanon, Aimé Césaire, Edward W. Said, Homi K. Bhabha, and Gayatri Chakravorty Spivak (see, e.g., Bhabha, 1994; Guha & Spivak, 1988; Said, 1979, 1993; Spivak, 1999). In general terms, there is an attempt to move us beyond an analysis of race/ethnicity alone to focus on the structural underpinnings of racism, and Eurocentrism in particular, resulting from Western colonialism and how these impact upon present-day racial inequalities (Chibber, 2013; Lazarus, 2011). The focus on taking theory 'into the field' such that postcolonial theory becomes a form of activism and potentially even a new social movement is important and distinct to many other theoretical developments. It is becoming increasingly rare to see 'progressive' scholarship, particularly when concerned with sexual and gender diversity that does not engage with postcolonial theory in some way. However, when it comes to postcolonial theory, and occasionally the associated activist arm of decolonization, I share the concerns of a number of other theorists (most notably Taguieff, 2001, 2020a, 2020b) regarding the need to think carefully and critically about this theoretical development.

Again, it is important to be clear from the outset that I am not defending historical colonization in my refusal to engage wholeheartedly—or, more accurately, uncritically—with postcolonial theory. To be crystal clear, I do not think colonialism was a good thing, nor do I think we should ignore the impact of such imperialism on contemporary societies. My concerns about employing postcolonial theory also do not represent a denial that there is value in critically examining the impact of colonialism and colonial thinking

INTRODUCTION 17

on the assumptions underpinning contemporary thought and practice. I am also not remotely interested in exploring—or defending—right-wing attacks on attempts at racial justice that are underpinned by modern (or ancient) racist ideology. Postcolonial theory provides valuable insight about the role of colonialism in historical, and to some extent present-day, structural inequalities. But, like intersectional feminism, it too has become overextended in the humanities and social sciences and at risk of creating unhelpful division rather than valuable analytic insight. It is also important to note that this criticism is not an attempt to engage directly with the full extent of postcolonial theory itself, where there has been considerable productive 'internal' critical debate (see, e.g., Lazarus, 2011, 2014; Parry, 2004). That level of critique is beyond the scope of this text. My focus here is much more limited. I aim only to raise a concern about the *uncritical importation* of postcolonial theory as an ideological framework when engaging in contemporary scholarship and activism on sex and sexuality (or indeed many other topics in the social sciences).

My concerns about postcolonial theory also extend to how this has been mobilized academically and politically as decolonization in contemporary scholarship and activism. Confusingly, postcolonial theory and decolonization are sometimes used as synonyms or as distinct concepts. Haslam (2016) describes the problem of 'concept creep', in which we see the semantic inflation of harm-related concepts such that they become all-encompassing. This is a particular problem with many critical concepts today, including notably postcolonial theory and decolonization. Calls to adopt a postcolonial position and engage in a project of decolonization can, for instance, mean anything from the practical overthrow of colonial oppression by Indigenous peoples; to better representation of POC in, for example, media or curriculum; to the application of postcolonial theory to all and every aspect of contemporary life, in which we see a somewhat strange neo-Marxism enacted where racial categories become individually and structurally reified, reviving—albeit in inverted form—an old-fashioned language and practice of biological racism (Taguieff, 2001).

One of the most pernicious aspects of concept creep and the tendency to resist tight definitions is that it shuts down argument. When concepts shift and change, with no clear definition, it acts to silence the other. The lack of clarity is itself part of the power wielded through these critical concepts, but that unfettered power is potentially dangerous. Who could argue with people overthrowing a colonial oppressor or there being better representation of

18   SEXUAL CITIZENSHIP AND SOCIAL CHANGE

POC in the media? That kind of decolonization is something relatively few would resist or argue against. But what about legitimate worries that the muscular reassertion of the language of biological racism needs to be handled with great care? Any attempt to voice such concerns can be and are met with incredulity that someone would wish to deny the wider project in question, especially among those on the progressive left. Such silencing—especially when connected with a particularly powerful moral accusation that the opponent is driven by prejudice—leads to a lack of dialogue and the opportunity for people to collectively explore, nuance, or resist these critical concepts.

With this in mind, I do not believe that we can or should seek to explain all contemporary life through the lens of postcolonial theory and decolonization. But this is becoming the norm very quickly within some strands of contemporary academic life, driven primarily by cultural circumstances and academic norms within the United States. Postcolonial theory and decolonization must be subject to the same level of critique as any other critical theory. We should not ignore the problematic elements of this academic theory (and associated activism), even if we share many of the underlying concerns about historical and present-day racial injustice driving the creation of these theories. It would be thoroughly unethical and of intellectual bad faith to do so.

There are three lines of criticism concerning postcolonial theory and decolonization that I will raise here. This will be necessarily brief given this is not the focus of the book but should still be sufficient to provide a sense of my reservations and an opportunity for the interested reader to follow up on these issues themselves. The point I am trying to make regarding these specific theories—and within the book regarding *all* critique—is quite simply that all critical theories have limits and must be subject to an equivalent level of critical scrutiny as the objects of their critique. To this end, all human beings must also have an equal right to voice such critique. To think otherwise is to risk the embrace of totalitarian ideology. And while those who think otherwise may sincerely believe they are acting on the side of the angels, I fear the devil is at their shoulder.

First is criticism of postcolonial theory from scholars sympathetic to the Marxist underpinnings of the various strands of theory but who object to how this project has become manifest, notably the work of Aijaz Ahmad (1992) and Vivek Chibber (2013). Ahmad (1992) provides a Marxist materialist critique of the postcolonial project, focussed particularly on Said

INTRODUCTION 19

and Jameson. Chibber (2013) offers a similarly powerful critique but specifically of subaltern studies, a particularly influential form of postcolonial theorizing, arguing that many fundamental concepts are based on historical and/or analytic mistakes. To this end, subaltern studies becomes the primary example used by Chibber in defence of his radical enlightenment vision that seeks to produce universal theory (e.g., regarding class inequalities) without a corresponding Eurocentrism or cultural reductionism. Whether we agree or disagree about the value and adequacy of their Marxist agenda, both authors highlight fundamental issues with postcolonial theory that bear serious attention. This is critique that stems from a genuine concern that postcolonial theory—and the associated political project—has lost sight of the original Marxist ambition.

A second line of criticism concerns the way that some postcolonial thinkers, like some advocates of intersectional feminism, refuse to engage with critique or indeed any dissent when operationalizing it in contemporary politics and/or activism. This is postcolonial theory as a new religion (McWhorter, 2021), all-encompassing, but also—within the context of contemporary 'cancel culture'—damning of anyone who refuses to uncritically accept this new belief system. At their worst, these theories become ideologies deploying critical techniques designed only to determinedly find what they are looking for, whether it is present or not. Key to this religious quality is how these theoretical perspectives serve to position their advocates—and opposition—within a moral and not just intellectual framework. The use of moral discourse is key to the power—and terror—of these theories. It is particularly acute right now with postcolonial theory and decolonization. Those advocating for these positions often—though not always, of course—argue their case such that an opponent is morally positioned as in some way complicit in the specific oppression being challenged. This is the avowed aim of third-wave antiracist literatures informed by postcolonial theory (e.g., Andrews, 2021; Kendi, 2019; see also DiAngelo, 2018). When it is something as morally charged and destructive as racism that can be levelled at any opposition, this will inevitably act to silence critical challenge to the intellectual project in question, no matter how warranted or well intended.

Arguably, there is also an all-too-eager uncritical importation of American political rhetoric within UK academia and activism, with surprisingly limited thought about how relevant it is in this very different cultural context. Recent fights within French academic and public life about postcolonial theory (and the associated project of decolonization) have been particularly vociferous

20   SEXUAL CITIZENSHIP AND SOCIAL CHANGE

in this regard but draw attention to important tensions often neglected in the UK context (in the English language see, e.g., Taguieff, 2020a, 2020b). In the light of this, a third line of criticism concerns the philosophical argument that postcolonial theory deploys—albeit in inverted form—the language of biological racism that was rightly cast aside some years ago. The work of the philosopher Taguieff (2001, 2020a, 2020b) represents one important part of an academic pushback within France against the uncritical importation of what is considered a uniquely American take on French philosophy, one that is also thought to be fundamentally at odds with the founding principles of the French republic.

In a detailed philosophical treatise, Taguieff (2001) argues that racism has transformed from a position that there are fundamental (biological) differences between the races, naturalizing inequality on the basis of bio-logical difference and fear of the other, into an argument about racialized cultures, thereby naturalizing historical difference and justifying a new 'pseudo antiracism' (focussed on 'Whiteness' in particular). The target of Taguieff's critique is the new antiracism centred on structural inequality, driven by postcolonial critique, in which Whites become guilty of racism simply through their 'Whiteness'. And, correspondingly, all POC become systemically innocent victims of racism. As Taguieff (2020b: 2) remarks:

> It follows that the attitudes and behaviors of individuals are entirely deter-mined by the 'system' and are thus dis-empowered. Individual responsi-bility is evacuated: it is 'the system' that directs everything, the thoughts, feelings, and actions of individuals being mere puppets. This militant definition of racism, known as 'structural' or 'systemic', further implies a dogmatic definition of anti-racism as the fight against white racism, and nothing else. And if said racism is 'systemic', then anti-racist action must aim at destroying the 'system' that produces racism by its very functioning. Definitional sleight of hand has thus removed the very possibility of anti-white racism and conferred a revolutionary final telos on the anti-racist struggle. This is why Marxists of all persuasions welcome these anti-racist anti-white mobilizations, in which they see the Revolution on the march.

The core of Taguieff's (2001, 2020a, 2020b) position is an appeal to a universal humanity, which is of course one of the founding principles of the French re-public. For him, postcolonial theory and associated activism, founded as it is on a revolutionary Marxism, albeit in cultural rather than materialist form,

INTRODUCTION 21

is fundamentally at odds with the French republican desire for equal rights and opportunities for all citizens, irrespective of culture. That is, postcolonial theory has a teleology, as befits its revolutionary Marxist origin, which is the overthrow of 'white supremacy', which to Taguieff means the overthrow of French (and Western European) culture itself, at least among the most vehement advocates of this position.

All that said, for my part, I think there is a need for balance. This book is inspired and informed by the work of Paul Ricoeur, and throughout his long and illustrious career, he demonstrated the value of an open-minded attempt to recognize the good in ostensibly opposed positions. He saw opportunity in opposition while always working to bring people and their ideas together. In my own small way, I shall attempt to embrace something of this same spirit.

With that in mind, there will be moments within this text when I draw upon contemporary critical theory where I believe it adds analytic value, albeit always being mindful of the need to engage critically with such critique.

Neoliberalism

A critique of neoliberalism has also become central in much contemporary critical cultural analysis, often as the ultimate distal cause of contemporary societal challenges. As with the discussion of intersectionality and postcolonial theory above, I am not seeking to avoid foregrounding a critique of neoliberalism because I stand in defence of this mode of economics. Indeed, in large part, I agree with much of the criticism directed at this economic model (see, e.g., Piketty, 2020). I do not subscribe to a Hayekian market economics as the foundation of the society I live within, nor do I wish that upon others: I was—and remain—a staunch critic of, for instance, Thatcherite and Reaganite politics. The critique of neoliberalism within the academy outside the discipline of economics that is on display in many contemporary books within sexuality and gender studies is, however, something I tend to find rather problematic.

The first problem is that the definition is terribly woolly, with the term 'neoliberalism' used as a shorthand for factors encouraging privatization and an unwanted individualism. As Venugopal (2015) notes, there is a lack of consistency and rarely any analytic thought about neoliberal economics per se despite the term being liberally deployed analytically across the social sciences, and I might add particularly so in studies of sexuality and gender.

22   SEXUAL CITIZENSHIP AND SOCIAL CHANGE

There is a general failure to discuss—or even define—neoliberalism vis-á-vis economic theory. Instead, it is used—with considerable disdain—as something akin to 'late capitalism' that somehow describes a social force responsible for a destructive privatization and commodification of contemporary life.

Downing (2019) is insightful again here, raising concerns about the tendency to reduce questions of individual and society into an unhelpful binary in which societal explanation is privileged above the individual, with the latter reduced to being the passive subject of 'neoliberal' forces only. She recognizes that many left-leaning cultural analyses 'presuppose that the forms of subjectivity produced under conditions of neoliberalism are inevitably and only negative, and that the antidote to "individualism" must be collectivism, rather than, for example, a restoration of the values of earlier modes of liberalism' (p. 12). In the specific context of feminism and arguments about the dangers of 'competitive individualism', Downing (2019) recognizes that while the effects of what many contemporary left-leaning critical thinkers refer to as 'neoliberalism' may well be pervasive, this line of power is not totalitarian. Noting that the notion of modern power derived from Foucault, which underpins many such critical arguments, also implicates 'a plurality of resistances', Downing (2019: 13) notes:

> I would argue that . . . it is incumbent upon women to question whether a given cultural current or trend works in or against their own self-interest; whether a strategy is worth adopting, using against the grain, or resisting. To deny this possibility (ethical exigency?) is to assume that living 'under neoliberalism' renders the individual entirely incapable of evaluating critically the materials encountered in daily life or of engaging in strategic deployment/rejection of the technologies with which one comes into contact.

The universal and the particular

All the concerns raised above, about intersectional politics, neoliberalism, and queer and postcolonial theories, that are central to much contemporary sexual and gender scholarship, speak to an older debate in political philosophy about the universal and the particular. As a number of contemporary authors have argued from a variety of political and disciplinary perspectives (see, e.g., Embery, 2020; Goodwin, 2023; McWhorter, 2021; Morson &

INTRODUCTION 23

Schapiro, 2021; Neiman, 2023; Özkirimli, 2023; Pabst, 2021; Stanley, 2021; Swift, 2022), ostensibly universal values are in danger from versions of contemporary 'progressive' identity politics that lead to ever further division. There is arguably a need to balance the universal and particular, just as we need to balance critique with tradition, as I discuss in this book. The endless atomization of—and an almost 'fundamentalist' obsession with—identity, something that could be argued to be the result of 'neoliberal' forces regarding, for example, consumption and individualism, risks robbing us of universal values like solidarity. That said, of course, as Mowlabocus (2021) and many others note, there has been value in the emergence of specific identity categories for political action and social moves towards greater equality. There is a balance to be struck here—which will remain my position throughout—but my fear is that we are now tipping over into a dangerously dystopian atomization of identity categories, with an associated divisive politics.

Scope, limitations, and context

There are some limits to the scope of this book, necessary I think but nonetheless important to note and acknowledge up front for the reader. First, I want to raise attention to the specific cultural context that informs this text. I write primarily about the United Kingdom, where I live, but will occasionally also move beyond the United Kingdom to include other territories, mostly European but also occasionally North American and beyond. This will inevitably be risky, but I think not unreasonable given much that I discuss is the result of a global—albeit Western-driven—trade in ideas and culture regarding sex and sexualities. I also hope the arguments herein have resonance for readers beyond the United Kingdom; the topics and debates I address are by no means UK only, and the principal theoretical argument being made is arguably universal. For readers unfamiliar with the United Kingdom, I will, however, outline some key demographics. This should help readers understand the specific nature of UK culture—given that is my primary focus—and, to some extent, help avoid assumptions that UK culture is inevitably the same as other ostensibly similar Anglophone territories, such as the United States.

The United Kingdom—and much of continental Europe—is very different from the United States in terms of race/ethnicity, for a variety of important

24 SEXUAL CITIZENSHIP AND SOCIAL CHANGE

historical reasons. Drawing on UK census data from the Office for National Statistics and data from the US Census Bureau at the time of writing, we find that 87% of people in the United Kingdom are White (as opposed to 59.3% in the United States), and 13% belong to a Black, Asian, Mixed, or Other ethnic group. The United Kingdom has a population that is only 3.4% Black (as opposed to 13.6% in the United States), with no recorded substantial Hispanic or Latino population (contrasted with 18.9% in United States), as of 2020. Of the 3.4% who are Black, about half are of Caribbean decent and about half African, and most are not decedents of the transatlantic slave trade but migrants to the United Kingdom. By contrast, the United Kingdom has a reasonably large Asian population of 6.9% (6.1% in the United States), made up of folk of (in population size order) Indian, Pakistani, Bangladeshi, and Chinese heritage, but also with a sizeable percentage from a variety of other Asian backgrounds.

The United Kingdom is also politically quite different from the United States. While many comparisons have been made about our (now former) prime minister Boris Johnson and the (for now former) president Donald Trump, they are mostly rather fatuous comparisons. While both are clearly populist politicians with rather 'colourful' personal lives, the similarity ends there as the political agendas they have enacted when in power have been quite distinct. Indeed, some within the UK Conservative Party that Johnson led were perturbed by the tendency of the Johnson administration to raise taxes to fund public services and engage in 'woke' policy regarding, for example, climate change. The United Kingdom also does not have a public sphere—at least at present—that has as strong a left–right distinction as can be seen in the United States (Goodwin, 2023). Strongly right-wing politicians in power do exist, but not to the same extent as in the United States, even within the ostensibly right-wing UK Conservative Party, with religious views underpinning political beliefs not so commonly expressed in the United Kingdom.

These rather basic facts are important in enabling us to recognize and reflect on how the different cultural situations may impact on the Anglophone trade in intellectual property and pursuits. They act as an important reminder that the wholesale importation of cultural theory and activism from one country to another requires appropriate critical gaze or risks the imposition of a peculiar form of contemporary US cultural colonialism by stealth.

It is also important to be clear that this book is primarily focused on sexual practices and identities rather than sex/gender per se. This is, of course, not an easy division to make, and there are times when I cross this divide. In the choice of topics that I focus upon, I have sought to ensure diversity, but the primary factor underpinning decisions about inclusion or exclusion stem from my determination about what is most important for the argument I am making. That said, I aim to be mindful of the historical tendency for particular categories of person to be excluded. For instance, I am acutely aware of the fact that the sexual practices of women have been traditionally ignored in academic theory (see, e.g., Doyal et al., 1994; Wilton, 1997, for early powerful interventions regarding women's exclusion from HIV/AIDS scholarship).

I try not to fall into the same trap. In discussions that follow about sexually diverse folk I focus on male and female experience. Furthermore, I also tackle recent debates around trans rights and gender critical feminism. This is obviously a debate very much centred on sex/gender rather than sex or sexuality per se, which is why the approach I take is limited to discussion of a politics of critique that is detached from tradition. When it comes to race/ethnicity, there has been a traditional bifurcation in which Black and Brown bodies are excluded, subsumed within White theorization, or otherwise brought into focus only in spectacular form (see, e.g., Cruz, 2016a, 2016b). This is a point that I seek to address directly in this book when I focus on how the 'downlow' has been conceptualized and in reflection upon the presence/absence of raced bodies in ostensibly radical and/or progressive sexual movements such as BDSM and polyamory.

Finally, I should note that this book is focused on adult consensual sexual practices and identities rather than acts of sexual violence or childhood sexuality. That said, I do approach nonconsensual sex through a critical analysis of the dangers of emancipatory language being—in my opinion—misappropriated in the context of 'minor-attracted persons'. This blurring of boundaries between consensual and nonconsensual, even within a framework that claims such desires are not acted upon, is deeply troubling and something I must address, even if my primary concern is with those sexual acts that fall as clearly, as any can do, within the boundary of consensual adult sexual practice. I find it problematic to see scholars deploy hard-fought-for emancipatory language (and politics) to defend and justify work with people who would like to have sexual relationships with minors or otherwise desire nonconsensual sex, regardless of their motivations. This marks the outer limit of citizenship where I think critique has become most dangerously detached from tradition.

Outline of the book

This book is a book of three parts. The first part (Chapters 1, 2, and 3) provides a detailed description of the theoretical underpinning for the substantive analysis that follows. The second part comprises three chapters (Chapters 4, 5, and 6) in which I explore the nature of contemporary sexual citizenship across a wide array of topics. The three chapters in this second section are designed to illuminate and exemplify my argument about the dangers of unfettered critique. I end the book with a final part in the form of a single final Chapter 7, in which I seek to develop my theoretical analysis further. I also look forward in this final chapter by outlining a positive strategy for how we might better frame our politics for the future.

In Chapter 2 I introduce the fundamentals of citizenship studies, moving from the foundational work of Marshall through to contemporary developments in feminist, queer, and postmodern theories. This includes consideration of work on activist citizenship by Engin Isin and ingenious citizenship by Charles Lee. Herein, I follow Ruth Lister and her arguments about citizenship as a 'momentum concept' that is useful for those of us in the social sciences interested in effecting sociopolitical change. The focus in this book is on sexual citizenship, in particular, and the ways in which the limits of belonging, as it pertains to sexual identities and practices, may be pushed and policed. My interest is in using (sexual) citizenship as a concept to facilitate discussion of stories of tradition and critique.

This chapter introduces the notion of sexual citizenship within the broader context of debates about the particular and universal in political theory. Citizenship in its most usual form, as political status within a polity, has been challenged by the growth of varieties of identity politics, particularly feminism. The particular as difference matters here as women's experiences have been—and continue to be—erased from the masculine public sphere of politics, hence the need for a feminist citizenship studies that properly accounts for this erasure. This work further inspired others, notably David Evans, to theorize sex and sexuality through a complementary focus on the particular experience of lesbian and gay identities. The tension between the universal and particular continues to be a challenge in political theory, with repeated attempts to articulate solutions. I conclude this chapter with some of my own thoughts about this tension, albeit reframed through Ricoeur as a debate between tradition and critique, and how a dialectical solution holding tradition

INTRODUCTION 27

and critique together within the social imaginary of political discourse may provide a valuable 'middle-way'.

These arguments about citizenship are followed in Chapter 3 with a discussion of the turn to narrative in the social sciences and, in particular, the narrative framework for understanding the social world espoused by the hermeneutic philosopher Paul Ricoeur. Key to the argument being prosecuted in this text is that in order to understand the boundaries of citizenship, we need to critically examine the narratives that underpin nascent and established claims for citizenship. That is, unlike some contemporary developments in citizenship studies that focus on what are effectively stand-alone events, and which are at risk of crystallizing contemporary politics into a dehumanized political present, the present analysis seeks to understand the contested nature of citizenship through the interplay of narratives being recounted by key 'actors' in a network or represented through key 'moments' or 'events'. To this end, this chapter introduces both the theoretical and empirical basis of narrative perspectives on sexual life within the social sciences.

The chapter begins by outlining and discussing Ricoeur's extensive theory about narrative. Ricoeur's philosophical work offers one of the most significant theoretical resources for understanding narrative and, most particularly, the turn to narrative within the social sciences. I discuss the importance of metaphor as semantic innovation, something shared with narrative, and how this semantic innovation within narrative comes about through the use of emplotment. This allows me to discuss the way that emplotment involves bringing together individual episodes of experience into some sense of a coherent whole. I also discuss the Ricoeurean idea that identity itself is brought into being through the narratives we create for ourselves as our 'narrative identity', a psychosocial concept offering a radical way of conceptualizing subjectivity.

Following this theoretical discussion, I move on to explore work in the social sciences concerned with narrative more generally and arguments therein about the need for the social sciences to give up any attempt to model themselves on the natural sciences. The arguments from Bruner, Sarbin, Polkinghorne, and others is that a narrative position, with its attendant theory and methodology, is the most appropriate way to make sense of human experience as a whole. Finally, I move on to discuss work on sexual stories and focus, in particular, on the seminal work of Ken Plummer. This work brings together theoretical and empirical understanding, with Plummer arguing that we are living in an age of new sexual stories that are not

28 SEXUAL CITIZENSHIP AND SOCIAL CHANGE

merely the production of individual storytellers but rely on coaxers, coercers, consumers, readers, and audiences. As such, sexual stories have their time and emerge within the 'social imaginary' of stories (Ricoeur, 1981), when the right combination of individual storytellers, coaxers/coercers, and receptive social world come together. This insight resonates throughout this book as an important way to understand sexual stories relating to claims for citizenship that engage states and wider publics. I finish this chapter by bringing ideas from Ricoeur about ideology and utopia, tradition and critique together with those about narrative. This section provides the theoretical basis for my argument that we need tradition and critique within a dialectic.

The three chapters of the second section of the book contain the substantive investigations into sexual citizenship that are designed to evidence and ground the theoretical argument I am advancing about tradition and critique. The three chapters each address a different problem regarding the dangers of unfettered critique. These cover the variety of ways that, I argue, critique can go awry. I begin in Chapter 4 with how critique can become dangerously detached from tradition, both where critique is forgotten and where it seeks to silence the other. The substantive concerns here are a series of school protests in the United Kingdom opposed to diversity education and the debate/fight between (some) trans activists and their allies and gender critical feminists. In Chapter 5 I highlight how critique may become distorted into something more akin to tradition as minority communities reproduce the language of their oppressors. To this end, I focus on the appropriation of a therapeutic narrative within BDSM communities and the tendency within polyamorous communities to embrace a discourse of love and eschew any association with sex. Chapter 6 involves critical examination of critique that—I argue— engages the spectacular, seemingly more in the service of theory than the lives of those it concerns. The substantive focus here is first on the 'down low', where we see ostensibly well-intentioned public health professionals embracing a racist discourse without empirical support. The second topic concerns how 'barebacking' and other 'spectacular' sexual practices have been deployed by queer theorists and others with insufficient focus on the lives of those implicated in such analysis. Finally, in this chapter I discuss the dangers of scholarship and activism concerned with what has recently been termed 'minor-attracted persons'.

In the final section and chapter of the book, I draw on ideas from Paul Ricoeur to help make sense of present problems. I also look to the future and outline a set of principles and practices, drawn again from Ricoeur's political philosophy, for how I think we might create a better sexual politics. Given that my argument is that we need to move beyond a reliance on critique only, I feel obliged to attempt, even in only some small way, to provide a normative ethical framework for the future. I argue that we need to move away from a pernicious 'either-or' politics and recognize the value of tradition *and* critique. I also highlight some potential dangers with an unfettered utopian politics, detached from 'real politics' (Geuss, 2008) and the ideological ground of everyday life for many people. Finally, I suggest that we might best engage with otherness—and envision a more productive sexual politics—by drawing on the model of translation and linguistic hospitality that Ricoeur outlined late in his career.

2
On sexual citizenship

Citizenship remains a contested term but traditionally concerns the ways in which persons may belong to and participate in a group or community with consequent rights and responsibilities. Over the last 30 years or so this concept has grown to become one of the central means by which political scientists, sociologists, and, most recently, psychologists interrogate the terms of membership of state and society more generally. It is also central to the change discussed in the previous chapter regarding greater acceptance of sexual diversity. Sexual minority communities have engaged in hard-fought-for rights claims over many years to gain greater acceptance and equality. After Hoffman (2004), Lister (2008: 48) argues that citizenship might be best thought of as a 'momentum concept' that can be repeatedly reworked to reveal additional layers offering greater egalitarian promise and, as such, may 'provide tools for marginalized groups struggling for social justice'.

One of the major changes in citizenship studies in recent years has been the gradual erosion of the more traditional state-centric models of citizenship, as scholars have sought to understand citizenship much more broadly (Nyers, 2008). Writing in 1999, Isin and Wood defined citizenship 'as both a set of practices (cultural, symbolic and economic) and a bundle of rights and duties (civil, political and social) that define an individual's membership in a polity' (p. 4). This move to recognize citizenship as both status (the usual focus) and practice has resulted in the concept of citizenship being pushed and pulled in many different directions, rife with theoretical difficulties but arguably still an important way of critically examining the boundaries of societal belonging.

In this section, I outline some of the fundamentals of citizenship studies for the reader new to this topic, examine the relationship with identity (another contested 'momentum concept'), and discuss more radical understandings of citizenship, particularly the notion of sexual citizenship that is at the heart of this work. The first section provides an overview of traditional theories of citizenship that seek to provide theories with universal application and so are ostensibly neutral to difference on the basis of abstract principles, whilst the

Sexual Citizenship and Social Change. Darren Langdridge, Oxford University Press. © Oxford University Press 2024.
DOI: 10.1093/oso/9780199926312.003.0002

second section provides an account of theories that attend to the particular. The tension between universal and particular is central to many debates in citizenship theory and is at the heart of the distinction between liberalism and communitarianism that is discussed below, along with the growth of difference-centred models of citizenship forged on the basis of community identity claims.

Theories of citizenship

The generally agreed-upon foundation of modern citizenship studies is the work of T. H. Marshall, notably his 1950 essay *Citizenship and Social Class*. His work has been extensively discussed and the subject of considerable critical commentary, which I will not reiterate here (see Isin & Wood, 1999, for a good account). What Marshall did was to formulate a historical typology of citizenship, exploring its relationship with class inequality. In his terms, citizenship is defined as the status given to all those who are full members of a community. Status and the rights that accompany it are gained through meeting the obligations of society, whether this is through voting or upholding the laws of the land. Citizenship in these terms comprises three sets of rights: legal, political, and welfare. Critics have focussed on its perceived universalism and the dangers of marginalization, notably through the way it excludes those who do not qualify as a citizen in any given state, that follow from his account failing to provide the means to account for difference (Plummer, 2003; Richardson, 1998, 2017). Given that much contemporary social theory seeks to work with difference—through analyses of gender, ethnicity, disability, sexuality etc.—and not just class, the civic liberal model of Marshall struggles to accommodate such difference-centred moves. The growth of identity-based claims to rights, in particular, pose a very real challenge to the Marshallian model, especially if one agrees with the linking of citizenship to identity (Isin & Wood, 1999) and the expansion of citizenship beyond rights and duties to include cultural, symbolic, and economic practices.

Three main perspectives on citizenship have been broadly identified in the extant literature: liberalism, communitarianism, and civic republicanism (Isin & Wood, 1999; Isin & Turner, 2002; Plummer, 2003). These distinctions are not hard and fast, with a number of key scholars either denying that they belong to a particular tradition or conducting work that

32 SEXUAL CITIZENSHIP AND SOCIAL CHANGE

does not easily fit into any one category. Isin and Wood (1999: 7) suggest that these perspectives might better be understood as 'ideal types' but with this distinction remaining a useful way of mapping out the terrain of much traditional work in citizenship studies. All three perspectives in their different ways seek to resolve the tension between universalism and particularism that underpins theoretical debates about citizenship.

Liberalism concerns the tradition in which individual rights, within the rule of law, act as the key marker of citizenship, with the state charged with preserving individual liberty and equality. Marshall's work can be located within this perspective with its emphasis on rights and obligations within a particular state. Classic liberal theories seek to protect individual freedom from intrusion rather than act proactively to promote freedom for groups that might otherwise be excluded. There is an ethical primacy to the individual as a universal ideal that involves their protection from social collectivism. That is, there is an a priori assumption of the equality of citizens that, as critics have argued (see Ellison, 1997), obscures differences in the capacity to participate as a member of the polity.

Communitarianism can be defined in opposition to liberal philosophy, as found for instance in John Rawls's (1971) *A Theory of Justice*. Communitarian philosophy is primarily concerned with positive rights, such as a right to a free education, and is staunchly critical of the atomistic subject at the heart of liberalism. There is a belief that with the perceived collapse of civil society, in large part as a consequence of the individualism at the centre of liberalism, governments should act to facilitate the growth of social capital (Putnam, 1995, 2000) and structures supportive of community cohesion. A common criticism of communitarianism concerns the way that the focus on positive rights violates the liberal principle of the protection of negative rights. For instance, insisting on universal health care violates the protection of individual property rights by requiring contribution to universal health care through taxation. Communitarians might respond by arguing that no rights exist prior to society and that everyone therefore has an obligation to contribute to society. While the liberal model does not require an active citizen, communitarianism demands at least a minimal level of participation for citizenship.

Civic republicanism stands apart from both liberalism and communitarianism through an attempt to recognize freedom within the context of mutual interdependence between persons (Honohan, 2002). As an older tradition than liberalism, civic republicanism derives from a long history of Western political thought concerned with the way in which freedom is related to active participation in self-government for the common good. The focus on the common good distinguishes civic republicanism from liberal theories whilst seeking to resist the homogenizing effects at risk in communitarianism. That is, the argument from civic republicans is that liberalism fails to appreciate the importance of the common good, particularly as it involves tensions between the public and private, whilst communitarianism results in too much authority being attached to existing social relationships in defining the common good. What is implied with civic republicanism, however, is that whilst individual freedom is preserved, there is also a 'civic identity' shared by all citizens in pursuit of the common good (Beiner, 1995). Whilst this may initially appear an acceptable compromise between the competing demands of liberalism and communitarianism, Isin and Wood (1999: 9) highlight the problem with civic republicanism thus: 'it assumes a unitary and singular conception of the political community . . . to claim that we all share a civic identity is inadequate to deal with deeply sustained forms of oppression and discrimination in society.' That is, increasingly we are seeing individuals and groups making claims to rights and recognition that are not necessarily tied to the common good, however that might be conceived, and it is here where civic republicanism may fail to meet the needs of the polity.

A series of alternative models of citizenship to the three above have emerged more recently that do not seek to resolve the tension between the universal and particular but instead recognize this tension as constitutive of the democratic process itself. Pluralist, poststructuralist, and postmodern approaches to citizenship that are focussed on the notion of difference have proliferated in recent years, offering a radical challenge to traditional perspectives (Mouffe, 1993; Phillips, 1991; Young, 1989). Key to these approaches is a challenge to the notion of a unitary subject and move towards recognition of subject positions within the context of debates about citizenship. These radical approaches undermine the need within liberalism for a self-regarding individual and the need within civic republicanism for a general commitment to the common good. Instead, there is a process of identification in which democratic demands emerge from different subject positions and identifications, whether these are grounded in common interests relating to gender, ethnicity, sexuality, or any other possible identification. Citizenship in these terms is therefore 'an articulating principle that affects the different subject positions of the social agent . . . while allowing for a plurality of specific allegiances and for the respect of individual liberty' (Mouffe, 1992: 237).

34 SEXUAL CITIZENSHIP AND SOCIAL CHANGE

The challenge for such postmodern positions on citizenship concerns the place of identities, the material-semiotic conditions surrounding them, and their role in rights claims to citizenship. That is, we see the dissolution of identity with a postmodern turn and the consequent loss of the potential power of identity claims. As I have discussed previously in the context of sadomasochism and citizenship (Langdridge, 2006), there remains power in identity claims that are endangered with such postmodern turns, power that comes from people uniting around a common cause that draws directly on their (arguably mythical but still psychologically significant) common history of oppression. Whilst postmodern conceptions may prevail in academia, in much practical politics identity claims prove a useful way of people on the margins engaging with the centre, where such understandings remain dominant. Lesbian and gay rights claims have tended to focus on lesbian and gay identities being core and coherent, equivalent to taken-for-granted heterosexual identities, and achieved considerable success and wider acceptance as a result. More diffuse arguments regarding, for instance, a desire to queer all sexualities—heterosexuality included—will likely struggle in comparison. That said, they may still serve a valuable role as disruptive acts of citizenship. As Grosz (1995: 56) states with reference to struggles in feminist theory:

> It is no longer a matter of maintaining a theoretical purity at the cost of political principles, nor is it simply a matter of the ad hoc adoption of theoretical principles according to momentary needs or whims. It is a question of negotiating a path between always impure positions—seeing that politics is always already bound up with what it contests (including theories)—and that theories are always implicated in political struggles (whether this is acknowledged or not).

Acts of citizenship

In an attempt to move beyond existing tensions concerning work on citizenship and as part of a project to reorient the entire field of study, Engin Isin proposes that we should focus on 'acts of citizenship' as the event through which subjects constitute themselves as citizens (Isin & Nielsen, 2008). This work is significant for shifting our understanding of the relationship between individuals, groups, and polities and aims to move beyond the citizen *as individual* as the object of study for citizenship studies. Isin and Nielsen (2008: 2) seek to recognize citizenship as both status and practice that is reducible to neither and 'to shift focus from the institution of citizenship and the citizen as individual agent to acts of citizenship—that is, collective or individual deeds that rupture social-historical patterns'. To this end, citizenship is reconceived from passive activities and repetition, such as voting, to attempts to engage in 'a political mediation between two sides of answerability that include the requirement to respond to challenges with a creative and unique performance that can claim no alibi, yet also defend an idea that is immanent rather than transcendent'. This approach concerns the moments when individuals and collectives find new ways of opening up the political, breaking from tradition in response to the failure of current modes of conduct within the social-political sphere. This is a radical project that takes the distinction between formal and substantive citizenship forward to ask questions of how subjects become claimants. Whilst recognizing that existing models within citizenship studies have enabled better understanding of how citizenship evolves over time, Isin (2008: 17) argues that there is little understanding of how 'subjects become claimants when they are least expected or anticipated to do so'. Even amongst relatively well-established social movements there have been turning points involving rapid change to established rights and wider public acknowledgement. From peaceful acts of civil rights resistance to innovative acts of challenge, the histories of social movements have invariably involved creative moments that rupture the status quo. Sexual citizenship, for instance, has involved formal claims for rights based on core identities alongside an array of acts of resistance and disruption. These acts have been—and continue to be—innovative and extensive, involving anything from drag performance to the public presentation of queer acts of relating and much more besides.

Through a sophisticated theoretical analysis, drawing on figures such as Bakhtin, Heidegger, and Levinas, Isin (2008) develops an ontology of acts that forms the foundation for the focus on acts of citizenship. The outcome of this analysis is three principles for the investigation of acts of citizenship (2008: 38–39):

1. Interpret them through their grounds and consequences, which includes subjects becoming activist citizens through scenes created
2. Recognition that acts produce actors that become answerable to justice against injustice

36 SEXUAL CITIZENSHIP AND SOCIAL CHANGE

3. Recognition that acts of citizenship do not need to be founded in law or enacted in the name of the law

There is a move here to explore and understand those moments in which acts constitute new activist citizens asserting rights and obligations, with such citizens newly emerging through these self-same actions and reactions.

> We define acts of citizenship as those acts that transform forms (orientations, strategies, technologies) and modes (citizens, strangers, outsiders, aliens) of being political by bringing into being new actors as activist citizens (claimants of rights and responsibilities) through creating new sites and scales of struggle. (Isin, 2008: 39)

Whilst I believe the notion of 'acts of citizenship' offers up a radical new framework for citizenship to better understand moments of change in which subjects constitute themselves as citizens, there remains a psychologically inadequate theorization of identity here, as elsewhere within citizenship studies. It is this lack that I believe may be best fleshed out using the hermeneutic philosophy of Ricoeur. That is, Ricoeur's notion of narrative identity provides a way of incorporating episodes of experience (that may include acts of citizenship) with a sense of personal continuity. So, for instance, a person's identity as lesbian, gay, or bisexual may often be understood through a series of episodes of experience that together represent their 'formal' identity, some of which may also involve acts of citizenship. Coming out is a good example, where the public declaration of a hitherto private experience serves as an act of citizenship in which the storyteller constitutes themself in these moments as a citizen demanding recognition and rights.

Furthermore, whilst the move towards acts of citizenship marks an important and radical shift forwards in citizenship studies—that is both theoretically grounded and practically useful—the focus on acts that rupture the social fabric may neglect the relationship between these and historical and cultural tradition. Ricoeur's attempt to locate ideology and utopia within a single theoretical framework serves to provide a way of locating acts of citizenship as utopian activities, creative moments of rupture (White, 2008) that are dialectically related to tradition through pre-existing ideological stances. In the substantive chapters that follow this theoretical introduction, I examine acts of citizenship but also seek to locate these acts within broader historically and culturally located narrative traditions. This includes, for instance, analysis of the clash of rights that emerges between school protesters acting to claim religious rights within the public sphere and teachers seeking to enact a liberal sex education, or the tension that emerges between activists seeking to enact a radical gender politics and those arguing for a more traditional biological understanding of sex. That is, I recognize acts of citizenship that bring new activist citizens into being as utopian moments against the backdrop of extant ideological traditions, within Ricoeur's framework of ideology and utopia as dialectic.

Ingenious citizenship

A further theoretical development of note, that is also in the spirit of Isin's work on acts of citizenship, concerns Lee's (2016) concept of *ingenious citizenship*. Lee explores citizenship in relation to a variety of 'abject' folk, from migrant domestic workers to suicide bombers, and seeks to identify the ways that subversive acts may constitute an innovative nondemocratic political act. It is valuable to situate the present work in relation to Lee's (2016) arguments about ingenious citizenship given his similar focus on thinking through the boundaries of citizenship, albeit in the context of a project that is not specifically focused on sexual citizenship. I pick up on the abject myself when I discuss spectacular critique in Chapter 6. There is considerable merit in Lee's arguments about the need to engage with the notion of ingenious citizenship and practices outwith traditional democratic politics. It is certainly true that citizenship needs to be understood beyond formal democratic processes and that it is vital we pay heed to ingenious practices that invoke citizenship in its various forms. But his is—at times—a rather negative and violent thesis that would arguably benefit by being rethought through the inherently more generous lens of Ricoeur's political philosophy.

The problematic at stake here is not about the fact that 'both sides contain their own insufficiencies' (Lee, 2016: 28) or that we require a 'methodological shift to decenter political philosophers and theorists and recenter an eclectic assemblage of abject subjects . . . as **resources** for a critical reinterpretation of political agency, citizenship practices, and social transformation' (p. 23), as Lee argues. Rather, it is about the fact that there is often merit to both positions and that people's everyday (antidemocratic) practices may provide us with valuable insights into how citizenship is being constructed through everyday actions. Lee adopts a rather combative strategy that even draws

38 SEXUAL CITIZENSHIP AND SOCIAL CHANGE

upon the thought of the kung fu legend Bruce Lee at one point. I think we will likely have greater success if we engage in a politics of recognition rather than one of conflict and violent struggle. That is, I think Lee is right that we need to recognize ingenious citizenship, but I'd suggest we build on the notion of recognition through feminist philosophy (Fraser, 2001) rather than revel in the ingenious but destructive politics that Lee (sometimes) seems to avow. This is then not a complete abandonment of formal politics—or 'politics without politics' in Lee's terms—but a case of expanding the terrain of politics to include those that are currently excluded such that we attend to their needs as we recognize their humanity.

Lee further falls afoul of the binary logic that sets formal politics against ingenious acts of citizenship when discussing the concept of critical contextualization. He argues that it may be necessary to abandon democratic politics and instead engage in 'ingenious' acts 'in order to achieve a de facto actualization of humane life for the abject in concrete situations' (Lee, 2016: 29). Why? Surely, the abject can continue to articulate a democratic claim to rights whilst also engaging in ingenious acts of citizenship. Why must it be either/or rather than both/and? Such claims may or may not have legitimacy, of course. There are boundaries to acceptability and permissibility concerning citizenship for good reasons, as well as bad. Ricoeur's theorization of ideology and utopia, which provides the theoretical foundation for this book, offers insight into how we might rethink the place of ingenious acts as part of the broader social imaginary—the web of stories—into which we are all thrown, where there is space for tradition (in the form of democratic politics and claims for rights) and critique (in the form of ingenious—utopian or even dystopian—acts that may effect social change with no attendant claim for rights).

One of the central aspects of this book is a positive approach—in the spirit of Ricoeur—to engaging with contemporary sexual politics. That is, in contrast to much contemporary writing on sexual politics, particularly that which draws upon contemporary critical theories, I do not seek to simply bemoan or criticize the neoliberal times we live in without paying due awareness to the positive elements of the political world that we inhabit. The Ricoeurean focus on tradition and critique—ideology and utopia—is concerned with identifying the good in ostensibly opposed positions, not the bad in everything that is currently present in the social imaginary. This does not mean we avoid critique, not at all, but rather that in the process of engaging in critique we do not throw the baby out with the bathwater in our own attempt to manifest our ideas in a blaze of glory upon the stage of academic life (or activism).

Too much critical theory is inherently destructive and engaged in an endless process of undermining what went before, very much in the spirit of most of the continental philosophy that provides the theoretical underpinning for the work. It appears that unless we proclaim the awfulness of the liberal state in Western democracies, and all that is associated with it, we are not radical enough, not critical enough, and not progressive enough. A hegemonic mode of politics has developed—somewhat ironically—in academic, and increasingly also activist, writing, in which there is no space for hope, engagement, or compromise (Goodwin, 2023; Pabst, 2021). The reality is, of course, that progress happens through engagement and sometimes argument but rarely simply the latter. Ricoeur's philosophy is founded on hope, and it is only through hope that I believe we can effect change and conjure up a better world for all. Hope provides space for recognizing the value of ingenious acts of citizenship, but crucially it also provides the motivational impetus to engage with the centre, with the mainstream of contemporary political life, in order to effect change.

Lee does recognize the need for positive engagement with liberal democracy despite the sometimes rather negative presentation of his case about the value of ingenious citizenship. For instance, he cites Ferguson (2006), who argues that the flows of global capital more often step over rather than manipulate Africa for gain, with Africans' themselves wanting to engage with global capitalism in the hope of enhancing their ways of life rather than being abused by its dehumanizing effects. Lee (2016) acknowledges the messiness and tension that is inherent in politics—it's 'fragility' in Ricoeur's terms—as he states: 'I also wish to emphasize that the messy webs of complicity and contamination do not spell doom or futility; rather, they formulate the instrumental conduits to create circuitous and nonlinear processes of social change' (p. 43). This is a positive vision and I think the best way to deploy the notion of ingenious citizenship. It is not a necessarily oppositional concept but can instead be a valuable way of thinking about those acts outwith democratic processes that may enact citizenship in (sometimes powerful) ways that may contribute to sociopolitical change.

40 SEXUAL CITIZENSHIP AND SOCIAL CHANGE

Citizenship and 'the particular'

Identity

Identity is a highly contested concept in the social sciences, for many years occupying an antithetical position to citizenship. Citizenship has traditionally been concerned with the universal and identity with the particular (Isin & Wood, 1999). However, with the growth of new social movements and rights-based claims based on affiliations around particular identities, the two have come together within the same social theoretical terrain. That is, claims to rights—and the consequent obligations that follow—have increasingly been mobilized around particular identities, and questions of identities have become a central issue for citizenship studies, as much as the broader social sciences. The expansion of the notion of citizenship beyond the state to include wider acknowledgement also places issues of identities more centre stage in contemporary discussions of belonging. From the claims of women to Black and ethnic minorities to lesbians, gays, bisexuals, and trans folk—to name just a few—there has been a shift towards a cultural politics of inclusion in which citizenship status concerns much more than simply legal rights (Isin & Wood, 1999): wider social acknowledgement is as important as equality before the law. As Plummer (2003, p. 59) states:

> Now, to speak of citizenship usually also implies an identity—a person, a voice, a recognised type, a locus, a position, a subjectivity—from which the claim of citizenship can be made. And such identities bring with them pasts, presents, and futures: a sense of our past histories, a defining 'other' different from us, and hints for future conduct based in part on this 'otherness'.

Within the social sciences there is continuing tension between essentialist and constructionist perspectives on identity. A great deal of work within the social sciences has treated identity as a relatively unproblematic expression of a person's sense of selfhood or group belonging. This has, however, been the subject of considerable criticism, with critical challenges from a variety of different theoretical perspectives, perhaps the strongest being those informed by postmodern philosophy and the move to embrace the notion of discourse as constitutive of meaning. Fundamentally, debates about identity concern sameness and difference or continuity and change within/across selfhood and social belonging. This tension is further complicated by the many different positions taken by those critical of essentialist understandings of identity. There is not one critical perspective but myriad, all drawing on different philosophical traditions to evince their case. In spite of the contested nature of identity, Hall (1996) maintains that it remains a useful concept for the social sciences, operating as a concept that is 'good to think with' and for which there is no better alternative: in Hoffman's (2004) terms, another 'momentum concept'.

Wetherell (2010) delineates three traditions of work on identity: identity as subjective individual achievement, social identity as group membership, and ethical and political aspects of identity. This categorization is—as any must be—a rough and ready way of understanding the terrain since there is a continual and necessary interplay between all three traditions, something I believe is particularly important for work in contemporary citizenship studies. Subjective individual achievement is familiar territory to most psychologists, and quite a few sociologists, with a focus on a personal sense of selfhood or identity. Whilst psychology has traditionally adopted a rather limited stance on personal identity, this tradition has expanded considerably, with work now much more often engaged with the psychosocial. Such psychosocial work seeks to bridge the artificial gap between the psychological and social through a variety of theoretical avenues, from psychoanalysis through phenomenology to narrative/discursive analyses. Many of these developments produce knowledge in which identity is no longer limited to essentialist understandings but inflected with the flavour of poststructuralist and postmodern philosophies. As Wetherell (2010: 4) states: 'Personal and subjectively felt identities are no longer studied as solipsistic, solitary and static individual achievements but have become seen as mobile, flexibly negotiated, practically oriented and jointly accomplished with others'. In many ways, this tradition of research has not been fully realized within citizenship studies, with the focus more clearly on the second two traditions in Wetherell's categorization.

Identity as group membership and ethical and political aspects of identity have been dominated by sociology and the political sciences, with the social much more strongly foregrounded than the individual. Within the category of identity as group membership the focus has been on questions of marginalization, exclusion, and segregation, with the study of social categories (woman, Black, gay) central to this work. Significant and sustained work has been conducted from feminist, queer, and postcolonial perspectives, to name just three. Work on ethical and political aspects of identity emerged

42   SEXUAL CITIZENSHIP AND SOCIAL CHANGE

from the civil rights movements of the 1960s and provides a clear link between academic analysis and activism. Here, issues of collective action, social movements, inequalities, and rights are centre stage. The field of identity studies cuts across disciplinary boundaries and is now a vast enterprise with considerable disagreement about the object of study and can therefore only be touched upon here in the specific context of citizenship and identity. That is, in Wetherell's words (2010: 4):

> The variety of often contradictory directions in identity studies, the heavy-duty reflexivity identity requires, scholarly unease about the significations and etymology of 'identity', and anxieties over definition and boundaries, mean that identity studies constitute a field of great theoretical and methodological complexity—a site of continuous unsettled argument. But, truly, would we have it any other way?

In the following chapter, I discuss Ricoeur's understanding of identity, one that is constructed through the stories we tell of ourselves, and argue that this provides us with a perspective that is reflective of the power of the social world to shape our sense of selfhood without abandoning the self—and particularly personal agency—entirely to social forces. Identity within this theoretical framework is both psychological and social, with space for understanding the impact of the social world on the capacity to make sense of episodes of experience through their narrative reconstruction. Further, this approach to identity is notable for the way in which it recognizes the personal need for a sense of continuity whilst resisting any essentialist reduction to inherent aspects of selfhood.

Feminist citizenship

Feminist social and political theorists have highlighted the ways that women have been systematically excluded from both the theory and practice of citizenship (Lister, 2003; Richardson, 2000b). Whilst citizenship may not on the surface appear to be a gendered concept, there is a long history of women's exclusion from both formal and substantive citizenship. This operates at multiple levels, from the most obvious and explicit historical exclusion of women from property ownership and voting, for instance, to more subtle acts of exclusion grounded in the gendered nature of theories of citizenship themselves. For instance, it was not until the mid to late 19th century in both the United Kingdom and United States that women were recognized in law as independent individuals, subject as they were to the coverture of their husband. Prior to these—hard-fought-for—legal changes, a woman would need the permission of her husband to purchase property or engage in any other contract, two elements central to the male-centred understandings of citizenship at that time. Coverture extended beyond control of contracts to control of a woman's body, with a husband having conjugal rights to his wife's body, a practice that continues in some countries even to this day. Vogel (1988, 1994) has highlighted the historical impact of married women's exclusion from the rights and duties of civil society in the form of a persistent image of women being unable to participate in citizenship fully. Even today in Western democracies the numbers of women at the higher echelons of power—whether this is in the political, legal, or business arenas—remains astonishingly low, with a pernicious and enduring perception concerning the suitability of these kinds of activities for women.

For some theorists, women's exclusion from citizenship appears to be nothing more than a historical aberration that is easily remedied by simply extending existing male rights to women. However, women's exclusion is not a simple historical artefact, not only because in many countries women remain disenfranchised, but also because the very foundations of citizenship themselves are gendered. One of the major contributions of feminist studies to citizenship has been to highlight how the model of the person underpinning contemporary liberal and civic republican notions of citizenship is in fact 'aggressively male' (Lister, 2003). Both liberal and republican models of citizenship require the subjugation of women (through coverture and labour within the private sphere, respectively) to produce the model (male) citizen engaged in the protection of others (extending to the ownership of other human beings) and/or active participation in the public sphere. As Lister (2003: 71) sums it up rather beautifully: 'The weave of the epistemological cloak, which has both hidden the man lurking behind the gender-neutral citizen and rendered invisible woman's absence, is so tight that it is difficult to disentangle the separate threads out of which it is fabricated.' However, central to the systematic exclusion of women from citizenship are two elements: (a) the distinction between the public and private and (b) the model of the citizen as abstract and disembodied. The 'private' has, of course, traditionally been the domain of women—and still is to a very great degree— and it is here where the qualities and activities deemed incompatible with

44   SEXUAL CITIZENSHIP AND SOCIAL CHANGE

citizenship are relegated. The citizen has been—and to some extent continues to be—the active, heroic 'warrior' of the public sphere. Furthermore, by assuming an abstract and disembodied citizen, through the refusal of particularity in liberalism or its transcendence in civic republicanism, there is a continual erasure of sex and gender (and also ethnicity, sexuality, disability, etc.). Whilst this abstract and disembodied citizen is ostensibly open to all, whether male or female:

> Feminist theorists have exposed the way in which abstraction has served to hide the essentially male characteristics of the individual *qua* citizen. Thus the qualities of impartiality, rationality, independence and political agency, which the citizen is expected to demonstrate, turn out to be male qualities in the binary thinking that informs traditional citizenship theory. In a classic double bind, women are banished to the private realm of the family, either physically or figuratively, because they do not display such qualities and because of their association with that realm, they are deemed incapable of developing them. (Lister, 2003: 71–72)

Issues of embodiment are also significant in the exclusion of women (and also many others) from citizenship. Key here is not simply the notion that women have 'weak' bodies but also the very identification of women with 'the body'. Men and masculinities have long been associated with the 'overcoming of embodiment', a necessary fiction to support the idea of male power/strength and to subjugate 'the power of the feminine'. Women have been distinguished from the transcendent (disembodied) male through being perceived as emotional, sexual, and, most significantly, the bearer of children. The body and all its messy emotional complexity is, consequently, relegated to the private realm, with space in the public sphere limited to the dispassionate, the disinterested, the disembodied. And this is far from historical, as any examination of the political elites in most Western democracies today will testify. There are exceptions, but these are notably exceptional precisely because they do not fit the civic republican model of the abstract—disembodied—warrior citizen leader (see e.g., Deweer, 2013). That said, there is not a single story of feminism or feminist critique, and other lines of feminist theory provide a strong counterpoint to this position (see, e.g., Downing, 2019).

Whilst feminist theory has highlighted the false universalism of the citizen as currently conceived, it has itself come under challenge for the false universalism of the category 'woman'. This has come about as the result of challenges within the feminist movement from Black and other groups of women whose particular identities have been subsumed beneath the veil of the universal 'woman', alongside those working from poststructuralist perspectives, suspicious of any notion of essentialism that might be expressed through stable identities. Black feminists have been particularly significant here in exposing the privileged nature of the White (often middle-class and able-bodied) feminist that has mounted the critique of patriarchy on behalf of all women, ignoring (or even excluding) other lines of oppression, such as those that are the result of race and ethnicity (see, e.g., Collins, 1990; Crenshaw, 1989; Davis, 1981; hooks, 1981, 1984, 1989). Such challenges have been followed by others including lesbians and disabled feminists, with a growing acceptance of the need to acknowledge intersections between gender, ethnicity, disability, sexuality, and so on (Laclau & Mouffe, 1985; Lister, 1997; Monro, 2005; Mouffe, 1993; Phelan, 2001; Richardson, 1998, 2000b; Yuval-Davies, 1997; Yuval-Davies & Werbner, 1999). That is, there has been a move away from universal critical stances (of the notion of a universal citizen) towards recognition of difference (Yeatman, 1993). The danger is, of course, that an incessant deconstructive stance towards the category 'woman' (or any other identity category) may lead to such fragmentation that political action against oppression becomes ineffective and increasingly divisive (Downing, 2019).

Iris Marion Young has produced one of the most important and successfully elaborated feminist interventions that rejects the idea of a unified polity, along with recognition of the need to challenge institutional oppression through a broadly communitarian 'vision of a heterogeneous public that acknowledges and affirms group differences' (Young, 1990: 10). Central to Young's thesis is the rejection of any notion of a unified polity, which inevitably results in a myth of impartiality. That is, any appeal to the universal in politics leads inexorably towards the projection of the position of the privileged onto all others and the effective silencing of difference. Her alternative is to espouse a position where oppressed groups are supported in their self-organization, the generation of policy, and their right of veto to policy that may have a direct impact on their members. However, here too we meet problems, some of which have been recognized by Young herself with her later work. Critics have questioned the perceived essentialism implied by the fixed and stable identities required to articulate a politics of group difference (Phillips, 1991; Mouffe, 1992; Wilson, 1993), with concerns raised about reifying particular identity categories, problems of competing identity groups, and people who may struggle to form coherent political groupings. In

46   SEXUAL CITIZENSHIP AND SOCIAL CHANGE

her later work, Young (2000) addressed some of these concerns, emphasizing that her notion of a politics of difference should not be confused with a politics of identity. That is, identity is not the constitutive component of group formation, with Young stressing the need for flexibility and a relational coming together on the basis of 'social perspective'. So, rather than identity providing the boundaries to group difference, this theory allows for a coalescence of interest based on the different social positioning that people may experience (of which some will undoubtedly be based on identity differences).

Many feminist theorists, whilst acknowledging the contribution of Young's theory, remain unconvinced that it is able to adequately account for fluidity and difference, foreseeing inevitable fragmentation and group struggles when there is competition for limited resources. Lister's (2003) development of 'differentiated universalism' is part of a tradition of feminist citizenship scholarship (see, e.g., Dean, 1996) that attempts to address the problem of the tension between universal and difference-centred models of citizenship somewhat differently. Key to all of these attempts are a version of the political subject that is fluid rather than fixed, able to recognize difference and intersectionality within and across groups; a 'framework agreement' outlining acceptable modes of conduct (Mouffe, 1992, 1993); recognition of the plurality of sites of citizenship (including those outwith traditional citizenship discourse, such as the home); and a commitment to dialogue. These feminist principles (a) provide the foundation for a difference-centred approach to citizenship that is cognisant of the dangers of the crass universalism that erases difference and (b) preserve the aim of seeking universal principles, in terms of moral commitment rather than impartiality (Dean, 1996; Lister, 2002; Young, 1990; Yuval-Davies, 1997). How possible it is to achieve this in practice is, in many ways, an empirical question and one that may become clearer as we see more practical experiments in living citizenship in feminist terms.

Richardson (2000b, 2000c) critically interrogates the notion of citizenship, and sexual citizenship in particular, through lesbian/feminist theory. She recognizes that bringing together sexuality and citizenship is complex and complicated through the respective histories and present-day understandings of these two concepts and spheres of life. Noting the neglect of sexuality in early feminist theorizing of citizenship, Richardson suggests this may be understood through the feminist critique of the public/private divide and how the public/private maps against citizenship and sexuality, respectively. The primarily feminist concern has been about the 'gender-blind' nature of citizenship such that other factors, like sexuality, have been marginalized. Richardson (2000b, 2000c) rightly highlights the challenge and complexity of intersectional thinking in the context of political scholarship and activism. She also highlights the erasure of lesbian citizenship in particular and the danger of a universal sexual citizenship founded on gay male experience. But—Richardson (2000b) argues—even this erasure can be productive, with lesbians not only claiming rights but also acting as radical 'outlaws' such that they might develop unique approaches to citizenship theory and practice. The tension inherent in a notion like sexual citizenship in bringing together the universal and particular (and also public and private) is not easily resolved, nor should it be. Arguably, holding the tension, aware of the respective pressures and limitations, is exactly what makes this concept so dynamically useful and is at the heart of the approach Richardson takes to citizenship (2000a, 2000b, 2000c, 2004, 2017, 2018).

Roseneil (2013), whilst acknowledging the value of this feminist tradition of work, is more cautious about the possibilities for feminist citizenship. Reflecting upon her own past struggles within feminist groups organized, at least in part, along anarchist principles, she highlights the inherent contradiction between state-centric models of citizenship and feminist allegiance with the anarchist critiques of state-centric models of governance. She describes the tension thus:

> Citizenship is a troubling proposition for feminism. Intensely luring in its expansive inclusionary promise, yet inherently rejecting in its restrictive, exclusionary reality, it is an ambivalent object for those of us committed to radical projects of social transformation. . . . Can citizenship transcend the gendered dichotomies on which it has historically rested: between public and private, reason and emotion, the cognitive and the embodied? . . . Might feminism's relation to citizenship be one of 'cruel optimism', in which our desire for citizenship is 'actually an obstacle to [our] flourishing', impeding rather than facilitating our aims (Berlant, 2011: 1)? Should we seek a different language to express our desires to belong, and alternative means to enact our yearnings for equality, justice and reciprocity? (Roseneil, 2013: Chapter 1)

This thematic question that Roseneil uses to frame the edited collection in which it occurs resonates widely. It is of particular relevance to sexual/intimate citizenship and all questions of citizenship in which the boundaries of

48   SEXUAL CITIZENSHIP AND SOCIAL CHANGE

belonging are in question. It is, therefore, an interrogative question of considerable relevance to the present book and the arguments I make herein and will serve to operate as a critical stance that must remain ever present, even if unlikely ever to be resolved.

The sexual/intimate citizen

The early feminist critiques of traditional Marshallian discourses (e.g., Lister, 1990; Philips, 1991; Walby, 1994; Young, 1989) paved the way for critiques based on sexuality, transgender, race, disability, and much more (Laclau & Mouffe, 1985; Lister, 1997; Monro, 2005; Mouffe, 1993; Phelan, 2001; Richardson, 1998, 2000b; Yuval-Davies, 1997; Yuval-Davies & Werbner, 1999). As discussed above, the emphasis with these difference-centred (Moosa-Mitha, 2005) models of citizenship has been on the ways in which markers of difference impact on the experience of citizenship, whether individual or collective, and public acknowledgement of such difference (Phelan, 2001). This has been mostly through an analysis of difference with regard to involvement in the wider public sphere (Hobson & Lister, 2002; Yuval-Davies, 1997; Yuval-Davies and Werbner, 1999).

Since the early 1990s the notion of sexual citizenship has gained widespread currency. The concept was initially employed by Evans (1993) as a way of focusing attention on rights to a range of sexual identities and practices linked to the state and the market. In particular, he sought to explore the commodification of sexuality, an issue remarkably relevant today, albeit now somewhat neglected. With this move to recognize the inherently sexual nature of citizenship, he argued strongly that existing models of citizenship were based on heterosexist patriarchal principles. While this and later work has been important for theoretically framing the debate, it is chiefly through the rights-based claims of lesbian, gay, and bisexual social movements in both the United States and the United Kingdom that the concept has assumed such prominence in recent years. There has been considerable theoretical work around this concept in the light of its central role in the development of such social movements.

Weeks (1998) identifies three aspects of social change that he sees contributing to the development of the sexual citizen: (a) the democratization of relationships, (b) the emergence of new sexual subjectivities, and (c) the development of new sexual stories. It is argued that the democratization of relationships arises in the context of the transformation of intimacy and increasing autonomy within relationships (Giddens, 1992). With this growing sense of autonomy come transgressions of the normative, which provide direct challenges to everyday expectations about sexual subjectivities. Weeks (1998) argues that all new sexual social movements are characterized by two moments: transgression and citizenship. The transgressive moment consists of inventive challenges to institutions and traditions that have sought to exclude this sexual other. These challenges stem principally from the creation of new sexual subjectivities, which transgress the norms of hegemonic patriarchal heterosexuality. However, this challenge is not simply an attack but also a call for recognition and respect and with this a demand for rights. This becomes the second moment of citizenship, a transformation of the other and a new sense of belonging. With belonging comes the other side to citizenship, responsibility, respect, and a new relationship with the wider sexual community. Weeks (1995) argues that both moments are necessary for each other, believing that without the transgressive challenge any call for citizenship is likely to be unheard, but that transgression alone cannot provide the recognition, respect, and rights that provide the impetus for the fight.

Ken Plummer (2001, 2003) has suggested that 'intimate citizenship', rather than sexual or feminist citizenship, may more appropriately act as the sensitizing concept for the analysis of the relationship between the personal and the public. Plummer (2003) suggests that the existing concepts of sexual and feminist citizenship are inadequate for the task since they fail to account for the key demands of the other. That is, sexual citizenship does not sufficiently account for gender, patriarchy, and feminist claims, and feminist citizenship does not sufficiently account for sexuality, heteronormativity, and lesbian, gay, bisexual, trans, and queer claims. This is undoubtedly true, although I believe Plummer (2003) overstates the case somewhat. In place of these concepts Plummer suggests that intimate citizenship recognizes a broader sphere of concerns. Plummer (2001: 243) is quick to recognize the dangers of such global terms and through a critical analysis of Habermas's (1962/1989) notion of the public sphere argues that 'the term "intimate citizenship" must learn to denote a plurality of multiple public voices and positions'.

While Plummer is undoubtedly correct about the limitations of sexual and feminist citizenship, I am not convinced he is correct in his solution. There are considerable dangers in clustering together very different people and practices

50 SEXUAL CITIZENSHIP AND SOCIAL CHANGE

and their attendant claims. Once again, there is a danger of rendering the sexual in sexual citizenship and patriarchy in feminist citizenship as background. As Richardson and Turner (2001: 333) state, 'We need specific sociological studies of the different formations of citizenship in different political and social conditions in order to understand systematic variations in social rights.' And while a global concept of citizenship may not prevent this, it certainly does not encourage it. Richardson and Turner (2001) recognize there is, of course, a danger in the proliferation of 'citizens' and 'citizenships', but the line needs to be drawn in such a way that crucial differences between gender and sexuality are not in danger of being conflated or ignored. Surely, a more sensitive way of dealing with the relative lack apparent in sexual and feminist citizenships is not to collapse these terms and lose what is most essential in both but instead to work with both dialectically, using them as necessary critiques for the other.

And, of course, we must not forget that citizenship is racialized, as well as gendered (Alexander, 1994; Anthias & Yuval-Davies, 1992; Yuval-Davies, 1997; Yuval-Davies & Werbner, 1999). Moreover, Richardson (2017) argues that there needs to be a decentring of the 'Western-centric' approach to sexual citizenship such that sexual citizenship might be more appropriately operationalized in ways suitable for both the Global North and South. She is undoubtedly right about the need for greater awareness of where the concept of citizenship is appropriate or not, and an urgent need to critically interrogate the concept such that its relevance in the Global North is not simply imposed in a normative manner in analyses focused on the Global South. Sabsay (2012, 2016) further articulates this point through a critical psychosocial analysis of liberal notions of citizenship. To this end, she argues for a more performative and relational notion of citizenship in order to escape the individual subject at the heart of the Western liberal project. This is derived theoretically through Butler and an array of continental critical theory. The case to critically interrogate the universal normative framework of citizenship especially in the light of, for example, colonialism is of course perfectly valid. I am, however, less sure that the end point need be one in which the individual liberal subject simply becomes completely erased from citizenship.

Where next for the sexual citizen?

There have been a variety of attempts to develop or transform thinking about sexual citizenship in recent years. Bell and Binnie (2000), for instance,

ON SEXUAL CITIZENSHIP 51

articulate a form of queer sexual citizenship that is much more radically transgressive than that found in Weeks (1998), Giddens (1992), or Plummer (1995, 2001, 2003). Bell and Binnie raise a wide set of concerns about the way in which appeals to sexual citizenship have involved compromise concerning acceptable and unacceptable ways of being a citizen. They recognize the history of such compromise but argue that a rights-based politics of citizenship is inherently marked out by compromise. This, they think, is especially true within the political climate at the time of their writing, which demands 'a modality of sexual citizenship that is privatised, deradicalised, deeroticised and confined in all senses of the word: kept in place, policed, limited' (Bell & Binnie, 2000: 3). But as Stychin (2001) and Cossman (2002: 487) both point out, things are not so clear cut as 'citizenship is never wholly disciplined' and there are often transgressive moments with claims to citizenship and moments of citizenship with acts of transgression.

In my 2006 paper on sexual citizenship, I explore the relationship between sadomasochism and sexual citizenship and, in the process, problematize many aspects of current models of sexual citizenship by highlighting how some practitioners want to foreground the sexual whereas others do not, some want to embrace a core identity whereas others do not, and some want to claim citizenship whereas others do not. This work highlighted what Carl Stychin (2001) refers to as the 'binary logic of citizenship'. However, unlike Stychin, I did not, and still do not, think the answer lies with a wholesale queering of the citizenship project, for this does not fully recognize the power of working with both the core and marginal in these debates. At present there is surely considerable value in working strategically with modernist and postmodernist politics and in particular working with the two moments described by Weeks (1998) of citizenship and transgression. By working with identity politics, we have the opportunity to directly engage with the inside in their own terms, where such conceptualizations dominate. The recent (qualified) successes of lesbian, gay, bisexual, and trans communities, in the West at least, with regard to progressive emancipatory legislative change clearly demonstrate the value of working with the inside. With a wholesale shift away from the dominant position we are likely to fail to engage with the inside and also lose many potential allies along the way. Such a move carries the risk that we lose what is valuable in the identity politics tradition. Elizabeth Grosz (1995) articulates the dilemma very well with regard to feminism and the tensions between feminist theory, and the desire for intellectual rigour, and feminist politics, focused on the liberation of women. Grosz argues that

52   SEXUAL CITIZENSHIP AND SOCIAL CHANGE

the 'criteria of intellectual evaluation' need to be more politicized and the goals of political struggle more theorized. To this end, she draws on Spivak's (1984/1985) notion of concepts as tools and weapons:

> It is no longer a matter of maintaining a theoretical purity at the cost of political principles, nor is it simply a matter of the ad hoc adoption of theoretical principles according to momentary needs or whims. It is a question of negotiating a path between always impure positions—seeing that politics is always already bound up with what it contests (including theories)—and that theories are always implicated in political struggles (whether this is acknowledged or not). (Grosz, 1995: 56)

A perspectival shift is required if we are to move beyond the apparent incommensurability of queer theory and identity politics. Both positions are impure, so the question becomes one in which we ask which strategy, at which time and in which place, is likely to be most effective in enabling us to achieve our political objectives, all the time remaining engaged in a critical reflection on that with which we are engaged. There is also a need to recognize more generally what is valuable in both tradition and critique, that both are needed to temper the worst excesses of the other.

There has, of course, been criticism of Weeks's arguments about the politics of sexual citizenship (Bell & Binnie, 2000), particularly concerning the perceived conservative (assimilationist) move from transgression to citizenship. Gamson (1995), like Grosz (1995) with feminism, recognizes the tensions between the lesbian/gay/bisexual/transgender and queer theories and movements, concluding that the communities need to engage with both identity movements and queer politics if they are to realize political success. There is no doubt that if Weeks (1998) is proposing a movement from raising awareness, through transgression, to rights and responsibilities, through citizenship, then there are legitimate political concerns about the conservatism of such a political strategy. However, there is an alternative way to understand Weeks's moments, where they are not oppositional but in a dialectical relationship with each other (Langdridge & Butt, 2004), as Weeks (1998) himself argues, both being necessary for the other. This dialectical relationship can be modelled on the relationship between ideology and utopia advocated by Ricoeur (1986), in which ideology is that aspect of the social imaginary concerned with identity preservation and utopia the aspect concerned with rupture, novelty, and difference. Here, the tools and weapons of transgression, simulation, and parody can be strategically employed, where and when they might be most effective, without directly disavowing sexual identities and oppositional identity politics even though they necessarily trouble such identities and politics.

There have also been attempts to radically transform thinking about sexual citizenship without recourse to queer theory, notably Plummer's (2015) argument in favour of cosmopolitan sexualities. This is an ambitious attempt to think globally about sexual diversity such that we might reach a universal ideal of 'living easily with diversity' (Plummer, 2015: 71). Plummer's utopian vision draws on a long tradition of thinking about cosmopolitanism, in which theorists envision a world where we are all 'citizens of the world'. This is grounded in a critical humanism in which—as Martha Nussbaum (2006) remarked—we should seek a primary allegiance to the worldwide community of human beings. Debates about cosmopolitanism continue to rage (see, e.g., Appiah, 2007; Brennan, 1997, 2001; Miller, 2002; Mouffe, 2005; Thaler, 2010), and it is a particularly bold move to focus on sexualities in this context given this is a topic in which there is arguably less global agreement about shared values than many others. Plummer (2015) recognizes the many criticisms of cosmopolitanism, dismissing some while accepting others, but still feels that—like democracy—cosmopolitanism offers the least bad option for sexual citizenship. His hope is a new global 'inclusive sexualities' underpinned by a set of rather abstract values—care, empathy, dignity, etc.— that few would disagree with but which become challenging when grounded in the local and specific.

While I have considerable sympathy with the positive vision laid out by Plummer, I am rather more uncertain this is either possible or even desirable. There is a risk of further erosion to local tradition when up against the cosmopolitan vision of a global elite, imbued with unparalleled communicative technological power, that has uncomfortable echoes of imperialism. Still, whether we agree with Plummer's (2015) argument or not, it may usefully operate—like varieties of queer theory—as a form of utopian critique. This would represent an almost completely opposite vision than that of the antisocial queer theorists, and perhaps that is where it is of most value. Critical arguments about change invariably differ and are sometimes incompatible, but regardless they all offer up challenges to the status quo. New perspectives that expand our thinking—and potentially also political praxis—are always valuable, even if we ultimately decide they are not the best way forward or even simply plain wrong. What is key, however, is the means by which we

54 SEXUAL CITIZENSHIP AND SOCIAL CHANGE

hold opposing views together in the public sphere such that we can engage in constructive debate as we work collectively but tentatively towards some shared utopian vision.

A dialectic of ideology and utopia

One possible way to engage in such productive political work is to recognize the value of a dialectic of ideology and utopia—or tradition and critique. For Ricoeur (1984, 1985, 1986, 1988), the social imaginary is the ensemble of narratives possessed by all societies that serve to mediate human reality. There is no starting point for human nature, no creative foundation, but instead a world of narratives (stories) into which we all enter. Narratives of meaning make up the social imaginary, with Ricoeur (1986) using this concept to understand and conceptualize the distinction between ideology and utopia. There is an important political role for the social imaginary since narratives can project and support distorted traditions as well as undistorted traditions. The role of narratives in projecting distorted visions of the world is well established. Marx emphasized the role of ideology in supporting oppressive distorted political structures (Marx & Engels, 1970). Ricoeur (1986) recognizes this but also seeks to identify a positive and socially necessary aspect of ideology. Ricoeur understands the positive aspect of ideology as the symbolic, which serves to bond human culture through identity and tradition.

Utopia, on the other hand, has tended to refer to a fantasy or dream, an escape, which is not, and cannot, be practically realized. Ricoeur once again recognizes this pathological aspect of utopia but seeks to find an alternative vision of utopia that represents what may be, a view from nowhere that projects a real possible future rather than a fantasy and therefore enables a critical vantage point from which to view ideology. Ricoeur's analysis is unusual because he attempts to locate ideology and utopia within a common conceptual framework. Traditionally, ideology and utopia have been treated quite separately: ideology the province of the critical social theorist and utopia the province of the literary. Ricoeur attempts to formulate a positive understanding of the relationship between the two concepts. He does this through a genetic phenomenology, that is, an analysis of the things in their appearing working backward from surface meaning/s to uncover the deeper meaning/s. I discuss this further in Chapter 3 where I discuss Ricoeur's philosophy and its relevance for a narrative understanding of sexual citizenship.

A dialectical relationship between citizenship (ideological tradition) and transgression (utopian critique) may provide a way of recognizing the different needs of community members in sexually diverse communities. That is, those who want recognition, rights, and responsibilities can make their claims for integration, identities, and citizenship and, with this, maintain the status quo or work to transform citizenship from within, while those who wish to remain outside, for the attendant thrill that this provides, can refuse citizenship completely or work to transform the project from the outside as transgressors or sexual outlaws. As Cossman (2002: 501) states:

> An alternative model of citizenship must encompass both the sexual outlaw and the encumbered subject, but need not conflate either with the neoliberal citizen. It must continue to displace not simply the heterosexual requirement of citizenship, but also the heteronormativity of sex, sexuality and sexual citizenship. It will not be enough to posit an essentialized gay and lesbian citizen to stand in contrast with the heterosexual one. Challenging the heteronormativity of the sexual citizen requires the deconstruction of the hetero/homo divide; it requires a recognition of the fluidity of sex, sexuality and sexual citizenship.

With such a dialectic we can be alert to the potentially distorting effects of citizenship and also the risks of unrealistic utopias—or even dystopias—that result from critique. The key is a need for a dialectical relationship between citizenship and transgression such that they act to temper each other.

As Weeks (1998) recognized, both are necessary for the current political struggle, but what he did not sufficiently highlight was how this might be achieved in such a way that there is not a necessary conservative assimilationist move from transgression to citizenship. The dialectical relationship theorized here is not and should not be a stagnant one, merely vacillating between citizenship and transgression. Ricoeur himself recognized the dangers of this in any oppositional relationship and suggested that a dialectical relationship must be spiral with, in this case, the critical imaginative variations that come from transgression providing the key movement upwards in the spiral, as all those concerned with extending or critiquing citizenship seek to engage in deliberative dialogue (Plummer, 2001) around such issues based on practical wisdom (Ricoeur, 1986), a theme that will be returned to in the final chapter.

This position needs to be tempered, however, by a more recent argument I made concerning power imbalances in dialectics of sexual citizenship with the consequent risk of assimilation within hegemonic institutions, such as those concerned with traditional notions of parenthood and family (Langdridge, 2013), or even hegemonic value systems, such as Western liberalism. So, for instance, work in queer theory concerned with the prosecution of 'the antisocial thesis' actively refuses citizenship. This body of work constitutes a queer subject that serves as the bitchy, fractious, and difficult critical other, who refuses to be assimilated within any notion of universal citizenship (Berlant, 1997; Bersani, 1995, Edelman, 2004). Edelman (2004), in particular, has advanced a broadly Lacanian thesis in which he advocates a rejection of 'reproductive futurism'. Reproductive futurism can be clearly seen within much citizenship discourse and involves the subordination of present desires (*jouissance* in Lacanian terms) to the always-deferred claim to meet the needs of innocent children. I argue that this can be most clearly seen with some recent claims for marriage and parenthood amongst LGBTQ people. In some of the arguments made by people, particularly in the United States, in favour of LGBTQ parenthood, we can see the production of an irresponsible queer other who has failed to grow up and embrace full membership of the wider (heterosexual) community through becoming a parent: hedonism is recast as irresponsibility. There is less and less space for jouissance as the power of family, aligned with axes of privilege, dominates the dialectic. In her discussion of transgender citizenship, expressing similar concerns to those of Roseneil (2013), Hines (2009: Loc 2278 of 6999 Kindle) summarizes the tension as follows:

> Radical gender and sexual movements such as *Queer Nation* and *Transexual Menace* act as a cautionary reminder of the dangers of a whole-hearted liberal approach to citizenship claims. Hence, those who remain 'different' are frequently constructed as 'difficult' and become further marginalized. In discussing a moment of citizenship, it must not be forgotten that most recent social movements divide on the desirability of citizenship as a political goal, with many arguing that the route inevitably leads to the subjugation of difference and transgression.

What we need to be alert to, therefore, is the power invested in different positions within dialectics and the possibility of both critique and tradition to sustain themselves in the face of the other. That is, we need space for people to embrace the traditional pursuits of liberal citizenship, such as marriage and parenthood, should they wish whilst also retaining space for others to embrace the antisocial and refuse such calls. Equally, we need space for localized modes of citizenship alongside calls for cosmopolitanism. A dialectical resolution to such conflicts can only be truly progressive if it offers up space for all of those affected to argue for their own personal and political desires, whilst also serving to effect broader sociopolitical change.

This is no easy option, however, as tradition and critique may not always sit comfortably together. There may at times be clashes and conflict, which may not be easily reconciled. We may also run up against limit conditions where we collectively seek to halt the critical moment of the dialectic. There must be an end point to critique, a moment when we no longer see value in transformation, or it becomes critique for the sake of critique only. This will require difficult—painful, even—conversations where those in opposition have to work hard to listen to and recognize the values of the other. This is a demand that must be placed upon all involved equally, those seeking to maintain tradition and those seeking change through critique. And, of course, there will always be dissenting voices, and that is something to appreciate and value rather than shut down or silence. We must always resist totalitarian thinking, whether that manifests through stories of tradition or critique. An awareness of the value and limitations of both tradition and critique, along with a generosity of spirit, will be needed to maintain any chance of a progressive dialectic for sexual citizenship. The risk otherwise is even more of what we have now, a culture war (Hunter, 1991), in which people seek to silence the other. While contemporary battles using this strategy may result in some victories, these will inevitably be temporary at best. Long-lasting change, and an end to this bitter culture war, will only happen when all those involved engage in constructive dialogue and through this come to recognize—if not agree with—the perspective and values of the other.

3

The narrative nature of sexual life

Key to the argument being prosecuted in this text is that in order to understand the nature of contemporary sexual citizenship, we need to critically examine the narratives that underpin nascent and established claims for citizenship. That is, unlike some contemporary developments in citizenship studies that focus on what are effectively stand-alone events, the analysis herein seeks to understand the contested nature of citizenship through the interplay of narratives founded on tradition and critique. This is within the context of a theoretical position where I resist eschewing the human individual whilst recognising the intrinsically socially and politically interwoven nature of subjectivity itself.

That is, in essence, this is an argument in favour of the return of the psychological, albeit accessible only through narrative, to the sociopolitical landscape, fully cognisant of the risk that one might simply reinscribe a neoliberal humanism onto the social world. Resistance to this risk in the analysis comes in the form of social theoretical critique through engagement with Ricoeurean critical social theory. The aim is to be sensitive to both the psychological and social and thereby develop a psychosocial political perspective on the boundaries of belonging as they relate to sexual citizenship. And I believe that an analysis of narrative best enables us to engage that particular sensitivity. It needs to be noted that this is not to position the arguments made here in opposition to developments such as the move towards acts and more performative modes of citizenship (e.g., Isin, 2008) described in the previous chapter, but rather that the notion of 'the act' is here reconceived as an 'episode' in Ricoeur's (1984, 1985, 1988, 1992) terms that then might be reconfigured into a narrative whole.

It is worth briefly discussing what is meant by narrative, as this is not necessarily clear-cut. There is a long tradition of narrative theory that has highlighted a wide variety of characteristics of narrative tradition in human culture. At the most basic level, a narrative will have a beginning, middle, and end (Becker, 1999), or at least the sense of an ending (Kermode, 1967). The chronological nature of storytelling is key, with narratives typically

Sexual Citizenship and Social Change. Darren Langdridge, Oxford University Press. © Oxford University Press 2024.
DOI: 10.1093/oso/9780199926312.003.0003

involving the ordering of events into some meaningful whole through a plot. Vladimir Propp (1969), a founding figure of the formal discipline of narratology, identified some 31 elements underpinning the fairy tale as narrative form. Many others have since built on this foundation to elaborate distinct theories of narrative structure and form (for instance, Elsbree, 1982; Gergen & Gergen, 1986), but it has been argued that

> attempts to create a definitive typology of plots have not been successful. The variety and combination of plot structures means that they do not conform to a categorical structure without intense abstraction of the specific features that give an individual story the power to supply a meaningful interpretation of experience. (Polkinghorne, 1988: 168)

Consequently, in this book, the body of work concerned with narrative structure and form will not be considered further. The focus is instead on broader social scientific understandings of narrative that serve the psychosocial needs of the thesis contained herein about sexual citizenship. Below, I begin by introducing the theoretical foundation for narrative being used here.

This primarily concerns the work of Ricoeur, one of the leading post-war philosophers in the West, a figure who has been enormously influential in the narrative tradition (Polkinghorne, 1988) and who provides a uniquely human philosophy of narrative that also encompasses the political. I discuss his arguments about metaphor and semantic innovation, and the importance of temporality in understanding the narrative basis of life. This brief outline of his ideas also includes his notion of narrative identity, which is part of his attempt to encompass human action within a narrative framework. I then move on to discuss social scientific, rather than exclusively philosophical, approaches to narrative, and notably the work of Theodore Sarbin and Jerome Bruner, who both sought to shift psychology from being a positivist discipline to a narrative discipline. Finally, I discuss the foundational work of the sociologist Ken Plummer on telling sexual stories alongside more recent contributions to the field. His work, alongside the arguments of Rubin (1984/ 1993) discussed in Chapter 1, forms an important part of the historical foundation for the ideas in this book. Plummer engaged in an empirical analysis of late-modern sexual storytelling and advanced a thesis about the elements that need to be in place for stories to have their time, a project that was—and remains—both radical and politically important.

The narrative basis of life

Unquestionably one of the most important theoretical resources underpinning a narrative approach to the social sciences is the work of the philosopher Paul Ricoeur (1913–2005). Ricoeur maintained a particular interest throughout his philosophical career in the creative power of language, seen through his interest in both metaphor and narrative. True to his hermeneutic and phenomenological roots, Ricoeur sought to uncover hidden meaning and open up new ways of seeing. With both metaphor and narrative there is creative potential as new interpretations and experiences are brought into being through language, or more properly discourse. Ricoeur has taken this further than many others, however, by extending his theory of language to account for human action as well. That is, building on his earlier work on the will, he argued that action can be understood much as we might seek to understand a text, for it is only through narrative that actions become intelligible. In order to understand narrative, it is, of course, necessary to understand the way that narratives might not simply represent some truth about experience but can also represent ideological distortions in the world. Ricoeur also offers something here to enable us to distinguish between true and false consciousness in the development of a critical theory (Kaplan, 2003).

Ricoeur (1977) argued that it is through metaphor that we can see new possibilities for existence. The split reference between the literal and figurative of a metaphor marks it out from the first-order reference of most ordinary language. In these terms, a metaphor allows us to imaginatively rethink (or 'redescribe') reality, much as we might do in fictional writing. Metaphors rupture language and, through this breaking apart, open up space for original thought rather than simply improving or adding to everyday communicative competence. This creative event only emerges, however, with 'live' metaphors where there is a novel bringing together of two previously disparate elements of language. A 'dead' metaphor, such as 'to grasp a concept', is where a previously original conjunction has now fallen into everyday usage and lost its creative power. There is value, therefore, when casting our analytic gaze upon the social world to look out for metaphors and, indeed, also to grasp the opportunity to engage in metaphorical declarations ourselves if we wish to open up new ways of understanding.

Narratives share a creative capacity with metaphors through the process of semantic innovation, a fundamentally human quality. Semantic innovation in narratives occurs through the agentic bringing together of characters, actions, events, etc. through the notion of a plot, whereby individual episodes are creatively configured into a coherent and meaningful whole. Key to understanding the significance of narrative in human meaning making is time: in the form of *cosmic time, historical time*, and *phenomenological* (or human) *time*. On the one hand, cosmic time is time on a universal scale, infinite and undifferentiated. This element of time is essentially unknowable on a human scale, meaningless to us as finite human beings. Phenomenological (or human) time, on the other hand, concerns our everyday understanding of time as lived. Here, time passes differently according to our mood and/or the meaning of any moment to us. Waiting for a train to go to an important meeting can feel like an interminable age whilst the very same temporal wait might be part of a positive anticipatory context when featuring as part of our holiday plans. Furthermore, particular moments in time are likely to be more important than others. Meeting a romantic partner or the birth of child will likely assume much more importance in how we view moments in time than other more mundane events. There is a profound rupture here, therefore, between lived (finite) time and the ungraspable (ostensibly infinite) time of the cosmos.

How, then, might we bridge the gap between cosmic time and phenomenological time? Ricoeur (1984, 1985, 1988) argued that we close this temporal fissure through the construction of historical time. That is, we bring these two perspectives on time together through the construction of devices like calendars and clocks, which allow us to inscribe our experience of lived time onto the cosmos and vice versa. Such devices are our way of leaving traces of existence upon the cosmos and thus reach out from the finite limits of human time towards the infinite sense of time of the cosmos. In order to make sense of action it is necessary to bring together lived time with cosmic time, such that we bring together the space of experience and the horizon of expectation:

> The present moment of historical time in which action takes place stands at the intersection of what Reinhart Koselleck calls the space of experience and the horizon of expectation. The space of experience is made up of past natural or cultural events that a person remembers and is influenced by in the present. It is the past now made present and thus it serves as the point of departure for a new decision or action. The horizon of expectation, on the other hand, is the unfolding of the array of projects that one can now

undertake, of paths that one can now begin to explore on the basis of this space of experience. It is the future made present. . . . Action, taken in the present, preserves the space of experience in a dialectical tension with the horizon of expectation. Without them, action would be impossible. But neither singly nor jointly can they fully determine action. Undoubtedly we are affected both by a past that is not of our own making and by the pictured future that our society presents. Nevertheless, through our initiatives we do make history and affect ourselves in the process of doing so. (Dauenhauer & Pellauer, 2012: 8)

And in order to articulate the historical present we need a form of discourse that can bring together individual episodes or events into a meaningful whole. It is through narrative that historical time becomes *human time*, as it enters the communicative realm where we are always inextricably in relation with others. Narrative is the means by which we articulate the psychosocial and thus bring together the individual and society. Narrative accounts better represent the action-oriented nature of life than other forms of discourse, operating as a model for understanding the connections between discourse, action, and interpretation (Kaplan, 2003).

Identity and narrative

As mentioned in Chapter 2, Isin and Wood (1999) note that citizenship and identity have traditionally been conceptualized as incompatible, with citizenship associated with the universal and identity with the particular. However, if we wish to move beyond this position and embrace some sort of differentiated universalism (Lister, 2003), then it is vital that we keep identity in mind when thinking through citizenship, albeit in a radically different form to its usual manifestation. Without some notion of identity, we may lose sight of the important differences that matter to people in the lived world. It is, of course, possible to move beyond identity in theory, but behind my arguments throughout this book is the principle that theoretical development alone will do little for the people practically engaged in the gritty reality of political life. So, whilst there might be considerable potential for contemporary critical theory—especially that seeks to further fragment present identity categories or move us beyond a politics of identity completely—to transform citizenship as we know it, this comes at the risk of doing serious

THE NARRATIVE NATURE OF SEXUAL LIFE   63

damage to the lives of people living within a world framed, at least in part, within a present 'identitarian' approach to politics.

Ricoeur (1992) offers us a different way of understanding identity, one that allows us to maintain some sense of personal continuity whilst recognising the influence of the social world, through the social imaginary of stories into which we are thrown. What remains central throughout Ricoeur's writing is a Kantian commitment to people as ends rather than means, with the consequence that we distinguish between people (as agents) and objects. If we wish to impute agency and responsibility, both critical for political life, it remains necessary to maintain such a distinction. Very much in the spirit of phenomenology, Ricoeur demonstrates that it is possible for people to exist and operate within two realms, the personal and social, and that it is not necessary to reduce one to the other or for that matter embrace any notion of ontological dualism. Central to Ricoeur's formulation of narrative identity is a distinction between two forms of identity: *idem*-identity (identity as sameness) and *ipse*-identity (identity as selfhood). This distinction emerges as Ricoeur grapples with the variety of Western analytic philosophical challenges to notions of identity, with him distinguishing between the 'what' (idem) and the 'who' (ipse) of identity through this process.

Idem-identity primarily concerns what Ricoeur refers to as numerical identity, in which we seek to identify the same thing as itself on more than one occasion. How do I know this person who stands in front of me now is the same person who was standing in front of me yesterday? The concern here is with permanence in time in a classic sense, the focal point for most Western analytic philosophy concerned with identity (such as the seminal work *Reasons and Persons* by Derek Parfit, 1984). This 'thing' (whether object or person) exists in this recognizable form over time and is thus identifiable when viewed on more than one occasion as the same thing. Secondary within idem-identity but irreducible to numerical identity is qualitative identity or extreme resemblance. Here, we see extreme resemblance used when there is uncertainty over the permanent recognition of an object in time. Ricoeur gives the example of two people wearing the same suit. It is clearly—in a literal sense—not the same suit but is so qualitatively similar that we take it as the same. In other words, we can interchange the items (the suit in this example) with minimal effect on our ability to recognize what it is. The experience of meeting twins might similarly conjure up concerns with qualitative identity and our capacity to correctly identify a person on more than one occasion.

64 SEXUAL CITIZENSHIP AND SOCIAL CHANGE

Ipse-identity, or selfhood, is where Ricoeur departs from more traditional Western philosophical understandings of identity focussed on the perma-nence of an 'object' through time. Here, permanence in time is connected to the question 'who?', rather than just the question 'what?', when considering our capacity to recognize people rather than inanimate objects. Ricoeur argues that the answers that might be found in response to the question of 'who?' remain irreducible to those found in response to the question 'what?', and that with ipse-identity come the two key expressions of selfhood de-manding a narrative answer: character and keeping one's word. With our own identity we are very likely to readily recognize our own character and capacity to keep our word in relation with others and thus these are central to answering the question 'who am I?'. But what is the relationship between idem-identity and ipse-identity, particularly with regard to character and keeping one's word? Ricoeur (1992: 118–119) states it as follows:

> My hypothesis is that the polarity of these two models of permanence with respect to persons results from the fact that the permanence of character expresses the almost complete mutual overlapping of the problematic of *idem* and of *ipse*, while faithfulness to oneself in keeping's one's word marks the extreme gap between the permanence of the self and that of the same and so attests fully to the irreducibility of the two problematics one to the other. I hasten to complete my hypothesis: the polarity I am going to ex-amine suggests an intervention of narrative identity in the conceptual con-stitution of personal identity in the manner of a specific mediator between the pole of character, where *idem* and *ipse* tend to coincide, and the pole of self-maintenance, where selfhood frees itself from sameness.

Character in Ricoeur's (1992: 121) terms is therefore the 'set of lasting dispositions by which a person is recognized', including all those aspects of idem-identity concerned with numerical and qualitative sameness, along-side an enduring sense of selfhood—through habits or other identifiable features of self—that we see with ipse-identity. But this is not the end, with us reducing selfhood to sameness through the permanence of character (or some expanded notion of personality, should we be thinking in the terms of contemporary psychology). Ricoeur (1992: 123) brings in the notion of keeping one's word, to promise, to enable him to distinguish between idem- and ipse-identity, for 'keeping one's word expresses a *self-constancy* which cannot be inscribed, as character was, within the dimension of something in general but solely within the dimension of "who?"' The promise is an agentic, personal, innovation in time that operates as the upper limit to a narrative dialectic between idem- and ipse-identity in which there is space for selfhood without sameness. When we promise we demonstrate constancy through our capacity to hold firm *in spite of* the passing of time and thus can be held accountable for our actions.

It is, however, only through a theory of narrative identity that we can properly reconcile the tension between idem- and ipse-identity or more concretely between a person's character and the keeping of their word. The model for understanding a person's identity in these terms comes from our understanding of fictional and/or historical texts. Fictional and historical narratives involve emplotment where disparate individual episodes are configured into a narrative whole, and it is through this plotted narrative that we come to understand the characters that inhabit such stories. That is, we come to appreciate the identity of characters in fiction and history primarily through the story we tell of the episodes of their lives. As Kaplan (2003: 90–91) puts it:

> Just as the story of a life unfolds like a narrative, the identity of a character also unfolds in a narrative. Because narrative theory articulates our temporal and historic constitution of the world, and because the self has a history, changes over time and yet maintains a constancy of selfhood by keeping promises, a personal identity can only be understood as a narrative identity. . . . And yet, the narrative function constructs an imperfect mediation, constantly changing as we change. . . . A narrative identity is constituted by whatever permits the identification and reidentification of a character as the same, which includes both public events and experiences that belong uniquely to someone. A narrative identity is a dialectic of personal experience and impersonal circumstance, or *ipse*-identity and *idem*-identity, selfhood and sameness.

The moral self, that is the primary subject of interest to the social sciences, whether psychology, sociology, or politics, can therefore be held to account by their identification through a narrative identity. In this book, this may involve a wide range of narratively constituted selves: the moral self that is ostensibly worried about the sexualization of children; the moral self that seeks to be inclusive of sexual and gender diversity; the moral self that believes they are having sex for 'good' reasons; the moral self that engages in sex that

66 SEXUAL CITIZENSHIP AND SOCIAL CHANGE

might put others at risk; or even the deliberately abject self that wishes to overthrow extant notions of morality. A moral self or narrative identity more broadly is not fixed, however, but is instead in flux, as the person continually configures and reconfigures the events of their lives. It might have been better for Ricoeur to refer to narrative identities in the plural to better capture the ongoing and dynamic process of identity construction than in the singular. Regardless, with narrative identity we have a way of working actively with the psychosocial within narrative theory, recognising the inherent relationship between the psychological and social, and therefore also the personal and political.

The narrative tradition in the social sciences

Within psychology, and the social sciences more generally, there has been a rapid growth of interest in narrative perspectives since the 1980s. In the case of psychology, there was growing disillusionment about the dominance of positivist methods, what has been termed 'the crisis' in social psychology, such that a number of theorists began to look around for inspiration for how they might create an alternative discipline. In sociology there has been a long history of research focused on storytelling, with Thomaz and Znaniekis' (1927) classic study of 'the Polish peasant' the most notable early example. This work was inspired by the Chicago School of Sociology, and the development of symbolic interactionism of course, where the analysis of stories remained important, but it was only in the 1980s and '90s that there was serious interest in narrative per se amongst sociologists. A number of key theorists provided the theoretical foundation that helped those early figures in the social sciences (described below) forge this turn to narrative, including, to name just four, Paul Ricoeur, whose work is described above; Hayden White, who's *Metahistory* (1973) demonstrated that history should be understood as narrative; Roy Shafer (1980), who argued that psychoanalysis should be understood as a narrative enterprise; and David Carr (1986), who demonstrated the power of narrative for understanding historical existence. The reader interested in historical discussion and debate about narrative approaches and the social sciences would be advised to turn to Polkinghorne (1988), who provides an excellent review.

In this book it is the work of Ricoeur that is central, with the work of these other primary thinkers less directly relevant to the present project.

THE NARRATIVE NATURE OF SEXUAL LIFE   67

The reason for the primary focus on Ricoeur herein is that Ricoeur almost uniquely amongst narrative theorists has a focus on narrative as a way of understanding human existence, rather than narrative as a means of describing the past (Polkinghorne, 1988). His work is also hermeneutic—grounded in a phenomenology of existence—rather than literary or historical and thereby provides a theoretical position that recognizes the critical role of embodied human subjects in narrative production, as well as an interpretative understanding of human nature grounded in narrative. And finally, his philosophy directly addresses the political, with his attempt to bring ideology and utopia together in a dialectic a unique intervention in critical social theory, one that is central to my argument in this text. That said, I now turn my attention to the work of some key thinkers on narrative in psychology.

Sarbin (1986) draws on the concept of the 'root metaphor' from Pepper (1942) to make the case for 'contextualism' rather than 'mechanism' as the root metaphor for the discipline of psychology. Pepper examined the history of metaphysics and concluded that any metaphysical position (or 'world hypothesis') is derived from a 'root metaphor'. This root metaphor allows and limits the available models for observation, classification and analysis. It is argued that a novel observation, for instance, calls out for classification if there is no pre-existing category for understanding it available, and it is only through a process of analogy that we can make sense of novel phenomena. The root metaphor in operation thus determines how we make sense of novel phenomena. This process of categorization through metaphor then provides a very particular framework within which we must now make sense of novel phenomena. Sarbin (1986) provides the example of the metaphor of the 'political puppet' that leads to a series of other (mechanistic) metaphors involving 'pulling strings', 'manipulating characters', etc. A key feature of metaphors is that whilst they provide the opportunity for creative processes of association and categorization, they also have the potential to lose their 'as if' quality (cf. Ricoeur, 1977). This move then risks the 'as if' quality becoming forgotten, and it being assumed that the phenomenon that is the object of the metaphor is being treated as if it literally were as compared. As Sarbin (1986: 5) describes this process: 'The once tentative poetic expression may then become reified, literalized. The reification provides the foundation for belief systems that guide action.'

Gergen's (1973) argument about social psychology and history figures large in this argument for the way that psychological theories must be recognized as historical productions rather than pronouncements on human nature that

68   SEXUAL CITIZENSHIP AND SOCIAL CHANGE

exist outside history. Consequently, if—as Sarbin, amongst others, argues—history is narrative, then psychology is narrative as well. Sarbin (1986: 8–9) further argues that narrative is the proper metaphor for psychology because of the way that it is fundamental to the human condition and the way that 'human beings think, perceive, imagine, and make moral choices according to narrative structures. . . . [T]he narrative is a way of organizing episodes, actions, and accounts of actions.' A narrative approach to psychology offers up a metaphorical position that is much more human than mechanical, one in which agency and the dramatic play a key role. Sarbin (1986) draws on a number of sources in support of his argument. This includes some early psychological studies by Michotte and Heider and Simmel that demonstrate the fundamental tendency of humans to make even randomly presented events into a more meaningful (narrative) whole, alongside the seemingly inherent tendency to make sense of historical/archaeological objects through narrative as a means of making the abstract nature of time more concrete (cf. Ricoeur, 1984, 1985, 1988).

In a similar vein, Bruner (1986) distinguished between two forms of thinking in science (and the social sciences): the paradigmatic mode (or logico-scientific mode) and the narrative mode. The former concerns the search for universal truths about the world, as we might see within a traditional mechanistic conception of natural science. For Bruner, this mode of engagement is entirely appropriate for the natural sciences but not for the human sciences. If we wish to understand humanity, Bruner argues, then we need to adopt a mode that is appropriate to the object of study, and with human beings as our object of study the proper mode is one founded on a narrative understanding. Key here is the way that we gain a sense of the whole of human nature rather than simply unconnected events: narrative understanding enables us to recognize the way that episodes of life become meaningful as a whole through their active construal. This is a radical move for psychology (Bruner's own discipline), as it is for many other disciplines in the social sciences, for this is a clarion call towards a distinctly human research focus that is clearly concentrated on narrative meaning and understanding.

Of particular significance for Bruner (1990, 2002) is the power of canonical narratives and the need to attend to those moments of narrative articulation in which the canonical is violated. Bruner (1990) argues that our world is dense with model (canonical) narratives that serve to structure our understanding, and that the need to articulate new narratives in the face of 'noncanonical' events is a fundamental human quality present even in very young children. That is, it is when we are confronted with events that do not readily fit the canonical narratives that provide the fabric of our culture that we must attempt to articulate a new narrative to account for the outlying event. An experience of same-sex desire in a teenager of the 1980s cannot readily be accommodated within the then ubiquitous narrative of girls, boys, men, women, dating, relationships, sex, marriage, and the family. In an echo of Ricoeurean claims about the power of metaphor, this is therefore a moment for imagination (see discussion of Plummer's work below) and the articulation of a new story of desire that is marked by similarity and difference. Bruner (2002), in collaboration with his colleague Anthony Amsterdam, refers to this as a 'dialectic of the established and the possible'. That is, he argues that the canonical and the possible are in an eternal dialectic and it is this dialectic that impels life itself:

> For tales of life—autobiography, self-referent narrative generally ('self-making')—have as their purpose to keep the two manageably together, past and possible, in an endless dialectic: 'how my life has always been and should rightly remain' and 'how things might have been or might still be'. A self is probably the most impressive work of art we ever produce, surely the most intricate. (Bruner, 2002: 14)

> Narrative fiction creates possible worlds—but they are worlds extrapolated from the world we know, however much they may soar beyond it. The art of the possible is a perilous art. It must take heed of life as we know it, yet alienate us from it sufficiently to tempt us into thinking of alternatives beyond it. (Bruner, 2002: 94)

And here we can see a link with Ricoeur's (1986) argument about the need for a dialectical solution to the problem of ideology and utopia that was touched on in the previous chapter. Ideological narratives bind us to tradition and with this support much of our everyday way of experiencing life within particular cultures. By contrast, our utopian imaginings offer up the possibility of a rupture in the ideological fabric of the social imaginary of stories that we inhabit and provide the glimmer of new possibilities. Neither can be—nor should be—separated from the other. Ideology and utopia must necessarily exist in tension, but this need not be unproductive. Taken together, they provide the foundation for a progressive dialectic in which we acknowledge both tradition *and* critique.

70   SEXUAL CITIZENSHIP AND SOCIAL CHANGE

In his *Lectures on Ideology and Utopia* Ricoeur (1986) argues that ideology and utopia operate at three levels in social life: as distortion, legitimization, and integration/identity (Ricoeur, 1986). They do not simply represent the social world as it is but function in differing ways in relation to praxis. At the most superficial level, ideology acts to distort reality, while utopia represents nothing more than a fantasy. At the next level, ideology serves to fill the gap between claim and belief by providing legitimization for authority. In contrast, utopia challenges the dominant system and advocates an alternative. At the deepest level, ideology functions in an integrative way to preserve an individual or group identity, while utopia provides a critical imaginative variation on this identity by forwarding practical alternatives that may be realized (see Appendix for a fuller account of this philosophical argument). In these terms, we can recast *ideology* as *tradition* and *utopia* as *critique*. The former is concerned with the preservation of what is, while the latter acts to rupture that foundation in the service of progressive political change.

There is an important political role for the social imaginary in that narratives can project and support distorted and potentially evil traditions as well as undistorted and positive traditions. The role of stories in projecting distorted visions of the world is well established. Marx emphasized the role of ideology in supporting oppressive distorted political structures (Marx & Engels, 1970). Ricoeur (1986) recognizes this but also seeks to identify a positive and socially necessary aspect of ideology. Ricoeur understands the positive aspect of ideology as the symbolic which serves to bond human culture through identity and tradition (see also Shils, 1981, and Stanley, 2021, for a recent and very readable defence of tradition). Utopia, on the other hand, has tended to refer to a fantasy or dream, an escape that is not and cannot be practically realized. Ricoeur once again recognizes this *pathological* aspect of utopia but seeks to recognize an alternative vision of utopia that represents *what may be*, a *view from nowhere* that projects a real possible future— critique grounded in praxis—rather than a fantasy and therefore enables a critical vantage point from which to view ideology.

The ideas of Bruner and Ricoeur further complement each other in their discussions of the making of selfhood and identity, respectively. Bruner's (1986) description of the narrative nature of selfhood provides a vision of subjectivity that beautifully matches the notion of narrative identity that Ricoeur (1984, 1985, 1988) articulates. In Bruner's (2002: 73) terms: 'Selfhood can surely be thought of as one of those "verbalized events", a kind of meta-event that gives coherence and continuity to the scramble of experience.' The

THE NARRATIVE NATURE OF SEXUAL LIFE   71

stories we tell of our lives, of our worlds, therefore serve to produce our sense of self, grounded in ideology and the stories that are culturally available but ultimately bound only by the limits of our imagination and power to articulate utopian possibilities.

Telling sexual stories

There is an important tradition of narrative work focused on sexual stories, the subject of this investigation, and here the work of Ken Plummer is particularly significant. Plummer (1995, 1996) argues that we are living in an age of new sexual stories that are not merely the production of individual storytellers but rely on an array of others for their telling including coaxers, coercers, consumers, readers, and audiences. That is, new sexual stories— like all narratives—rely on an interactive social world ready to receive and help reproduce the story: 'tellings cannot be heard in isolation from hearings, readings, consumings. When can a story be heard, and most especially, how is it heard? A voice with no listener is silence' (Plummer, 1995: 25). Sexual stories, therefore, 'have their time' and emerge within the 'social imaginary' of stories (Ricoeur, 1981), when the right combination of individual storytellers, coaxers/coercers, and receptive social world come together.

Plummer (1996) recognizes the influence of Foucault in understanding how sexuality has been thoroughly reconstructed in modern times but argues that his work is 'too opaque' and 'strangely undifferentiated' (p. 38). That is, for Plummer, Foucault fails to attend to the details of people's lives and the way they reveal their lives to us through the very particular stories they tell. Furthermore, he argues that power operates to expand and empower some choices (citing the example of coming-out stories) whilst closing down others through control and domination (citing pathology/victim tales). The key, therefore, is to focus in on the stories of sexual life that are being told in more detail, to ask questions about why 'specific stories have their specific times, whilst others do not' (p. 38). A central element here is recognition of the change in communications technologies since the 1960s and 1970s and how these technologies have facilitated the increase in telling of new sexual stories. But this is not all for Plummer, as he argues that consumerisms, particularly those related to the post-war rise in youth cultures, also play a key role in the proliferation of new sexual stories within the context of global capitalism. This rise in storytelling has been accompanied by the creation

72 SEXUAL CITIZENSHIP AND SOCIAL CHANGE

of an infrastructure of 'cultural intermediaries' (p. 40) that serve to support and encourage the telling of these stories. Here, we see media figures, advertising and 'para intellectuals' acting within the context of the continuing rise in therapy culture (see also Furedi, 2004) to encourage the telling of these stories. We might note that all of the above has grown exponentially in the last 10 years with the rise of social media and growth of global capitalism where a ready audience for one's story, no matter how particular, can always be found within the global world of consumers.

Plummer (1996: 41–45) advances his 'formalist account' of the storytelling process in an attempt to provide an account for why stories have their time. He describes five generic processes that I think remain valid even with the recent changes in communications technology: (a) imagining—visualizing—empathizing, (b) articulating—vocalizing—announcing, (c) inventing identities—becoming storytellers, (d) creating social worlds/communities of support, and (e) creating a culture of public problems. This process represents a move from the private to the public, from dialogue within one's 'inner world' to the public world in which individual stories become part of public discourse.

The first stage of 'imagining—visualizing—empathizing' concerns the moment some private, individual, feeling, or experience comes into focus as a story. This may be conscious or not but involves the awareness of 'trouble' revolving around some challenge to what is currently taken for granted. Stories are often conjured up from the world of stories that we inhabit but may also be newly created as a product of the imagination. The classic coming-out story is one of the most well known. In this story a sense of one's sexual desire not being quite the same as everyone else's results in a feeling of difference and potentially stigma—often in one's teenage years—that requires a new story to help make sense of one's desires. Without the availability of this story, same-sex sexual desire was the 'love that dare not speak its name'. Individual, often highly personalized, stories are significant for the person in question but socially inconsequential if they fail to enter the public domain in any serious manner, if they fail to be taken up by others. The second stage of 'articulating—vocalizing—announcing' is critical for the making of new sexual stories. A new story must be articulated and a new language found to make sense of the early moment of individual imagining/experiencing. It is necessary to find the right language and a space identified where this can be articulated and announced. Without this space, a nascent story will be nothing but a whisper. It is easier than ever to find a space today with the rise

THE NARRATIVE NATURE OF SEXUAL LIFE   73

of social media, but it was not always the case and prior generations may have had to move to a city or find a community where they could begin to speak the story they were struggling to articulate. Given the right space, an emergent story may become a 'language explosion'.

The third stage, 'inventing identities—becoming storytellers', described by Plummer involves storytellers coming to public attention, whether through writing or other media. Individual storytellers have to tell the stories of their own lives to garner the interest of others and facilitate the creation of a community willing to hear the story. These stories will need to resonate with others or risk floating around with little take-up or engagement. Stories will also conjure up particular identities—the 'lesbian', 'gay', or 'bisexual'; the 'survivor'; the 'kinkster'—expressing sameness and difference, and the foundation for a politics of identity (Calhoun, 1994). The fourth stage, 'creating social worlds/communities of support', involves the story moving out beyond an individual storyteller to a receptive community. This community may already exist or be newly formed through the coming together of storytellers and others for whom it resonates. These communities may well be segregated, with stories kept separate—at least initially—from others (family, friends) outside this circle. The more powerful the community, the more resources it has ready to deploy, and the more likely it is that the story will be told and heard beyond the particular limits of the community. The final stage in Plummer's scheme is, therefore, when the story enters the realm of the public proper and becomes part of the culture of public problems that demands a response. The nature of the story is critical, for given the right conditions, the story will attract allies but may also need to fend off foes. Stories whose 'time has come' will involve (Plummer, 1996: 44–45):

(a) a large number of people willing to claim it as their own;
(b) a willingness to tell the story very visibly so that others can identify with it;
(c) the presence of alliances who do not claim the story as their own but who are keen to give it credibility and support.

The relatively recent emergence of new sexual stories coincides with the rise of 'life politics' (Giddens, 1991), where we have witnessed the evolution of the politics of emancipation into life politics. Plummer (1995: 147) describes it thus: 'a radical, pluralistic, democratic, contingent, participatory politics of human life-choices and differences', and he sees one axis of this new politics in issues of gender and sexuality and the creation of 'intimate citizenship'. Giddens (1992) argues that these changes have been facilitated by new technologies that have resulted in the separation of sexuality and reproduction. For Giddens (1992), technological advances, such as the contraceptive pill, combined with feminist arguments have freed women from the inevitable link between sexuality and death that occurred as a result of disease and multiple (often unwanted and dangerous) pregnancies. This 'transformation of intimacy' (Giddens, 1992) has provided the foundation for the emergence of new sexual stories and the boundary battles for inclusion/exclusion that necessarily follow. What is missing from Plummer's argument, quite understandably given the period when it was written, is how emergent narratives are themselves shaped through and by technology, which is itself part of a wider economic system. The technology and media giants become key actors here in serving to shape and form such claims in often unacknowledged ways.

While Plummer's work provided an insightful approach to understanding sexual lives, it is not without limitations. The model outlined by Plummer (1995) is a peculiarly modern story of individual discovery about some inner 'truth' that is then shared publicly, a story of our time but not necessarily a universal story, across cultures or even within modernist Western cultures. There is increasing evidence of new stories that offer up a profound challenge to this model of telling, at least with regard to sexuality and 'coming out' (see, e.g., Anderson, 2009; Cohler & Hammack, 2007; McCormack, 2012; Savin-Williams, 2005, 2011). Not all individuals feel the need to tell their story in such an idealized manner or engage with a specific sexual community, especially where they do not view their sexual identity/practice being personally significant. And, of course more generally, developmental stage models tend to be problematic for being idealized descriptions that may not reflect the reality of sexual storytelling or an end point of a developmental process (Langdridge, 2016).

More recent work on sexual storytelling notably includes the collection on sexual identity edited by Phillip L. Hammack and Bertram J. Cohler (2009). This work brings together an extensive collection of essays, empirical reports, and more personal accounts about sexual identity development across the life course. Unlike much previous work on sexual identity, particularly from psychology, this book places narrative understandings of same-sex sexual identity development centre stage. A central theme in this collection is the argument from Hammack and Cohler (2009), very much in the spirit of Bruner's thinking, about the need to place personal narratives within a broader historical and discursive context. They use the historically situated nature of the story of 'coming out' as a key example. That is, the well-known post-Stonewall story of 'struggle and success' (Cohler & Hammack, 2007) that describes the process of a teenager grappling with feelings of same-sex desire against a backdrop of social stigma is increasingly being called into question, in certain communities in the West at least. Increasing numbers of younger people, albeit often within quite privileged communities, are refusing this story and creating new stories of queer sexual desire beyond straightforward identification as lesbian, gay, or bisexual that do not engage with notions of stable identity or social stigma (Cohler & Hammack, 2007). Hammack and Cohler (2009) use this example to highlight the need to attend to the historical context of personal narratives and how people inhabit a particular 'identity space' that frames the discourse available to them to make sense of their experience. As such, they argue that a life course perspective is critical for understanding sexual identity and avoiding the seemingly irreconcilable tensions between essentialist and constructionist notions of sexual identity development.

The life course perspective acknowledges both the influence of social structure, with development being a socially situated process, and individual agency. With this in mind, Hammack and Cohler (2009) further introduce the concept of 'narrative engagement' as a way of bringing agency and structure together. They argue that we should not privilege structure over agency or vice versa but instead see them as 'reciprocal and co-constitutive' (p. 11). The life course perspective alerts us to the need to be attentive to the way that discourse is, at least partly, framed in generational terms with culture and identity in a reciprocal relationship (Hammack & Cohler, 2009) but also subject to agency and individual choice (engagement). The generational cohort that is socially and historically located, therefore, becomes a significant unit of analysis within this historical context:

> As individuals navigate the discursive waters of a given social ecology, as they come to recognize the meaning of the social categories of identity available to them in a given cultural context, they must make decisions (conscious or otherwise) about the relationship between their own sexual desire and the discourse available to make sense of that desire (Hammack, 2005). That is, individuals form their sexual identities through a dynamic

76 SEXUAL CITIZENSHIP AND SOCIAL CHANGE

engagement with the discourse of sexual desire that characterizes their sociohistorical location (Foucault, 1978). (Hammack & Cohler, 2009: 13)

A (critical) story about queer critical theories

The story of queer politics, as traditionally conceived, invokes a notion of radical transformation, a tearing up of the sexual status quo. Queer theory emerged some 20-odd years ago as a reaction to tensions within (and outside) activist communities and academia (Seidman, 1996). It was and continues to be heavily influenced by French poststructuralist thought and particularly Lacanian psychoanalysis, albeit often articulated through North American academic culture (e.g., Butler, 1990; Fuss, 1991; Sedgwick, 1990; Warner, 1993). Queer theory has multiple—and contested—meanings but in general refers to a body of work, mostly from English/literary scholars, which challenges the notion of stable identities. It emerged from the recognition that the homosexual–heterosexual binary, like most binaries, is constructed on the basis of one being normative and the other not, one being 'inside' and the other 'outside' (Fuss, 1991). This binary inevitably leads to that which is outside (e.g., homosexuality) being defined in opposition to that which is inside (e.g., heterosexuality), as that which is different from the (normative) inside, excluded, and therefore problematic. Queer theorists have sought to trouble this binary, undermining and/or refusing the notion of stable identity categories (e.g., homosexual, heterosexual) as the foundation for political activism or scholarship in the process.

> Queer theorists view heterosexuality and homosexuality not simply as identities or social statuses but as categories of knowledge, a language that frames what we know as bodies, desires, sexualities, identities. This is a normative language as it shapes moral boundaries and political hierarchies.... Queer theory is suggesting that the study of homosexuality should not be a study of a minority—the making of the lesbian/gay/bisexual subject—but a study of those knowledges and social practices that organize 'society' as a whole by sexualizing—heterosexualizing or homosexualizing—bodies, desires, acts, identities, social relations, knowledges, culture, and social institutions. (Seidman, 1996: 12–13)

This story has proven to be one that is clearly having its time within academic and (some) activist communities, despite being controversial (see Seidman, 1996, for a good if now somewhat dated selection of positions on queer theory from the social sciences). Queer theory is not, however, a story of sexual life that is (as yet) hegemonic or even that widely heard or retold beyond some very particular communities. That is, the story of sexual politics that still engages mainstream politics most effectively is a traditional story of identity, with change occurring in an incremental rather than radically transformative manner. But this is changing, with recent trends in gender and sexual diversity politics being heavily influenced by ideas from Judith Butler, in particular. Add in other contemporary critical theories, such as post-colonial theory, and there is a plethora of critique being operationalized within and beyond the humanities and social sciences, with knock-on effects on contemporary activism. Furthermore, some recent elements in queer theory, often influenced by Lacanian theory, have taken a turn towards the 'anti-social'. Edelman (2004), for instance, argues that queers must necessarily stand outside contemporary politics and abandon any claim to 'a viable political future' (p. 4). This new tradition of critique can and does lead to rather 'wild' scholarship and activism, as can be seen most recently in some work on trans queer theory (see, e.g., Chu, 2019; Lavery, 2022). Donald E. Hall (2009: 12), amongst others, takes issue with these 'anti-social' (and more generally 'a-political') queer theories/theorists and argues instead that 'we desperately need an approach to sexual identity that motivates, that embraces the "politics" in identity politics, and that articulates a vision for the future.' I'd add that we need care regarding all critique and not just that which is a-political or anti-social.

Hall's (2009) book *Reading Sexualities* is in many ways the literary companion work to this one, with him advancing a number of arguments that resonate with those contained herein. His theoretical framework is also similar in that he adopts a hermeneutic position to explore stories of sexual identity, albeit primarily Gadamerean (1989) rather than Ricoeurean and focused on the literary text rather than sociopolitical sphere of citizenship. He argues that, in contrast to the destructive claims of (some) queer theory/theorists, sexuality studies needs to recognize the incremental nature of change whilst attempting to project a positive vision for the future. A Gadamerean sense of dialogue and an openness to experiment (and critically, difference) are crucial for Hall (2009) in the lifelong development of desire and (incremental) sexual change. This is coupled to a pragmatic notion of political engagement,

78 SEXUAL CITIZENSHIP AND SOCIAL CHANGE

where theoretical purity is put aside in the project of effecting incremental, and often hard-won, social and political change in the world today.

The position being taken herein is that tradition and critique both have a part to play in how we make sense of sexual diversity and effect political change to better serve minority communities. However, as I highlighted in Chapter 1, arguments for a better kind of progress that is more nuanced and inclusive—'proper progress' rather than 'mere tolerance' or conservative accommodation—are already plentiful within scholarship on sexual diversity, or at least with regard to LGBTQ identities anyway (see, e.g., Duberman, 2018; Mowlabocus, 2021; Signorile, 2016; Walters, 2014; Yoshino, 2007). What is less common and what I address here is the importance of tempering critique with tradition. Critical theory when left to its own devices can get dangerously out of hand, as we are starting to see, and as I will evidence in the following chapters. Critical theories—like queer theory—can be useful for challenging extant ideology, providing a critique to traditional stories that have become ideological, opening up new ways of thinking or rupturing the status quo, but the key is linking tradition and critique together in a dialectic, as Ricoeur (1986) argues. Maintaining that link is crucial or there is a risk that critique becomes mere utopian fantasy detached from everyday life, as vital traditions are in turn erased, with people and communities mourning this loss or otherwise fighting to prevent change. As Shils (1981: 329–330) wisely remarks:

It should be remembered that, once a particular tradition or belief or conduct is jettisoned and has remained in relegation or suppression for an extended period, it might fade away entirely or nearly so, leaving an unfulfilled place, which will be felt as a gap and then replaced by a poorer belief or practice. . . . A tradition once it has receded from regular usage cannot be deliberately restored. . . . What I would like to emphasize here is that great circumspection should be exercised and that traditions should be taken into account not just as obstacles or inevitable conditions. . . . A mistake of great historical significance has been made in modern times in the construction of a doctrine which treated traditions as the detritus of the forward movement of society. It was a distortion of the truth to assert this and to think that mankind could live without tradition and simply in the light of immediately perceived interest or immediately experienced impulse or immediately excogitated reason and the latest stage of scientific knowledge or some combination of them.

We might also add that political change itself can also emerge from within ideology, not only from utopian critique. Tradition is itself dynamic, not static, and in large part self-correcting (Shils, 1981; Stanley, 2021). As Stiver (2019) argues in the context of Ricoeur's work on ideology and utopia, while Ricoeur was himself focussed on the way that ideology not only distorts but also preserves, there remains a creative potential within ideology itself. All traditions are built upon a foundational utopian aspiration such that change can, and does, emerge from what Stiver refers to as a 'period of effervescence', in which this original aim provides the imaginative stimulus for critique and renewal. Carelessly discarding tradition risks not only the loss of something that was actually better, as Shils (1981) argues above, but also the possibility of transformation from within. Stories of sexual citizenship, given the intrinsic tension between the universal and particular underpinning this concept, are—not surprisingly—at the vanguard of contemporary challenges regarding the role and value of tradition and critique. There is an attendant and urgent need to take this very seriously and think through the challenge with the utmost care.

SECTION 2

SECTION 2

4

Sexual citizenship and a clash of rights

Critique can go awry most obviously through becoming completely detached from tradition. And this can manifest in different ways. It can disappear entirely, such that there is no critical political resistance to new incarnations of old prejudices. Or it can become hegemonic, with tradition silenced, and thereby lose sight of the value of tradition to challenge or nuance arguments. The first issue I explore in this chapter could be framed as part of the need for further progress with respect to equality for sexually (and gender) diverse folk. This is a problem that has emerged in recent years in the United Kingdom of religious (mostly Muslim) objection to the teaching of sexual and gender diversity within state schools. I think, however, that this issue is better understood as a distinctly new challenge for sexual citizenship rather than simply a continuation of older battles between conservative and progressive positions. This is because it involves a clash of rights and notable absence of resistance to the reimposition of an older problematic tradition, with the teachers (and students) involved left—in the main—to fend for themselves. This is the result of a powerful narrative—within the left, in particular—around causing offence, in this instance in the form of Islamophobia/racism, to minority religious communities.

This first case involves a clash of values in which we see a particular religious worldview and LGBTQ rights in direct conflict, a conflict in which there is a failure of recognition. The case in question revolves around schools in a large multicultural UK city, Birmingham, and a protest mostly involving Muslims (some parents but many not) opposed to diversity education for primary school children. I focus on this case because it stands as a stark reminder of the dangers of complacency when it comes to LGBTQ rights, wider acknowledgement, and recognition, and also speaks to a failure of institutions and minority communities themselves to be able to deal with such activity. When we unpack this case, it is frighteningly clear how this clash of cultures involves a pushback against the liberal embrace of difference and diversity, an attempt to return sexual and gender diversity to the closet. This resurgence of tradition is not isolated either. I fear that in the context

Sexual Citizenship and Social Change. Darren Langdridge, Oxford University Press. © Oxford University Press 2024.
DOI: 10.1093/oso/9780199926312.003.0004

84 SEXUAL CITIZENSHIP AND SOCIAL CHANGE

of the culture wars, the LGBTQ movement has lost sight of its original ambition and in this instance in particular abandoned the fight for fear of the accusation of being Islamophobic or racist. The result is a troubling lack of engagement between tradition and critique. More generally, in the current cultural climate, there appears to be a bifurcation of critique such that it either disappears entirely or becomes all-consuming when there is a difficult cultural battle to be faced. This case highlights how—particularly erstwhile radical—politics struggles to deploy a necessary critique when the object of this critique appears to be one that also suffers oppression. Citizenship claims regarding equality with respect to the education of children about sexual and gender diversity run up against the rights of parents to determine what they choose to tell their children and associated religious objection. The tension between LGBTQ claims for equality and religion—particularly religious views from ostensibly oppressed communities—has not been seriously addressed, and such battles are only likely to grow if ignored.

The second case offers up a very different contemporary cultural battle-ground but one that demonstrates a similar political problem to the previous example, in the form of a lack of constructive engagement between tradition and critique. In this second example, I seek to show how critique may become detached from tradition through a 'cancel culture' politics and how—I fear—this results in unnecessary anger and the risk of unwarranted political pushback. And, like the previous example, this case also demonstrates how things can go awry when there is a clash of rights. In the fight between trans activists (and allies) and gender critical feminists (and allies) occurring in the United Kingdom (and elsewhere), I believe we are witness to the danger of a critique that is not engaged with tradition in a meaningful way. The result is considerable emotional heat but, sadly, less progress than might otherwise be achieved should the political strategy be rethought. Contemporary claims for trans citizenship run up against objections because, at least in part, such claims are multiple and complex. There is a basic and relatively simple claim here to be treated as equivalent to women/men that has echoes of claims from LGB communities to be treated in an equivalent manner to heterosexuals. This claim requires treating people with kindness, accepting them in good faith, and ensuring prevention of discrimination across an array of public settings. There appears to be a general acceptance in the United Kingdom that this is right and deserved for trans folk (Morgan et al., 2020), and I very much agree. There is, however, a stronger claim being advanced by some trans activists and their allies that is becoming all-consuming. This

SEXUAL CITIZENSHIP AND A CLASH OF RIGHTS 85

is captured within the claim that 'trans women are women' (and vice versa, for men). This seemingly innocent rhetorical move demands a societal shift from sex to gender as the primary means by which we categorize men and women. As a result, this claim inculcates others in the demand, most notably those women who now identify as gender critical feminists. The further demand—advanced by some advocates making this case, including powerful UK advocacy organizations such as Stonewall—that this not be debated or even discussed adds additional problems, as there is then no space to work through the sex/gender division. Replacing a biological concept with an entirely psychological one is a significant demand, one that moves considerably beyond the basic claim to be treated in an equivalent manner to everyone else. This stronger claim has implications for many different people—not just trans folk—and regarding many different aspects of life. Of course, individual trans folk have rightly had quite enough of needing to explain or warrant their existence, and no one should be required to do so. It is deeply unfair that often vulnerable folk have become caught up in such a toxic fight. That said, I worry that without further engagement by trans folk and their allies with those who are critical or simply interested in thinking through the implications of such a profound cultural shift, there will likely be continued anger and little hope of fair resolution. This requires considerable generosity of spirit on all sides, genuine compassion, and a lot less anger and accusation.

So, while my personal position is supportive of trans rights, in the discussion of the topic in this chapter I will focus on the dominant political strategy being deployed by some trans folk and their allies in the public sphere and argue that this may be ultimately unproductive. That is, a key argument running throughout this text is that we need to resist the contemporary tendency to engage in critique without paying equivalent attention to tradition. New demands to substantially transform how we make sense of ourselves with respect to whether we primarily understand ourselves as sexed bodies, framed through a canonical biological narrative, or as gendered persons, framed through a psychological narrative, necessarily implicate tradition. Many of these claims are themselves underpinned by ideas from critical social theory, notably the queer theory of Judith Butler (1990, 1993), which itself may be contested. There are few cultural traditions stronger than that of the binary divide between men and women underpinned by the language of biology. My aim is not to adjudicate this debate but rather to highlight how the move to eschew having the debate entirely and seek to only engage in critical utopian thinking regarding the replacement of sex with gender is, I believe,

86 SEXUAL CITIZENSHIP AND SOCIAL CHANGE

unfortunately but inherently problematic. And this is especially so when the eschewal to engage also, at times, involves an aggressive 'cancel culture' strategy designed to silence the other. Cancel culture leads only to the most shrill and extreme voices being heard, with reasonable discussion and debate increasingly silenced. To this end, and because my focus in this book is on sex and sexual practice, rather than gender diversity per se, I'll only mention one or two substantive issues regarding trans rights that I think exemplify the need for respectful discussion and debate rather than simple acceptance or violent disagreement, but not engage in the now very wide array of topics that are currently being extensively discussed—sometimes productively and sometimes not—by others (see, e.g., Barnes, 2023; Brunskell-Evans, 2020; Faye, 2021; Hemmings, 2020; Joyce, 2021; Lavery, 2022; Mackay, 2021; Soh, 2020; Stock, 2021).

Religious (in)tolerance and a clash of cultures

In this first section, I discuss a particularly difficult and very recent moment in UK sexual history, one that involves a clash of cultures—and associated rights—and clear attempt to police the boundaries of acceptability and permissibility of contemporary sexual life. This revolves around an attempt to police 'the deviants' and most specifically stop the spread of the 'homosexual menace' and their propaganda to innocent children, the historically naturalized binary opposite to the dangerously sexual queer (Bech, 1997). The case involves an attempt by predominantly Muslim individuals and groups to stop primary schools from teaching diversity education that includes mention of sexuality and gender diversity. For these campaigners, the claim is that this is not about homophobia but instead a need to protect children from their sexualization. Whilst this is a familiar old trope used against LGBQ folk, the nature of this campaign is particularly pernicious, with the schools involved—teachers and children alike—under siege by protestors trying to stop the teaching of a diversity education programme. This campaign is challenging for how it brings an otherwise underdiscussed clash of cultures into sharp focus. This has led to a reluctance to intervene, in a manner that is itself uncomfortable given the now known historical failure of UK authorities to intervene in abuse cases where there was perceived to be racial sensitivities (see, e.g., Jay, 2014). There is a risk of homophobia (and transphobia) going unchecked not because of the demands of freedom of

SEXUAL CITIZENSHIP AND A CLASH OF RIGHTS   87

speech but rather due to fear of addressing tensions between competing societal values regarding sexuality and gender and traditional—homophobic and heterosexist—values of some members of religious minorities.

This case, now involving protests at multiple schools, emerged in response to a diversity programme called 'No Outsiders' created by Andrew Moffat from Parkfield Community School.[1] The programme includes a variety of lesson plans designed to encourage an appreciation of diversity and inclusion. The tagline for the programme is 'Everyone is welcome in our school. No one is the same but everyone is equal.' Stated core values underpinning the programme include:

- Respect for diversity through education in schools
- Commitment to community cohesion through understanding and acceptance of difference
- Promotion of dialogue to counter fear and hate in society

Diversity here includes the major characteristics recognized within most Western democracies including race and ethnicity, religion, disability, gender, and sexuality. The programme started in Parkfield Community School but has also been adopted elsewhere as a way of encouraging acceptance of diversity within early-years teaching. The controversy has arisen in this instance due to the inclusion of material concerned with sexuality, notably that focused on recognizing same-sex relationships. There is, for instance, material on two male penguins who raise a chick together.

The protest that arose in complaint at these materials was ostensibly a protest by parents seeking to refuse—on religious grounds—the promotion of homosexuality and the 'sexualization of children'. That is problematic enough given the United Kingdom has a legislative (and wider attitudinal) position that fully accepts same-sex relationships as being equal to opposite-sex relationships. Discrimination on the grounds of sexual identity is illegal in the United Kingdom (Equality Act, 2010). But the matter is even more complex and sinister. The fact is that many people concerned with these protests, beginning at Parkfield School and then moving to Anderton Park, also in Birmingham, are not parents but instead random figures within the Muslim community opposed to discussion of same-sex relationships of any kind in schools. Indeed, the campaign spread to schools in Nottingham and East London, where there are large populations of Muslim people, in part due to activists seeking to challenge the teaching of this aspect of diversity in schools. A man centrally involved in the protest in Birmingham led the assault against a Nottingham School likely, at least in part, because he was subject to an injunction banning him from protesting at Anderton Park School. There have also been reports of imams encouraging the protests on the basis that the schools are encouraging 'paedophilia'. Whilst these protests have been predominantly driven by Muslim religious objection, targeted at Muslim majority schools, there have also been recent reports of a traditional Jewish school encouraging parents to request that their children be removed from diversity classes involving discussion of same-sex relationships, with the head teacher openly expressing their opposition to the teaching of lessons on sexual and gender diversity.[2]

Teachers at Parkfield and Anderton Park have come under intense pressure over many months of continuing protest, with them feeling isolated and vulnerable. Whilst it might have been hoped that key authorities like the Department for Education (DfE) might have come out in support of the schools, it was reported that pressure was applied by the DfE to halt the teaching of these diversity lessons in order to diffuse the tensions.[3] The lessons did indeed stop for some time, but the protests continued. There was some support for the schools involved from the local mayor and Member of Parliament (MP), but even these individuals were subject to considerable harassment when they visited the schools in support. The crowds protesting sought to intimidate all those seeking to gain access to the schools. Eventually, the local city authority, encouraged by the mayor and MP, sought a legal injunction on the protest at Anderton Park School, which had continued and was most fraught. This was initially granted as an interim injunction moving the protest away from the school gates, with a high court judge (Mr. Justice Warby) finally ruling (in November 2019) in favour of a permanent exclusion zone around the school. The court heard about the stress affecting teachers (with 21 off sick due to stress) and the lies being told about the programme on social media—that it was, for instance, teaching the children how to masturbate and a paedophile programme.[4]

The arguments against sexual diversity by these protestors have been strongly framed within a contemporary discourse of 'sexualization', with LGBTQ individuals narratively figured only as sexual subjects that are therefore threatening to children: the quintessential 'homosexual menace' or 'predatory paedophile' providing the canonical narrative. At a very simple level, this is palpably not an accurate representation of the teaching at these schools or this particular 'No Outsiders' diversity programme, as stated by the high court judge himself in his judgement about the case presented for an exclusion zone. The aims and the implementation of this programme are—as presented above—rather innocent and certainly not concerned with sexual practice, whether same or opposite sex. The teaching is designed for UK primary age children (5 to 9 years) and so not focused on sex education per se but rather general matters of inclusion and diversity, including diverse identities, relationships, and family forms.

The core conflict here stems from a strongly held prejudice in much Islamic faith against sexual and gender diversity (Clements & Field, 2014; Curtice et al., 2019; Jaspal, 2012; Jaspal & Siraj, 2011; Siraj, 2012; Watt & Elliot, 2019). It goes without saying that not all Muslims are prejudiced against sexual and gender diversity—of course not. But this particular prejudice is endemic within UK Muslim communities, as it is within some fundamentalist Christian communities. This is evidenced through British social attitudes surveys consistently showing a stubborn sexual and gender prejudice within strongly religious communities, notably including Muslim communities, and also the experience of LGBTQ Muslims themselves who sadly continue to face a terrible struggle in many cases should they dare to come out (Jaspal, 2012; Jaspal & Siraj, 2011; Siraj, 2012). Islam occupies a complicated place within contemporary UK culture. There is general acceptance of Islam within the context of people within the United Kingdom seeking to embrace diversity, particularly amongst those on the left of the political spectrum. Indeed, the London Mayor at the time of writing is Sadiq Khan, a former Labour MP who positively embodies a thoroughly modern Islam, with a ready embrace of diversity clearly a central passion. But there is also a strong tradition of Islam in the United Kingdom that does not embrace diversity, especially when it comes to issues of gender and sexual diversity. The usual expectation that those on the left will critically challenge prejudice, offer up their critique, and engage in an associated activism, as has historically been the case for sexual and gender prejudice in the United Kingdom, is also further complicated in this instance due to a particular left-wing reluctance to criticize Islam. This recent reluctance stems, I think, from two sources. First, there is an understandable desire to resist what has been termed 'Islamophobia', prejudice against Muslims, particularly from those on the far right of politics. Second, the resurgence of a harder left-wing politics in the United Kingdom has brought with it a long-standing anti-Israel stance, one that has tipped over into anti-Semitism at times (Rich, 2016). What is often ignored is that this stance in support of the Palestinian Muslim community may also mean that criticism of Islam quickly becomes off limits on the left. Leaving it to the far right is not likely to result in a terribly sophisticated or sympathetic conversation about the tensions between some Islamic faith beliefs about gender and sexuality and the rights of sexual and gender minorities.

The recent embrace, particularly on the left, of the term 'Islamophobia', often within a cosmopolitan multiculturalism, whilst driven by a perfectly understandable desire to stop prejudice against a particular community, may also inadvertently serve to silence those of us who may wish to raise questions about the Islamic faith as it is practiced by sections of the UK and global community (Embery, 2021; Goodwin, 2023). The charge of being 'Islamophobic' may therefore act as a cover for religious bigotry against sexual and gender minorities. This is about a specific religious form of 'intolerant Islam' and associated figures. People can hold whatever beliefs they wish as individuals, derived through their religious convictions or not, but within public (and private) schools there is a requirement that all children receive appropriate sex and relationship education, and LGBT sex, sexuality, and relationships are an appropriate (and necessary) part of such education. Being LGBT is a protected characteristic in the United Kingdom through the Equality Act (2010), same-sex partnership (civil and marriage) is provided equally to opposite-sex partnership, and this therefore forms the cultural norm against which we should measure such challenges. And yet, where is the resistance? Where is the critique? Individual heads of schools and teaching staff have been put under siege for months from angry protestors with very little support from people we might have expected to see as allies.

This issue is itself further complicated by the problems facing LGBTQ people who are also Muslim, in the United Kingdom and most other places in the world. In the United Kingdom, as elsewhere in the West, LGBTQ life is associated mostly with Whiteness. Walters (2014: 167) describes the tendency—in the context of making an analogical case between sexuality and race—to view sexual identity and race in bifurcated terms: 'the analogy can't help but reassert the troubling assumption of gayness as whiteness and blackness as heterosexual.' Furthermore, LGBTQ life in all its forms is also frequently framed as a White Western obsession or even perversion—at least that's the hegemonic discourse within some UK Muslim communities. It is unwelcome, and so those people with same-sex desires (and/or nontraditional gender identities) who are born and raised in such communities struggle to belong. The idea that everything is okay for LGBTQ folk, as if the struggle to identify and then come out is entirely historical, is a peculiarly

White discourse. Of course, there will be welcoming Muslim families embracing their children's identities, but in many cases there will not be, and Muslim LGBTQ people often face a very difficult struggle (Jaspal, 2012; Jaspal & Siraj, 2011; Siraj, 2012). There are some green shoots to show that things might be improving, but there still seems a long way to go before Islam within the United Kingdom undergoes a wholesale reconstruction regarding sexual and gender norms. In the meantime, the bravery of those who do come out in these circumstances needs to be recognized and embraced by the wider LGBTQ community. In the United Kingdom we have recently seen the first LGBTQ Muslim Pride festival, where LGBTQ Muslims stood proud in their declaration that being a Muslim does not need to equate with sexual and gender prejudice.

The claim that diversity education is about the sexualization of children is complex, however, due to the danger of a growth of discourses of respectability for LGBTQ people. That is, there is an inherently conservative story being pitched against the charge of sexualization from the Muslim community here, and this story risks the loss of LGBTQ sexual subjectivity within the public sphere. A key element within this stance is the way that politics are increasingly a politics for the child rather than the adult (Berlant, 1997). Decisions and discourses about teaching sexual and gender diversity within school should not automatically shy away from more difficult discussions about how we teach children about the nitty gritty of contemporary sexual life, to inform and protect. But as soon as that sexual life includes LGBTQ life, we witness the need to background the sexual and foreground the relational only, amongst the critics and advocates alike. This reluctance to face the charge of 'sexualization' head on has been apparent in this case, with (ostensibly supportive) allies defending the diversity programme consistently and repeatedly dropping into a discourse that denies a sexual life—at least in public—to people who are LGBTQ. The assumption that emerged time and time again in this case was that children should know about LGBTQ life but not too young and certainly not with any hint that this life might include sex between the parties involved.

There is also a more systemic problem here. Key authorities have not resolved the issue, at least not with any sense of urgency. There has been remarkably little support from authorities (police, politicians, local authorities, etc.) and remarkably little campaigning by LGBTQ groups resisting this assault on contemporary UK values and representation for a specific minority community. A former government equalities 'tsar', Dame Louise

Casey, argued that ministers were silent,[5] leaving it to the beleaguered head and her teachers to fight mostly alone. It is apparent that the Department for Education simply wanted this to go away rather than engage in a fight to defend the teaching of sexual and gender diversity in UK schools, in spite of claims to the contrary.[6] Perhaps even more worrying is how it appeared that LGBTQ communities similarly avoided this conflict. A potential clash between two stigmatized cultures appears to have stopped any necessary activism, and critical engagement with an old but newly resurgent ideological tradition, dead.

The Gender Wars

By contrast with the events discussed above, the next case I discuss is one in which critique is central but where—I fear—it has also becoming worryingly detached from its opposite, tradition. This concerns what has been termed 'the gender wars' (Mackay, 2021; Suissa & Sullivan, 2021), in which claims for trans rights are being challenged by an array of others but most particularly in the United Kingdom by a group of people identifying loosely under the umbrella of 'gender critical feminism'. The central fight in these 'wars' is over the move to shift societies from sex-based to gender-based understandings of the categories of man and woman, and all associated sexed/gendered public provision, being promoted by some trans folk and their allies. This is a form of radical critique that goes considerably beyond a request for equality under the law and wider public acknowledgement. This topic is undoubtedly sensitive, but that does not mean it should not be discussed. Indeed, my argument here—and throughout the book—is that it is vital that we talk about sensitive topics like this if we are to effect long-lasting change and avoid the myriad dangers associated with both unreconstructed tradition and unfettered or distorted critique. For my own part, I see no problem with including transmen as men or transwomen as women in most instances. And most importantly, I think we need to get beyond the story of trans people as threat. This is an old trope, akin to the pernicious notion, still promoted by some though thankfully relatively few people today, that gay and bisexual men are a threat to children. This really shouldn't need to be said, especially to those from the critical left who claim to embrace diversity, but sadly this must still be stated given the way threat has been mobilized in so much contemporary discourse on this topic. My point here is that I am someone who has supported—and been supported by—trans folk since I came out as a gay man more years ago than I care to remember, and I still do.

That said, I think there are some issues regarding contemporary trans politics that need further thought, research, and discussion. It is unfortunate that so often this is framed such that you are either in favour of every claim currently made by (some, remember) trans folk and their allies, especially on Twitter, or you are a transphobe. There are some aspects of trans politics that undoubtedly require further investigation and public discussion, just as we had—and continue to have—with respect to rights for people who are lesbian, gay, or bisexual. I know the argument I am making here will be attacked—note, not just disagreed with but attacked—by some trans folk and their allies, regardless of my own history or intent. This is a shame but only serves to prove the point that there is a damaging tendency among some advocates of critique to shut down debate as part of a contemporary 'cancel culture'. The aggressive attempts to cancel are now legion—I see new examples daily, particularly on social media—with a dangerously totalitarian politics in play. The accusation of 'fascism' and even 'genocide' is now equally ubiquitous and frankly ridiculous. The gender wars have become a topic increasingly only whispered about in private because of the fear of being cancelled or otherwise attacked, and yet this is a topic that desperately needs to be discussed openly, with honesty, compassion, and respect.

I also need to say something about my use of terminology here. The UK advocacy organization Stonewall, as of 2022, defines the term 'trans' as follows:

> Trans is an umbrella term to describe people whose gender is not the same as, or does not sit comfortably with, the sex they were assigned at birth. Trans people may describe themselves using one or more of a wide variety of terms, including (but not limited to) transgender, non-binary, or genderqueer.

There has clearly been quite a change in a very short time from the categories that were previously used to address this topic, such as transsexuality and transvestism (two very different 'phenomena'), which were far more specific and encompassed far less diversity. Perhaps this change is a good thing, perhaps not, but it does complicate matters as very loose definitions like that above can result in it being difficult to have a coherent discussion about a topic. Few would consider transsexuality and transvestism to constitute the same experience or represent similar claims for citizenship, and yet they are increasingly treated as equivalent. Still, I shall use the term 'trans' here in the sense described above and not dwell on potential difficulties further. I shall also use the term 'gender critical feminist' rather than 'trans exclusionary radical feminist (TERF)' for those espousing concern about some of the claims regarding trans citizenship. I am aware that some may find this problematic, but if we are to move beyond mere shouting then we need to stop calling people fascists, and TERF has become a term used in that manner, albeit now increasingly reclaimed. It is also worth noting that there is a relatively broad array of folk who are raising concerns about (some) trans claims that are being called TERFs, many of whom are definitely not radical feminists. As such, I will use the term 'gender critical', which has been embraced by what appears the larger grouping of those critical of a shift from sex to gender that they perceive within recent trans claims regarding citizenship, and who are not simply right-wing reactionaries opposed to all and any progress for sexual citizenship.

With all that now stated, I want to open a space for the difficult conversation that we really need to start having on this topic. In particular, we need to talk about the aim to replace sex with gender, possible implications, and the associated political strategy being advanced by some, but by no means all, trans activists and their allies. The trouble with so many contemporary fights about trans rights is that—often vulnerable—trans lives are being lost to a much bigger fight. This is a tragedy. The fundamental claim for equality, respect of difference, and societal acceptance for trans folk has become caught up in a much bigger critical ambition to completely rethink the societal category of sex. This overthrow of tradition is not something that has been fully thought through, with even internal inconsistencies among those in support of the move. In many ways the radical claim has garnered support indirectly because people really do want to support trans people, which must not be forgotten (see, e.g., Morgan et al., 2020), but often don't recognize or understand the bigger issues at stake here. Resistance that has emerged from, for example, gender critical feminists has come about in large part because of fears about the implications that follow from this radical cultural change. The backlash that is now happening from those opposed to the bigger transformation—and not necessarily opposed to support for trans folk per se—means trans people being caught up in a much bigger fight, which was not necessarily of their own making. Much of the most aggressive fighting involves 'allies' as much as trans folk themselves. The use of 'no debate' and an aggressive 'cancel culture'–style policing—a phenomenon enabled and

Sex versus gender identity

intensified by social media in particular—further exacerbates the problem, as it offers few opportunities to separate these issues out from one another and think them through productively.

Sex versus gender identity

Traditionally, women and men have been defined on the basis of biological sex. And biological sex has been understood as a binary in which you are born female or male, with this determined initially, at least, by a doctor, nurse/midwife, or other party attending the birth, based on observable genital characteristics (or simply by a mother herself where no other party is present). Obviously, with the growth in scanning technologies, such a determination may now arise prior to birth. The growth in genetic technologies expanded this notion to include identification of sex on the basis of genotypic difference between men and women (specifically, whether a person has an XX or XY chromosomal makeup), but this is not routinely examined unless there is some medical reason for such an investigation; a visual inspection of primary and secondary sex characteristics usually suffices. More generally, it is accepted that males are the sex that produces small gametes (sperm) and females produce large gametes (ova) (Byrne, 2018; Coyne, 2018; Goymann et al., 2023; Soh, 2020; Stock, 2021; Wright, 2021, 2023). There are almost no biologists who would dispute these facts, with the notable exception of Anne Fausto-Sterling, who has promoted a dissenting view in which she argues that sex should be understood as a spectrum rather than binary. She is an outlier, however, despite being adopted by trans advocates to argue against the notion of binary sex. Her argument, like all advocating a spectrum view, is primarily driven through the existence of intersex and other disorders of sex development (Fausto-Sterling, 2000), now generally referred to as differences in sex development. Fausto-Sterling, as lead scientist but in an article with her students (Blackless et al., 2000), claimed that 1.7% of people are intersex, after previously claiming it could even be as high at 4%, though even the lower figure is an exaggeration as the calculations included numerous errors (Hull, 2003) and she conflates intersex conditions with those that are not usually recognized as intersex by clinicians (Sax, 2002). The reality is that if the correct criteria and calculations are used, only 0.015% of people are born intersex (Byrne, 2018), almost 100 times lower than Fausto-Sterling's estimate—just under 50,000 people in total in the United States, as opposed

96 SEXUAL CITIZENSHIP AND SOCIAL CHANGE

to some 5.6 million if Fausto-Sterling's estimate were to be believed. On this basis, along with a few other arguments such as reference to the biology of other species, she makes her case that the classification of sex is arbitrary and better understood as a spectrum rather than binary. This is an idea that she has actively promoted and has been readily embraced by those who take succour in the notion that sex might be understood as something of a rainbow. It is also worth noting that the erroneous 1.7% figure and even the earlier 4% figure continue to be deployed by activists. Byrne (2018, 2020, 2021, 2022, 2023), Dembroff (2020), Goymann et al. (2023), Heartsilver (2021), Stock (2021), and Wright (2021, 2023) all ably engage with the various biological and philosophical debates that are occurring about how sex is determined and categorized (see also Nussbaum, 1999).

Within the phenomenology of everyday life, sex continues to work reasonably effectively as a binary construct for most people, fully accepting that this is not perfect or completely uniform. At the most basic level, human life requires binary sex for reproduction, and this obviously remains important for large numbers of people wishing to have children, as well as the future of humanity more generally. Beyond reproduction alone, human health and health care more broadly are also deeply inflected by a binary biological sex. Disease manifests in sex-based forms, and an associated sex-informed health care is vital, for cis and trans folk alike, especially if we are to move beyond existing sexual inequalities in current provision (see, e.g., Gribble et al., 2022; Mauvais-Jarvis et al., 2020). This does not mean that sex need determine how we structure all of medicine, let alone all of society, nor does this mean we should not consider whether a spectrum model might be better than a binary classification system in some circumstances. But before we overthrow this long-standing tradition, we may wish to pause a moment and think carefully about what might be lost as well as gained. That is, this is a tradition that is inherent to much everyday life—for good and bad—from reproduction to sexual object choice, as well as science, medicine, sport, the law, and much else besides. Many people are invested in this tradition at a personal level, in most, if not all, countries throughout the world. Overthrowing something so foundational needs considerable thought and discussion and needs to involve many more people in dialogue than just one or two biologists and a relatively small number of gender scholars and activists. And yet there has been precious little discussion to date, particularly in the context of people promoting a 'no debate' culture around this topic.

Beyond the radical view of Fausto-Sterling about human biology, the other argument used to undermine the acceptance of a sex-based understanding of human life stems from folk who embrace the arguments of Judith Butler (1990, 1993), a professor in the department of comparative literature at Berkeley, University of California. Butler, like Fausto-Sterling, also operationalizes intersex folk in their argument that sex is performative—constructed rather than observed—in the same manner as gender. Butler has become immensely important to (queer) gender scholarship and particularly the strand of trans activism seeking to undermine the place of sex within contemporary culture, even if other significant philosophers have serious doubts about their philosophy, particularly the lack of materiality therein (see, e.g., Nussbaum, 1999, and Paglia, 1994, for a critique of this entire genre of scholarship). Gender is a term that involves considerable conceptual confusion but is key in understanding what is occurring with claims that seek to position sex and gender as equivalent constructs, albeit with the latter considered by advocates a better way to make sense of the sexed/gendered patterning of individuals. Gender traditionally referred to the social norms regarding sexual roles for men and women, effectively being a structural concept that served to explain the patterning of society with respect to gender, with some linking it with sex while others do not. Confusingly, it has also become commonly used as a synonym for sex, likely due to some sense of embarrassment around use of the word 'sex' and its associated dual meaning, which may account for at least some of the embrace of the term 'gender' rather than 'sex' in everyday discourse. But, more properly, gender—as opposed to biological sex—acts as a concept that seeks to explain how society works to inculcate people born men into masculinity and people born women into femininity.

The seemingly quite innocent claim that 'transwomen are women' (and vice versa for transmen) and that there is 'no debate' about this continues to be made by the leading UK LGBTQ advocacy body Stonewall and has been adopted by many, if not most, activists too. It has become almost totemic for trans rights. Many folks will undoubtedly be happy to consider transwomen as women in many, maybe most, situations (and vice versa, for transmen), but this statement also implies an equivalence that some find problematic. That is not my primary concern here, even though it is undoubtedly important, but this statement also implies a redefinition of the category women (and man) such that we see these terms now founded on gender identity—an inner felt feeling—rather than sex. It is only when we replace sex with gender that this statement starts to make sense, albeit even then it can be contested

(Byrne, 2020, 2022). If it is a felt sense, some inner emotional perception, rather than a biological characteristic that underpins the definition of man and woman, then we are free to determine the boundaries of these terms as we see fit. Now, whether we think this move is a good one or not, it does suggest—once again—quite an overthrow of tradition and perhaps warrants some serious thought and discussion, especially around the limits to such a transformation of citizenship.

For some gender critical feminists (e.g., Brunskell-Evans, 2020) this move represents a muscular reassertion of patriarchy, while others disagree strongly (e.g., Mackay, 2021). For others (e.g., Soh, 2020; Stock, 2021; Wright, 2021, 2023) it involves the denial of science and objective truth, while others disagree (e.g., Fausto-Sterling, 2000; Faye, 2021; Hemmings, 2020; Mackay, 2021). Others fear the consequences of such a shift for a variety of additional reasons. For instance, most recently, Biggs (2022) has discussed his concerns about the shift from sex to gender in the context of English prisons, while Sullivan (2020, 2021) has raised concerns about this in the context of the UK census (see also Suissa & Sullivan, 2021, and Biggs, 2023), and Barnes (2023) raises serious concerns about child safeguarding in the context of gender services for children. This does not seem a time for 'no debate', regardless of the sensitivities. Indeed, given the lack of evidence, complexity, and apparent disagreement about this topic, along with the singular foundational importance of sex/gender within all societies, it seems that this topic demands discussion more than most. To give just a few further examples concerning sex/sexuality, which is the focus of this book.

We might want to discuss the implications of a shift from sex to gender with respect to sexual orientation/identity. Stonewall has arbitrarily shifted its definition of being lesbian or gay from being a sexual orientation founded on same-sex attraction to now being founded on same-gender attraction (Stonewall, 2022). I'm not sure where or when the consultation happened with the wider community on this important change in meaning, but I don't recall ever being asked whether I was comfortable having my sexuality redefined without my consent. It seems rather unfortunate that the leading UK LGBTQ rights organization has taken it upon itself to unilaterally redefine our identities and eschew tradition entirely with respect to same-sex desire. And yet this new definition is now being used as the norm in workplaces and other organizations across the country, in large part because of this organizational initiative.

SEXUAL CITIZENSHIP AND A CLASH OF RIGHTS   99

This change in definition also has implications for sexual desire itself, with divisive concepts like the 'cotton ceiling'—the difficulty trans people experience when seeking sexual relationships—now being deployed by some to argue that, given the primacy of gender rather than sex in sexual identity, lesbians should be willing to have sex with transwomen and vice versa for gay men and transmen. Now, I'm sure some lesbians and gay men will be open-minded about their choice of sexual partner—lots of us have been for many years—but to frame any resistance to including trans folk as partners, which includes people who are anatomically unchanged from birth, as an equivalent to the glass ceiling is deeply problematic. This positions a desire for same-sex as opposed to same-gender people as inherently discriminatory rather than simply reflective of the diversity of human desire, and has worrying echoes of older homophobic narratives, especially around lesbianism. Given that some initial empirical work also suggests that in everyday language people using the terms 'men' and 'women' are generally referring to biological sex rather than gender identity (Jarvis, 2022), it suggests we are witness to the imposition of gender identity upon communities rather than a grassroots drive to effect this change. Furthermore, do we really want communities, and potentially even public or private authorities, policing our sexual desires and practices to this extent? This is already happening with dating apps. Is the threat of a cotton ceiling, and the fact that some will not want to or be able to overcome this sexual difference, however unfair that may feel, so important that we wish to invite others in to police this most personal aspect of our lives?

Whether one is in favour of a shift towards gender identity or not, there also appears to be a serious commodification of identity happening with the increased diversity that attends to gender identity (and, for that matter, recent sexual identities too) as opposed to sex. The proliferation of sexual and gender identities, ably encouraged by the California tech sector, among others, risks trivializing hard-fought-for recognition and undermining the foundation upon which political claims are made. Indeed, one might claim this as an excellent example of the dangers of 'neoliberalism', should that be one's chosen form of critique. The claim that there are 72 gender identities as of 2023, up from 58 gender identities only a year earlier, according to Meta (e.g., Facebook), is a good example of the dangerous interplay of an increasingly reductive identity politics. We may also see risk with the growth in ideas like 'xenogender', a rather novel identity category that has emerged within some sexual and gender diverse communities where

100 SEXUAL CITIZENSHIP AND SOCIAL CHANGE

a person may identify with other species (or objects), such as 'catgender'. This obviously extends the notion of gender to a level most would probably consider absurd, and yet these gender identity categories have even—albeit temporarily—been incorporated within UK university 'pronoun guides'.[7] The complete atomization of gender within certain sections of contemporary society also risks ultimately undermining the notion of gender as an alternative to sex. Putting aside any claim that we are in the realm of the ridiculous, the extension of gender identity to include animals, and beyond, extends a concept that is conceptually important—if it is to replace sex, at least—beyond utility. Such moves may themselves bring down the notion of gender as a replacement for sex. But whether it does or not, it is good evidence that there is considerably more thinking needed before we simply replace sex with gender.

We might also argue, for instance, that the shift towards gender, an internally held feeling, as opposed to sex, an observable physical characteristic, in many ways represents the continuing embrace of 'psychological man' within the present historical era (Rieff, 1959). Psychological man is the term Rieff (1959) used to describe the human type that emerged at the time of Freud who is forever anxious and insecure, preoccupied with self. Drawing upon the concept from Rieff (1959), Lasch (1979) further articulates a rather dystopian vision of the cultural consequences of a shift from 'economic man' to 'psychological man' in contemporary life. This work is now rather old-fashioned and yet also strangely prophetic, with the current period arguably ever more constituted through individual anxiety, insecurity, and narcissism (Pabst, 2021). A variety of forces have played a role in this cultural transformation. But given continuing concerns about the narcissism of the present era, perhaps it might be time to pause and reflect on whether psychological man is the best foundation for humanity.

In other words, there is an awful lot to think about. But the need for further thought on the relationship between sex and gender need not—must not—be framed as an argument for or against support for trans people. The problem is that the sole emphasis on critique in much contemporary discourse on this topic—aided and abetted by the casual importation of critical theory—so often loses sight of the phenomenology and the everyday lived experience that matters. It also too often reproduces a peculiarly privileged and atomized version of individual lived experience, with precious little recognition of individual and collective responsibility. As Byrne (2018) has remarked:

> That sex is not binary is evidently something that many progressives dearly wish to believe, but a philosophically sound case for treating everyone with dignity and respect has absolutely no need of it. . . . To those struggling with gender identity issues, it might seem liberating and uplifting to be told that biological sex in humans is a glorious rainbow, rather than a square conservatively divided into pink and blue halves. But this feel-good approach is little better than deceiving intersex patients: respect for autonomy demands honesty. And finally, if those advocating for transgender people (or anyone else) rest their case on shaky interpretations of biology, this will ultimately only give succor to their enemies.

This is so true. There is no need for trans lives to be caught up in a radical campaign to replace sex with gender or indeed to change or undermine understandings of sex itself, unless they themselves choose to do so, of course. Citizenship for trans folk need not be predicated on such an overthrow of tradition but could, for instance, rely instead on the more traditional, and now canonical, universal claim to human rights, in an equivalent manner to previous—and obviously still ongoing—campaigns for equality from people of colour and sexual minorities. This is for trans folk to decide, but if we can separate out trans rights from this bigger battle over sex and gender, accepting of course that some will not want this, then those who do want to pursue the battle against sex in favour of gender—or otherwise overturn these traditions entirely—can do this openly and honestly by engaging with opponents, with less risk of collateral damage.

The problem of critique as political strategy

So much of the problem here relates to the political strategy being adopted by leading advocacy organizations and many of the most vocal activists on this topic. It is the tendency towards 'cancel culture' as political strategy, which is by no means simply a fiction of the right wing (Ungar-Sargon, 2021), rather than open discussion and debate that really exacerbates the tension at the heart of the gender wars. This also masks many of the issues I have sought to pick apart above, and this is by no means a comprehensive assessment. A recent incident in the United Kingdom with the Equality and Human Rights Commission (EHRC) is a good example of the dominance of cancel culture as the default political strategy being adopted by (some) folk advocating for

102 SEXUAL CITIZENSHIP AND SOCIAL CHANGE

trans rights, notably in this instance the leading UK LGBTQ rights charity Stonewall. This incident was prompted by an EHRC intervention in 2021 to the Scottish plan for legislation in support of trans self-identification within Scotland (Gender Recognition Reform [Scotland] Bill). In a submission to the Scottish Government, the EHRC raised concerns about possible clashes of rights (e.g., regarding the use of single-sex spaces such as women's shelters) and advised the government to consider this matter carefully before engaging in legislative change. The EHRC recognized the need for urgent improvements to gender services in the United Kingdom (Scotland included), but in this intervention it recommended a 3-month pause in which there was time to seek consensus and reflect further on a range of issues in which it perceived there might be some challenges (e.g., with respect to data collection, participation in sport, and practices within the criminal justice system).

We can agree or disagree with this intervention, but it is a position that can be legitimately argued. Some might say it would be useful for there to be more open discussion and reflection on such matters prior to legislative change regarding self-identification to avoid negative impact on vulnerable women. Others may say that self-identification offers no risk, already operates in other countries, and should go ahead regardless. As an intervention, it was—to my mind, at least—a request to pause and reflect rather than anything more determinative or damaging. The Scottish Government has the power to press ahead if it wishes, albeit it would generally be unwise to simply ignore the view of the EHRC given its role as the statutory national human rights body charged with enforcing the UK Equality Act (2010).

However, this intervention by the EHRC has been claimed by Stonewall to be an attack on rather than defence of equality. Here too one could argue that this is also a legitimate position to take. Stonewall has every right to make this case and convince all interested parties that the concerns of the EHRC are unfounded and their intervention unwarranted. As an advocacy organization they support self-identification for trans folk and believe legal change to allow this will not result in harm to anyone else, vulnerable women or otherwise. But instead of engaging in debate about the issues at stake, which are otherwise being endlessly debated in the UK media, Stonewall—in alliance with a number of other bodies—once again attempted to shut down the debate completely, in this instance by attempting to have the EHRC itself shut down on the grounds they are not politically neutral.[8]

A claim of political neutrality or not is complex, not least in the case of the trans versus gender critical debates. Surely, both sides of such a debate are politically engaged and must necessarily be so? This issue does not simply fall into a disagreement between those with left- versus right-wing viewpoints either. It was, for instance, the centre right government of then Prime Minister Theresa May that first sought to enact new self-identification legislation for trans people in the United Kingdom. That same government remains in power, as of 2023, albeit now under a new prime minister, and there has recently been considerable rollback on the plan for self-identification, in England at least. Many, if not most, gender critical feminists would also politically identify with the left. The Scottish Government responded to the EHRC intervention by saying that the planned legislation did not provide substantive new rights for trans people or exceptions to the single-sex provision in the Equality Act. But Stonewall did not respond similarly or seek to engage in debate about the issues identified. Instead, backed by the Good Law Project, it drew up a submission to the Global Alliance of National Human Rights Institutions, calling for the EHRC to lose its 'A rating', such that it would be unable to make representations at the United Nations and elsewhere. It lost the case.

It is exactly this kind of action that is stifling much-needed—considered and respectful—debate on this topic. Stonewall's political practice may ultimately help to push through their position with respect to self-identification, but at what cost? The public debate about such matters has not been undertaken; the public—where they are even aware of these matters—have not being persuaded of the validity of the case. An Ashcroft poll in 2023 found just 22% of Scots supported the Gender Recognition Reform Bill. This is sadly the stuff of the culture wars and not a war in this instance being led only by a regressive right-wing agenda. Such actions risk resentment or even angry backlash. To disavow tradition with respect to sexed bodies versus a critique that privileges gender identity in such a cavalier manner is a high-risk strategy, to say the least. And sadly, there are numerous other examples, including far too many that involve vile personal attacks, from individuals and organizations likely to do much more harm than good: instilling fear is not an effective tactic for winning hearts and minds.

If we contrast this strategy with earlier LGBTQ protest, the strategic change is striking. To give just one trivial example, I recall being part of a mostly young activist student network fighting homophobia (and later biphobia) when at university. We had a local MP who was an arch homophobe, and who would likely have also been a transphobe, but such matters were only infrequently discussed outside queer circles at that time. We did not seek to silence him or produce leaflets threatening to kill him (see recent cases at Sussex University with Stock, Essex with Phoenix, and also now Cardiff[9]). No, we invited him to debate with us, and we mobilized the masses to protest directly to him. No doubt the odd letter sent his way will have been offensive, but the tenor of the engagement was never intended as such. We instead sought to win the debate. We knew that we were unlikely to persuade this individual character, but that was not the point. We sought to win the argument with the political class and wider public more generally. We wanted to preach beyond the choir. These debates also helped us hone our argument and identify issues with the claims being made. We became a more powerful force through this engagement, much surer of our arguments, and much more aware of the consequences of the change we sought to bring about. The connection with tradition also ensured that we never detached ourselves from the beliefs of those who had doubts about our claims, some of which were fair minded, some of which were not. That link with tradition, no matter how uncomfortable at times, was crucial for effecting lasting change.

The current strategy of 'no debate', 'cancellation', and old-fashioned threat of violence in some instances may effect change in the short term, but I fear it may not be long lasting. We are already witnessing a backlash against Stonewall, and trans advocates more generally, and not just by the usual suspects. The 'no debate' political strategy, allied to the determination to 'cancel' all and any opposition, also acts to recruit otherwise neutral or uninterested parties to the fray, driven to intervene by a sense that something is amiss here in the aggressive way gender ideology is being advocated and policed. When old allies turn against you, it speaks to a failed political strategy that needs to be reflected upon before further damage is done. The irony here is that the 'no debate' position reduces complex cultural change to a divisive binary: 'you're either with us or you are against us.' It allows no room to think through the complexity inherent in such change. Nor does it allow space to have those difficult conversations about sex versus gender or the opportunity to explore and alleviate legitimate worries and doubt. It is the very antithesis of an ethos of diversity and yet framed entirely within the present paradoxical incarnation of that notion.

Conclusions

In this chapter I have sought to raise a particularly thorny issue, which concerns a clash of cultures in which those involved are themselves marginalized. We are going to have to be a little braver if we are to address some of the remaining—intrinsically difficult—cultural challenges required to improve the situation for sexual (and gender) minority people in the United Kingdom and elsewhere. The tension between some kinds of religious faith communities and sexual and gender diverse folk cannot be ignored in the hope that it will simply go away. The protests at UK schools, mostly among Muslim individuals (not just parents), because of the teaching of sexual and gender diversity is alarming. Head teachers have found themselves in an intolerable position but have bravely stood their ground, despite limited support from key authorities. The UK Department for Education, which we might have expected to play a key role in resolving this situation, was noticeably absent. The state was not present to support sexual and gender diversity when the challenge presented to it was perceived to involve a clash of cultures. Absent too were many LGBTQ people and organizations offering a counterprotest and critique of the narrative of sexualization, as if our ability to mobilize has been lost, captured by fear, or at least temporarily forgotten. The lack of passion for protest, with a move to accommodation instead, at least when it concerns a category of persons the left currently deems particularly vulnerable, opens up space for others to draw upon older traditional narratives, rise up, and protest against us without resistance.

The narrative deployed here is an old trope in which the overly sexual queer is positioned in opposition to the figural image of the innocent child. This pernicious narrative is operationalized through another contemporary narrative concerned with the sexualization of children and one of freedom of religious expression. The former contemporary concern has been cleverly deployed here to ward off the charge of being homo-, bi-, and transphobic. This is not about sexual and gender diversity but about protecting children from overly sexualized queers, emerging within an overly sexualized culture. The latter is an old trope but one that has not been challenged, even among those opposed to the protest. Indeed, supporters of the diversity programme sought to distance themselves from any notion that there was anything sexual in the programme or that this represented a battle between two incompatible ideological positions. What we saw instead was either the removal of the programme or action to get the protest moved farther away from the school entrance and dialogue between staff and parents to calm down their fears about the content. There was little evidence of drawing a line in support of sexual and gender diversity or critique. Tolerance is a particularly pernicious narrative in this regard. Walters (2014: 148) shows how the 'tolerance trap' is sabotaging the fight for equality: 'By framing social justice and equal rights as a kind of "gift" bestowed upon "us" to a minority "them."' Tolerance is, after all, the acceptance of something that we otherwise would rather not encounter. The story of tolerance that underpins much discourse concerning sexual and gender diversity may at times become pernicious in constructing a sexual subject that remains marginalized, with the normative centre untouched in any meaningful way by this dangerous otherness (see also Mowlabocus, 2021).

The other political context at play here concerns the notions of homonationalism (Puar, 2007) and/or homocolonialism (Rahmen, 2014), where we see the deployment of sexually diverse lives by critical theorists as evidence only in an argument against Western imperialism. Both Puar and Rahmen rightly demonstrate how discourses of sexual equality can be deployed to further demonize the non-Western other, as a continuing form of imperialism. The danger here though is how contemporary critical theorists now increasingly only discuss sexually diverse lives in this context, as if equality in the West is all over and done with. Goal achieved, we can now turn our attention fully and without reservation to the next issue and pursue the critical agenda yet further. This has two possible negative consequences. First, it is underpinned by and/or leads to an assumption that sexual equality has been achieved within Western democracies, something that has been shown to be palpably untrue. Second, this discourse may be in part to blame for an apparent reluctance on the part of the LGBTQ and allied community of scholars and activists to challenge sexual (and gender) prejudice in non-Western communities. The clash of cultures in the school protests is a good example of this, as a specific example of a more general issue where progressive politics fails because it faces a genuinely hard question about a clash of cultural values.

The situation is similar but arguably even more challenging in the fight between trans folk and gender critical feminists, and other associated actors. Here too both groups can justly claim disadvantage, and both genuinely feel that they are under attack. The 'gender wars' are primarily being conducted among folk from the left of the political spectrum in the United Kingdom;

SEXUAL CITIZENSHIP AND A CLASH OF RIGHTS   107

this is not about right-wing conservative religious opposition. Instead, we have a battle between the (still as yet) unfulfilled promises of a strand of feminism regarding sex-based rights and a new utopian critique seeking to shift the societal focus away from sex-based rights towards gender-based rights. If we are to avoid vulnerable folk being caught up in a battle not of their own making, further resistance, or even backlash against progressive change towards equality, then we must speak openly about this issue. This topic needs compassionate and reasoned debate urgently; the call for 'no debate' is hugely problematic, and also thoroughly disingenuous. The charge of 'bothsideism'—a tendency to treat policy debate as if both sides are equally valid, regardless of the evidence—is likely to be levelled at this call for dialogue. This is a dangerous concept, however, that risks tipping into totalitarianism. Who gets to decide the validity of opposing arguments such that they may be legitimately heard or not if they are not themselves subject to public discussion and debate? A claim of individual and community vulnerability cannot be used to force through radical change without due reflection, discussion, and debate. To resist the move from sex to gender need not mean those involved seek the erasure of trans lives or do not support claims for equal citizenship. We need to work hard to ensure that everyone understands that trans lives matter regardless of how we conceive of sex and gender. These folks are human beings deserving of equal rights, support, and compassion, just like any other citizen.

That said, there are undoubtedly aspects of the claims being made by (some) trans folk and their allies that might be perceived as problematic—and may indeed be problematic—by equally well-intentioned others, especially where these demands involve change to long-held and -valued tradition. This needs to be discussed and unpicked properly; claims for citizenship are always complex and multiple and rarely resolved through single-issue—'you are for us or against us'—politics. There might be legitimate concerns that need to be researched and/or thought through further, particularly regarding things like health care, to avoid inadvertent harms. The use of an aggressive cancel culture politics to silence opposition leads to reasonable discussion and debate being pushed underground, with the public sphere occupied increasingly by those with the most strident and uncompromising voices. Critique is vital for challenging tradition, enabling us to imagine a different future and effect progressive change. But unfettered critique that has become detached from—and disrespectful of the value of—tradition may also be dangerous at times, especially when allied to a political strategy designed to silence the

108 SEXUAL CITIZENSHIP AND SOCIAL CHANGE

other. What is utopian to one community may well be dystopian for another. The current anger about this topic, where all those concerned might otherwise seek to be kind, inclusive, and supportive of minorities, is a very good, albeit tragic, example of the very real danger of a politics of critique that has lost sight of the value in maintaining a dialectical relationship with tradition.

Notes

1. https://no-outsiders.com/
2. https://www.bbc.co.uk/news/education-50566453
3. https://www.bbc.co.uk/news/uk-england-birmingham-49110151
4. https://www.bbc.co.uk/news/uk-england-birmingham-50557227
5. https://www.thetimes.co.uk/article/ministers-too-silent-on-lgbt-school-protests-says-former-adviser-louise-casey-dsrzbzm6n
6. https://www.bbc.co.uk/news/uk-england-birmingham-49755250
7. https://www.independent.co.uk/life-style/catgender-bristol-university-pronoun-guide-b2010087.html
8. https://www.bbc.co.uk/news/education-60331962
9. https://freespeechunion.org/letter-to-jeremy-miles-ms-minister-for-education-and-welsh-language-concerning-a-campaign-of-violent-threats-and-harassment-against-several-of-our-members-who-are-all-academics-at-cardiff-universit/

5

Conservative claims for citizenship

There is another version of critique within sexual citizenship that turns the relationship between tradition and critique completely on its head. This is where critique leads to sexual minority communities embracing what appears almost identical to previously oppressive tradition within the context of an ersatz performative radicalism. This is distinct from the well-discussed issues of political assimilation and homonormativity that might be seen in the embrace of traditional notions of marriage and the family within sexually diverse communities (see, e.g., Bell & Binnie, 2000; Duberman, 2018; Mowlabocus, 2021; Warner, 1993, 2000). This is instead critique that has become so distorted as to appear indistinguishable from the very thing that these self-same communities sought to resist or overthrow. And what distinguishes this form of citizenship from simple assimilation is that the people reproducing tradition as critique more often than not seek to position their practices, identities, and attendant claims for citizenship as radical and progressive. The examples I draw on to evidence this argument are bondage and discipline, domination and submission, sadism and masochism (BDSM) as therapy and polyamory as love.

Before I go any further, I want to be clear that this argument should not be read as criticism of individuals in these communities who understand their own experience through narratives of tradition (or critique). It is not for me to judge individual choices about how people make sense of their own sexual desire. My aim is to focus upon community advocacy in favour of these narratives and the work of communities to encourage the telling of certain stories over others (cf. Plummer, 1995), albeit recognizing that individual stories are necessarily intertwined with community discourse and so a focus on one necessarily implicates the other. This is about the stories that are being spoken by individuals and then coached into the public sphere by activists and their communities, stories of citizenship that are becoming canonical.

The problem with critique as the reproduction of tradition is that it effectively mimics the language and practice of (present and former) normative sexual life. With the rise of a therapy narrative within BDSM communities,

Sexual Citizenship and Social Change. Darren Langdridge, Oxford University Press. © Oxford University Press 2024.
DOI: 10.1093/oso/9780199926312.003.0005

we are—I will argue—witness to a peculiar community reproduction of psychiatric thinking about this sexual practice. It risks production of a dominant narrative in which BDSM is once again associated with pathology in need of cure, the only difference being the absence of the professional psychiatrist (Barker & Langdridge, 2009; Langdridge & Barker, 2013). And with polyamory, we see activists deploying the language of love in the public sphere, reproducing stories akin to Hollywood movies, even if this is not necessarily reflective of much everyday life. This may appear harmless, maybe even simply reflective of the focus among polyamorists on love rather than sex. But there is a tension here too. Stories of polyamory are beginning to eclipse all other stories of relationships beyond the dyadic, silencing alternative stories of sexual citizenship, notably those that serve to bring more obviously sexual subjects into the public sphere. And this is happening within minority communities as well as within society more generally. Key to this canonical narrative is a naturalizing discourse in which polyamory is promoted—ostensibly in contrast with monogamy—as the natural, normal, and healthy state for human relating (Willey, 2016). The reproduction of such a naturalizing discourse serves to ground polyamory in a pernicious biological foundationalism that undermines agency and implicates the practice/identity in the attendant problems of biological foundationalism (Willey, 2016).

The copying of present or former hostile discourse, apparent with BDSM and polyamory, speaks to the philosopher Rene Girard's (1966, 1986) belief that at the heart of desire is mimicry. Girard argues that we imitate other people's desires and, as such, come to desire the same things as the other, with the risk of rivalry as two people (or communities) strive for the same object. Mediation is the process by which a person influences the desire of another, with the person being copied becoming the 'mediator' or 'model' when their desires are imitated (Girard, 1966, 1986). This process is not conscious, however, but operates outside awareness as a fundamental part of human nature. Girard (1966, 1986) further argues that mediation becomes more commonplace as societal hierarchies lessen, something that has been particularly acute when it comes to contemporary Western cultures. Mimetic desire may develop to such a degree that the person ultimately wants to become their mediator. The mediator becomes the 'obstacle' to satisfying the desire, resulting in a rivalrous competition that is addictive, impossible to resist, and outside conscious awareness and control. This 'obstacle addiction' involves people acting to hide their addiction from themselves through any means possible, to avoid giving any sense of reward to those being imitated or fuelling their own humiliation.

The stories of BDSM as a therapy and polyamory as a love story both speak to this sense of mimetic desire, the former desirous of the power of psychiatry and psychology and the latter desirous of the power of a naturalized heteronormative marriage and the family. This is not assimilation but rather a rivalrous appropriation of the tools of the oppressor. The language of tradition here is also imbued with power. The language of the 'psy' professions is the language of the current age, ever expanding in scope (Furedi, 2004; Lasch, 1979). The language of marriage and the family is an even older and more pervasively powerful tradition, even if it is one that has undergone some rather fundamental changes in the last few hundred years (Coontz, 2004). And in both instances, and for very good reasons, hierarchies have lessened. The untrammelled power of the medical profession has been moderated by patient empowerment, greater shared knowledge of medicine, and so on. The hierarchies concerned with marital love and family life have also been eroded, initially through the shift to marriage founded on love in the 18th century, with effective contraception, feminism, LGBTQ activism, etc., to follow (Coontz, 2004). It is perhaps not surprising that the present era becomes a time in which former obstacles—canonical narratives of tradition—become embraced by those they used to oppress, hidden from self and other within narratives of tradition masquerading as critique.

BDSM, psychiatry, and the growth of a therapy narrative

BDSM—a compound term for a range of sexual practices, including bondage and discipline, domination and submission, and sadomasochism—continues to occupy a liminal space within the social imaginary of sexual citizenship. Here we can find a story of progress but one that also needs some qualification, even more so than the story of contemporary LGBTQ life in the United Kingdom. BDSM is variously narrated as a form of psychopathology in need of treatment and cure, an activity involving violence and abuse in need of legal sanction, a thrillingly decadent and transgressive counterculture in which people can explore self and other in ever more fantastical and (sometimes) extreme ways, or simply part of the natural variation of sexual desire (see, e.g., Beckmann, 2009; Brown et al., 2020; Califia, 1994; Cruz, 2015, 2016a, 2016b, 2021; Downing, 2007, 2013; Langdridge & Barker, 2013;

112 SEXUAL CITIZENSHIP AND SOCIAL CHANGE

Langdridge & Parchev, 2018; Moser & Madeson, 1996; Newmahr, 2011; Simula, 2019; Weiss, 2011). Consequently, people who practice BDSM may be constructed as pathological and inherently troubling subjects or sexual adventurers pushing the boundaries of personal pleasure, albeit more commonly the former rather than the latter. These very different narrative understandings are shifting and changing all the time.

Medicalization and pathology

There has been an ongoing challenge towards practitioners of BDSM from the medical professions, particularly the psychiatric profession. Sexual sadism and masochism have been listed in the psychiatric nosologies of the American Psychiatric Association (APA; *Diagnostic and Statistical Manual of Mental Disorder*, fourth edition, text revision [DSM–IV–TR]) and the World Health Organization (*International Classification of Diseases*, 10th edition [ICD-10]) for many years. The consequences of psychiatric classification are significant. Not only may individual BDSM practitioners encounter a pathologizing psychiatric (and broader mental health) profession, but also the medical categorization impacts on legislation and experiences of the legal system, as well as wider public understandings. But things are changing for the better here with substantial progress regarding the status of BDSM within the latest edition of the APA diagnostic manual (DSM-5).

The latest edition of DSM has been published (as Version 5) following a long period of consultation about changes to diagnostic categories by the APA task force charged with rewriting this document. The APA claims that the DSM is and should continue to be 'neutral with respect to theories of etiology' (APA, 2000: xxvi) rather than grounded in psychoanalysis, as it was when first created. However, as Kleinplatz and Moser (2005) point out, this assumes that science can be value free. During the process of construction of the new APA diagnostic manual, a number of organizations, academics, and activists sought to petition the APA to have sexual sadism and masochism removed since, it was argued, they do not meet the criteria for categorization as a psychiatric disorder (e.g., distress and dysfunction) or where they do it is because of discrimination rather than individual pathology (see Baggaley, 2005; Kleinplatz & Moser, 2004, 2005, 2006; Moser, 2016; Moser & Kleinplatz, 2005a, 2005b). These arguments and others from key clinicians in the field, along with the campaigning efforts of the National Coalition for Sexual Freedom (NCSF[1]), had an impact, and the DSM-5, which was published in 2013, no longer considered BDSM a disorder per se.[2] That is, the diagnostic criteria were changed such that BDSM interests and activities are not in and of themselves sufficient to warrant a psychiatric diagnosis, a major change from the previous editions. BDSM practices may still lead to a psychiatric diagnosis but now only where there is distress and impairment in everyday living.

The breakthrough in declassifying BDSM as pathology in need of psychiatric treatment is undoubtedly important, and there is already emerging evidence that it is having a positive impact on the lives of people who engage in BDSM. The NCSF reports that there has been a substantial drop in the number of people having their children removed from them on the basis of their sexual preferences. The number of discrimination cases dropped from 600 in 2002 to 500 in 2010 and, following the change to DSM, to around 200 in 2015.[3] The change to this diagnostic manual that resulted from the campaigning efforts of a dedicated group of people has had a profound impact on the lives of BDSM practitioners already in the United States. It is also likely to make a difference to the lives of people beyond the United States given the widespread use of the APA DSM in world psychiatry and the fact that the other widely used diagnostic manual, the World Health Organization ICD-11 (11th edition), has followed the lead of the DSM-5 in adopting the same model of moving from diagnosis on the basis of paraphilia alone to one based on paraphilic disorder and individual distress not caused by prejudice. This is undoubtedly a story of progress in which one line of resistance to sexual freedom and equality has been pushed back.

There remains some way to go with regard to BDSM and the medical professions, however. It will take some time for the changes to the psychiatric manuals to change psychiatric practice. Psychiatric and psychotherapeutic training courses are also frequently poor when it comes to sexual (and gender) diversity issues (Davies & Barker, 2015). There will often be just one or two sessions on LGBTQ issues with rarely anything on sexual and gender diversity more broadly. As a specialist working therapeutically in this field myself, I still see far too many clients who have had their interests in BDSM categorized as pathology by other therapists, most often these days as a form of sexual addiction. The addiction model has been in the ascendency for some time so perhaps it is no surprise to see it being deployed here, but it is deeply troubling nonetheless (see Ley, 2012; Reay et al., 2015). It may be

114 SEXUAL CITIZENSHIP AND SOCIAL CHANGE

that addiction forms the foundation of the next twist in this tale of sexual pathology; time will tell.

BDSM and the rise of the therapeutic narrative

Notwithstanding the changes outlined above designed to extricate BDSM from the psychiatric profession, within BDSM communities there has been a noticeable rise in the telling of a narrative of BDSM as psychologically therapeutic (Barker, Gupta, & Iantaffi, 2013; Barker & Langdridge 2009; Cruz, 2019; Lindeman, 2011). This narrative appears to offer a valuable way of articulating the experience of BDSM practice for a growing number of people. It frequently involves some notion of BDSM being healing and a journey from mental illness to psychological health, as in the film *Secretary* (2002). Central to many of these stories are accounts of how people use BDSM to take control over their bodies, as we can see in the documentary *Sick* (1997), or otherwise rework past trauma (Barker & Langdridge, 2009). Scenes are created and worked through in order to process some troubling sense of self. We see people engaging in BDSM to release pent-up emotions that would otherwise overwhelm, to atone for past wrongdoings, or to be released from the responsibilities of contemporary life.

So, what is the harm? Why are these community tales of health and healing through sexual practice problematic? Well, first, BDSM has historically been associated with trauma and abuse within the medical profession (Langdridge & Barker, 2013). Despite empirical evidence suggesting it is incorrect (see, e.g., Brown et al., 2020; Moser & Kleinplatz, 2006, 2020), a common assumption is that people who engage in BDSM have suffered abuse (trauma) in some way in their childhood and are then re-enacting it later in life. There is obviously a psychoanalytic root to this story, and it is pervasive, with people outside and within BDSM communities adopting the story with often quite troubling consequences. It has been argued that the use of therapeutic narratives can be seen as an attempt to wrest the story of pathology from the medical profession, to radically rework it, and to take ownership of it (Barker, Gupta, & Iantaffi, 2013; Cruz, 2019; Hammers, 2014). That is, by deploying a narrative of healing through BDSM practice, these folks deny the medical profession control of their bodies and instead forge a nonmedical alternative for thinking through their mental health and well-being. The narrative of therapy is therefore not only a way of phenomenologically describing

CONSERVATIVE CLAIMS FOR CITIZENSHIP   115

the experience of BDSM for some people but also a political rejection of the increasing biomedicalization of our bodies (cf. Clarke et al., 2010). This does sound like a positive position, and a radical one too. However, as I have argued elsewhere, I continue to fear that the negatives outweigh the positives, at least in political rather than personal terms (Barker & Langdridge, 2009). The use of a narrative that implies that people engaging in BDSM need healing combined with the increasingly hegemonic nature of the therapeutic narrative risks reinscribing pathology within this community whilst shutting down other voices. So, whilst we might want to welcome people articulating their experiences in whatever manner makes most sense to them, this carries political consequences when amplified by a community beyond that individual and their experiential process.

Lindeman's (2011) analysis of professional dominatrices ('pro-dommes') in New York and San Francisco helps us think this through further as her participants deployed the language of therapy, at least in part, to make sense of their work. In this study of 66 female pro-dommes, the participants describe their work—in Lindeman's terms—as 'an alternative to repression, a mechanism for atonement, a device for confronting past trauma, and a psychological reprieve from the pressures of postmodern life' (p. 168). They argue that the essence of what they do is offer a safe and nonjudgmental space in which their clients can work through their needs, in which BDSM activities are construed as psychologically healthy. This is obviously in direct opposition to the traditional—albeit now changing—psychiatric discourse of BDSM as inherently pathological. However, the stories of these pro-dommes are complex. For instance, there are examples where the pro-dommes draw directly on notions of pathology underpinning a client's need and therefore reinforce rather than undermine the link between pathology and BDSM. They also talk of BDSM practices as 'recuperative' and so invoke a notion of cure, and therefore end point, which is resonant with the notion of pathology but not a returning client engaged in a consensual sexual relationship, and so is counterproductive for client and pro-domme alike. The shift in narrating their work as therapy rather than sex work speaks to a particular issue about how people make sense of their experience through the stories they tell about it. These women appear to want to distance themselves from the more stigmatized notion of being sex workers and instead embrace the more acceptable notion of being (mental) health care workers. This is, of course, understandable in the Western context where the canonical narrative of therapy is laden with power and privilege, and undoubtedly seductive. The danger is

116 SEXUAL CITIZENSHIP AND SOCIAL CHANGE

how this narrative of therapy may operate at a cultural level to imbue a sense of vulnerability, or dysfunction even, to the clients whilst elevating the professional dommes (and male doms) to a privileged (nonpathologized) status.

Hammers (2014) investigated the experience of women BDSMers who were survivors of sexual violence and engaged in 'rape play', where they re-enact consensual scenes of sexual violence. The women in Hammers's (2014) study reported engaging in rape play in order to effect bodily change, notably shifting a sense of somatic dissociation resulting from their experience of sexual violence, in order to gain a greater sense of control and bodily integrity. Hammers (2014: 73), drawing on the notion that BDSM may involve a 'fusion of bodily horizons' (Langdridge, 2007), argues that rape play allows participants to gain recognition and affirmation for their embodied pain such that

> in this moment of recognition, shame, that overriding negative affect, is contested and transfigured into bodily affirmation thus triggering somatic (re)connection. Rape play interrupts the doubt and disabling that had held the body hostage. It is through this sharing—a consensual type of dumping—that the somatic pain loosens its grip on the victim, unleashing in turn the becoming process.

The accounts that underpin this claim provide powerful evidence of the value of this practice for these women and its therapeutic value. It is unclear whether this is a process that resolves the sense of somatic dissociation once and for all or not, but regardless the ability of these survivors of sexual violence to take control of their assault experience and work through it has value for them personally.

Another place where BDSM has been perceived to have therapeutic potential is with people of colour (and others) engaging in 'race play'. Cruz (2019) offers important insight regarding the potential value of BDSM in offering a space for reworking race-based trauma, in multiple and complex ways. Race play involves BDSM scenes in which people enact racially charged experiences. This may include, for instance, Jewish people being interrogated by Nazis or themselves acting as Nazi guards and people of colour enacting scenes of slavery. Like rape play, this form of BDSM practice is controversial, particularly so given the general Whiteness of many BDSM communities. Cruz (2019: 55) identifies race play as a deeply problematic but also potentially powerful practice for Black women, with her arguing that race play—by contrast with much other BDSM practice—'does not exhibit a disavowal of racial hierarchies or material institutionalizations of racial domination; it recognises them'. That is, while much BDSM practice claims a warrant through the ability to undermine existing structural inequalities, e.g., through a parodic distinction between reality and fantasy, that claim should not be made for race play. Instead, Cruz (2019: 56) argues that race play is

> a way to fuck and fuck *with* racism: a potential parody or mimetic re-iteration that exposes the fabrication of race and challenges and reifies racial-sexual alterity and racism and a sexual relationship with these 'racialisms'—a pleasure in their enactment, a getting off on, a fucking.

This is especially complicated because—by contrast with much of the theatre of BDSM—one's race cannot be chosen when wanted or simply walked away from when the scene is concluded:

> While I agree that this tension between fantasy and reality becomes a productive dichotomy in the labor of BDSM . . race play does not exhibit a disavowal of racial hierarchies or material institutionalizations: it recognises them. . . . Mollena Williams's statement that 'I do race play whether or not I want to' is relevant here. . . . Her words testify to the always alreadyness and perdurability of race play for black women. (Cruz, 2019: 55–59)

This distinction is profoundly significant given that so much BDSM is performative, focussed on the temporary possibility of transcending everyday life for a theatrical alternative within agreed-upon boundaries that provide the necessary sense of safety to push one's limits. While this opportunity exists (ostensibly equally) for people of colour, Cruz (2019) highlights how they cannot escape present-day racial discrimination no matter how they choose to 'play'. As such, race play speaks not only to the potential for the enjoyment of perverse pleasure and/or perceived therapeutic value at an individual level, like rape play, but also the 'enduring power of the black/white binary, the history of slavery, and racism itself' (Cruz, 2019: 73).

Notwithstanding these powerful examples of the potential benefits of BDSM as therapy, there is value in interrogating the language being used by BDSMers themselves here. Within BDSM communities, the psychological benefits of BDSM have been part of the story of BDSM for many years. That is, BDSM has long been associated with transformative experiences that act

118 SEXUAL CITIZENSHIP AND SOCIAL CHANGE

in powerful ways to provide new psychological insight through embodied practice (Califia, 1994). Perhaps the growing use of the language of therapy is not grounded in a change to the lived experience of BDSM practitioners per se, but rather in the stories that are available to make sense of this experience and the forces that serve to support some stories over others within the public sphere. Stories of transformation and healing, whether sexual or not, are increasingly being narrated through the language of (formal and credentialed) therapy rather than through the language of religious or spiritual practice, and it is this canonical therapeutic story that is gaining traction within and beyond BDSM communities. Califia (1994) argues that shame is very hard to eliminate from sex, and this may account for the apparent need among some to warrant their sexual desires through a claim to something seemingly more significant, whether that is enhanced spirituality or—as in the present context—healing potential. As Califia (1994: 238) insightfully remarks, 'Sex does not need to be justified. Pleasure is a virtue and virtue is its own reward.' I do agree, but regardless, the point I want to make here is that while individuals may engage in BDSM in ways that feel therapeutic, it is the reproduction of these experiences through the language of therapy within the public sphere—as part of a claim for sexual citizenship—that may inadvertently harm members of this community. It risks a return to BDSM being a story of pathology, with other stories marginalized and external criticism reinforced. Such stories may be read externally as pathology in need of professional intervention and may very well invite a return of unwanted psychological scrutiny that has only just started being pushed back.

To give just one example, I will briefly discuss a legal case in the United Kingdom that involves a rather sinister attempt to police the sex life of a man on the basis of unacceptable sexual fantasies. In echoes of the dystopian future presented in Philip K. Dick's *Minority Report* in which people are identified as criminals in advance of committing any crime, this case involves a variety of legal and medical professionals severely restricting a person's (sexual) liberty on the basis that he might commit a criminal act in the future. John O'Neill from York in the north of the United Kingdom was found not guilty of rape in 2015, but a magistrate court, following advice from the local police force, issued a 'Sexual Risk Order' (under the Anti-Social Behaviour, Crime and Policing Act, 2014), which meant that O'Neill must inform the police of any intention to have sex or engage in a relationship with a woman 24 hours in advance. The police can then inform the woman of their concerns about O'Neill, despite him not having a conviction for any crime. If he has sex without first notifying the police, he could be sent to prison for breach of the Order.

The grounds for the Order stem from O'Neill revealing information to a psychiatric nurse and his local doctor in which he expressed suicidal thoughts along with thoughts about killing and choking partners, including a statement that he 'thought it might have gone further than she expected'. This evidence is contested by O'Neill, who claims he was speaking about his fantasies only, but it appears the accounts of these two health care professionals remain sufficient for the courts, and his attempts to appeal the Order have repeatedly failed. The old story of BDSM as pathology in need of medical or legal intervention is clearly the canonical narrative operating here. Investigation by the press has revealed that UK police forces have issued sexual risk orders on at least 50 occasions in the 2 years since they were introduced in 2014 (Sky News, 2016). It might be argued that it is appropriate to oversee the actions of a dangerous person, but there is no evidence as yet that this man is actually dangerous—he has not been convicted of any crime. He has also not been detained under mental health legislation for being a danger to himself or others, but—based on two brief meetings with a psychiatric nurse and general medical practitioner in which he argues he simply expressed his sexual fantasies and depressive thoughts—he has suffered the loss of sexual rights available to every other UK citizen.

> The government says Sexual Risk Orders are given in cases where a person has 'done an act of a sexual nature' which has given officials 'reasonable cause to believe that it is necessary for an order to be made', even if the person 'has never been convicted'. So these individuals aren't criminals; they've just had sex in a way the authorities don't like. The authorities have gone from punishing sex crimes to punishing sex, slapping orders on people for behaving in a way that was presumably a little strange, possibly perverted, but not criminal. Through these orders, our rulers have invited themselves into the realm of sex, into what happens between non-criminal, consenting adults. Even the most intimate act that two (or more) grown-ups can engage in is now not free from the prying eyes of officialdom.[4]

This disturbing case raises the spectre that the old narrative trope that BDSM is an expression of pathology is still very much active within the medical and legal professions, in spite of recent changes in psychiatric classification. Individuals and communities seeking to embrace a version of this narrative,

120 SEXUAL CITIZENSHIP AND SOCIAL CHANGE

even when radically reworked, may inadvertently act to reinforce such understandings.

It is important to understand this BDSM narrative within the context of a growing culture of therapeutic storytelling in society (see, e.g., Furedi, 2004). The therapy narrative deployed within BDSM communities reflects a wider cultural trend in which individuals and communities appear to be adopting a peculiarly US-driven psychotherapeutic discourse. The risk is that this becomes totalizing. Previously, narratives of transcendence were popular for explaining the ways that BDSM might be experienced beyond the contained self, in ways that were felt to be healthy—even therapeutic. Powerful narratives, such as the narrative of psychotherapy, tend to dominate as more and more people coax and coach, tell and retell, such stories (Langdridge, 2006, 2013; Plummer, 1995; Weiss, 2006; Wilkinson, 2009). It is difficult to sustain marginal stories in the face of narratives that speak to wider cultural understandings that are themselves imbued with power and privilege. A story's fit within the social imaginary is critical for its reception, and with the growth of mass (and social) media, narratives circulate cross-culturally more and more. This has huge potential for opening up new ways of making sense of sexual life but also carries considerable risk if the only stories that are told become tales of therapeutic sex or Hollywood romance, as I discuss below. The key here is how we must think critically about the lines of power operating through narratives and whether they will become hegemonic and shut down other possibilities. In the case of the therapeutic narrative of BDSM, this is a worry. Not only does a therapeutic narrative carry connotations of pathology and the need for healing—with all the associated risks that this entails regarding unwanted legal and medical intervention—but also it desexualizes BDSM practice. BDSM in these terms is no longer a pleasurable sexual pursuit, a form of serious sexual leisure if you will (Attwood & Smith, 2013; Newmahr, 2010, 2011), but is instead another desexualized part of the reflexive project of self (Giddens, 1991, 1992), a way of coping with personal vulnerability and uncertainty in these risky and uncertain times (Lasch, 1979).

Polyamory as love

There has been discussion of multiple-partner sex within sexual subcultures for many years, albeit with relatively little wider societal acknowledgement.

The exception is probably the notion of 'free love' in the 'swinging sixties', but even that is rather more of a fiction than reality for most (Jeannin, 2021). My focus in this section is specifically on polyamory, a compound term for 'many loves' ('poly' from the Greek for several/many and 'amor' from Latin for love), which has been embraced by people wishing to engage in intimate relationships with more than one partner at the same time (Barker & Langdridge, 2010a, 2010b). I focus on polyamory primarily because stories about this form of nonmonogamy are in the ascendency, eclipsing all other stories of multiple-partner or nonmonogamous sex. Polyamory is also interesting for how it involves claims about having radical potential to shake up heteronormativity through an attack on dyadic relating but which often instead—at least in much public presentation—adopts a curiously neoconservative narrative tone in which sex is very much background to an 'ethical' love. I should note that by contrast, a good amount of the community literature on polyamory is focused on the possibilities for untrammelled sexual adventure (see, e.g., Hardy & Easton, 2017), and there are others—mostly academics—who seek to deploy poly as part of a wider radical political project. For instance, Sabsay (2016) uses this practice to model her desire to destabilize the neoliberal subject. These radical academic projects tend to be detached from everyday life, however, focussed predominantly on cultural critique, with limited reflection on how this might impact on the lives of those it touches, something I discuss further in the next chapter.

Polyamory and the denial of (sexual) desire

Polyamory is a relatively recent term that has been embraced to describe the practice—and for some also identity/relationship orientation—of engaging in consensual nonmonogamous relationships (see, e.g., Barker & Langdridge, 2010a, 2010b; Ferrer, 2022; Haritaworn et al., 2006; Klesse, 2007, 2014; Scoats & Campbell, 2022; Sheff, 2014). I focus on polyamory in particular because it has in many ways become the dominant story of nonmonogamy in recent years, at least within the United Kingdom, Europe, and the United States (Barker & Langdridge, 2010a, 2010b; Barker, Heckert, & Wilkinson, 2013; Cardoso, 2019; Sheff, 2014). Hitherto popular stories of open relationships, 'fuck buddies', and swingers—albeit mostly in the form of sensational media accounts and late-night documentaries within the wider public sphere outwith these communities—now appear to be receiving much

122   SEXUAL CITIZENSHIP AND SOCIAL CHANGE

less attention, whilst the story of polyamory is in the ascendency. This sadly does appear to be a zero-sum game. And it is the very particular nature of this story with its increasingly singular focus on love rather than sex—a story that is becoming hegemonic for all intimate relating beyond the dyadic—that I focus on here.

Notwithstanding the growth in stories of polyamory, the many campaigns within much of the Western world for same-sex marriage have dominated recent public discourse on sex and relationships beyond the heterosexual norm (Mowlabocus, 2021). And nondyadic sexual relationships of all kinds have been quickly jettisoned by many of those involved in campaigns for same-sex relationship recognition. Marriage for multiple-partner relationships has proven to be a step too far for many marriage equality activists/advocates it seems. Furthermore, multiple-partner relationship forms, including polyamory, have often been positioned by critics of same-sex marriage within a 'slippery slope' discourse as a potential risk of legal equality (see Klesse, 2007, and Rambukkana, 2015, for discussions of these arguments). In this cultural context, nonmonogamies represent both a perceived threat to ongoing efforts for 'equal marriage' rights and a critical challenge to the hegemony of monogamous dyadic relating at the heart of all such claims. This tension offers an opportunity for productive interventions on the part of those advocating for nonmonogamous relating but only if these emergent stories can connect with an appropriate audience to hear them and encourage them further.

Polyamory has been heralded as a radical alternative to dyadic monogamy by those who act as public advocates for this particular form of nonmonogamy (Barker, Heckert, & Wilkinson, 2013; Cardoso, 2014; Haritaworn et al., 2006; Klesse, 2007; Rambukkana, 2015). It has been argued that polyamory acts as a form of resistance to the dominance of what has been termed 'mononormativity', the commonly held assumption that monogamy is the normal and/or proper way of engaging in intimate relationships (Pieper & Bauer, 2005). Monogamy is further entrenched through contemporary notions of 'the family', with monogamous coupledom for parents the expected norm and all other parental forms relegated to second best or worse (Sheff, 2014). Polyamory offers up a challenge to mononormativity, given that it presents the possibility of having an intimate relationship with more than one person at a time, and supposedly also one involving open negotiation, with it sometimes referred to as 'ethical nonmonogamy'. Much polyamory advocacy/lifestyle literature presents polyamory as superior to monogamy on the basis that it involves greater self-awareness and emotional sophistication

CONSERVATIVE CLAIMS FOR CITIZENSHIP 123

(e.g., through resisting notions of competition and possession) and negotiation within relationships (e.g., Anapol, 1997). Underpinning theories to warrant this apparent claim to superiority also abound, ranging from therapeutic enlightenment to critiques of neoliberalism (Barker, Heckert, & Wilkinson, 2013; Barker & Langdridge, 2010b; Klesse, 2007; Rambukkana, 2015). Polyamory has also been drawn upon to provide a story of relationship anarchy beyond intimate relationships through a move from 'multiple lovers' to 'multiple loves', to include not only friends and others but also the environment and planet (Barker, Heckert, & Wilkinson, 2013; see also Ferrer, 2022).

Clearly, there is a lot resting on the story of polyamory! Sadly, however, the disruptive potential of polyamory has been somewhat underrealized to date. It is important to highlight the ideological risks attached to the dominant narrative of nondyadic relationality associated with polyamorous practices, identities, and communities, a narrative that appears to eschew anything sexual and is anything but radical. My concern revolves around the way stories of polyamory may be speaking to a conservative norm as much as—if not more than, in some instances—radical progressive change. Here, with these nascent claims and newly formulated stories of identities and rights, we can see a real risk of internalizing and reproducing a potentially problematic story that is at heart conservative and exclusive. This is a story that may lead to some gains but carries the risk of considerable loss and division through the reproduction of acceptable, age-old tropes about nonsexual romantic subjectivities in contrast to the risk associated with the unacceptable aberrant sexual subject.

In contrast to the variety of other forms of nonmonogamies, the primary focus in the public expression and representation of polyamory is on love, not sex. This is perhaps not surprising given the meaning of polyamory ('many loves') itself but nonetheless presents a potential problem. In contrast to the stories of nonmonogamy that foreground sex (e.g., open relationships, fuck buddies, and swinging), the story of polyamory is gaining ground (Barker & Langdridge, 2010a, 2010b; Barker, Heckert, & Wilkinson, 2013; Cardoso, 2019). There is an audience ready to hear this story, quite likely because of the way that stories of polyamory sit more comfortably with our culturally normative sex negativity. The emphasis on love and care in stories of polyamory are—at least at a superficial level—thoroughly respectable. Rarely will a popular representation touch on sex much beyond a playful picture of three people in a bed, all appropriately covered up of course. The de-emphasis of sex also involves stories of polyamory that draw on the hegemonic story of

124   SEXUAL CITIZENSHIP AND SOCIAL CHANGE

parenthood to help justify this form of nonmonogamy. The rhetorical move in question asks that the audience equate polyamory with parenthood, and how natural it is for a parent to love more than one child, hence loving more than one adult in a relationship being equally natural. This curious rhetorical move would in most other circumstances be dangerous—the child is deployed almost exclusively in opposition to sexuality, and adulthood more broadly (Berlant, 1997)—but the de-emphasis on sexuality within polyamory clearly makes this odd comparison acceptable.

Haritaworn et al. (2006: 519) highlight three primary issues with stories of polyamory:

> First, the produced discourses are frequently unaware of their capacity for setting up their own regimes of normativity. Second, they tend to endorse an abstract individualism at the expense of critiquing the structural power relations around race/ethnicity, gender, sexuality, and class. . . . Third, the posited universalistic model of affect ties in with an imperialist model of the West as sexually and emotionally advanced and superior.

The first of these criticisms is particularly relevant to the arguments in this book. Drawing on the extensive ethnographic investigations of Klesse (2007) and Sheff (2014), we can see how the focus on love sets up a regime of normativity based on an opposition to 'unacceptable' stories of sex and nonmonogamies. Not only is there a de-emphasis on sex within stories of polyamory, particularly those in the public sphere, but also this is not 'neutral' but rather one that involves rhetorical distancing from any association with 'promiscuity' or 'casual sex', akin to traditional narratives of marriage and the family. This is especially notable for how community members engage in dividing practices regarding their 'ethical', 'responsible', 'loving' relationships to distance themselves from clearly less acceptable and permissible stories of casual gay sex ('cruising') and swinging ('wife swapping'), in particular. This may even extend to a complete refusal of anything sexual being involved in their multiple loving relationships such that they are not nonmonogamous at all (Klesse, 2007; Sheff, 2014). The focus on a superior love, perceived and articulated as very different to those nonmonogamies focused on sex, may act to reinforce existing pernicious sex-negative narratives. Much of this distancing discourse feels unpleasantly class based, grounded in educational privilege among those practicing their 'superior' sexuality. Rambukkana (2015) further picks up on the second and third lines of criticism from Haritaworn et al. (2006) to highlight and critique polyamorous communities for their failure to engage adequately with privilege and structural inequalities. Although at times a little harsh, Rambukkana (2015) rightly points out how there has been (a) a failure to attend to power (and intersectionality) such that we can see a systematic othering within polyamorous writing and—it is assumed—communities and (b) the creation of cultural spaces that are themselves privileged and restricted.

Finally, I should mention that there have also been endogenous community claims about polyamory being an identity akin to being lesbian, gay, or bisexual. That is, there are narratives of polyamory emerging from communities that make a claim that polyamory is 'hard wired', an essential element of their sense of selfhood (Barker, 2005; Klesse, 2014). This position has even been used within legal arguments in the United States, in an attempt to include polyamory within workplace antidiscrimination legislation through comparison with LGB identities (Tweedy, 2011). Klesse (2014: 92) argues that this is a further move involving a potentially conservative and normalizing narrative:

> The promotion of sexual orientation models of polyamory will strengthen one-dimensional poly identity political currents in the wider field of politics around consensual non-monogamy. The equation of polyamory with sexual orientation may undermine the disruptive potential of the category polyamory, achieve only selective protection under the law, obstruct the ability of poly movements to pursue broader alliances, and foster a politics of recognition at the expense of a more transformative political agenda.

There is undoubtedly a good deal of truth in this criticism (see also Willey, 2016), although there may well be strategic value in such identitarian moves, albeit also risk if they serve to exclude other voices and stories. Finally, we should note, especially with the claim to a polyamorous identity/orientation in mind, those who engage in polyamory are rather lacking in diversity. Like many contemporary sexual subcultures, especially those involving media-savvy vocal activists, the poly community is very White, educated, and middle class (Klesse, 2007; Sheff, 2014; Sheff & Hammers, 2011). This is not in itself grounds to condemn poly communities per se, as long as they are serious about encouraging more diversity and mindful of how this lack of diversity may impact on the construction of community norms and narratives. I think the jury is out on this, but time will tell. If polyamorous communities are just as White, educated, and middle class, deploying the same story of superior intimate relationality, in 5 years' time as they are now, then I think it'd be safe to say there is a serious problem.

My aim, however, is not to simply offer a critique of polyamory and attendant—albeit still nascent—claims for citizenship rights and wider societal acknowledgement. Perhaps not surprisingly, given the political aims (and educational backgrounds) of those involved with polyamory, there has already been plenty of critique, especially as this identity/practice relates to contemporary sexual politics (see, e.g., Ferrer, 2022; Klesse, 2007; Rambukkana, 2015). Instead, I want to draw attention to the ideological narrative framework that limits polyamorous narratives whilst also recognizing utopian potential where it exists. Thinking of polyamory through traditional either/or critical theoretical discourse, where it must be either a political failure because it is insufficiently critical (see, e.g. Rambukkana, 2015) or the radical solution to all the perceived problems of monogamy (see any of the many popular books written by advocates: e.g., Anapol, 1997; Easton & Liszt, 1997), is both unfair and the product of an unhelpful dichotomous—specifically, either/or—mode of thinking. This is a mode of thinking that is, of course, in stark contradistinction to the Ricoeurian theory that underpins this text, and which argues that we seek out the best from ostensibly opposed either/or philosophical positions. Ferrer (2022) adopts a similar transtheoretical mode of thinking, albeit in an attempt to rethink the non/monogamy binary itself rather than political tradition versus critique.

Polyamory and its practitioners—like all sexual practices and identities—may be both conservative and radical; some may identify their activities as a deliberate critique of mononormativity, while others seek instead only to live a lifestyle beyond the constraints of monogamy (Ferrer, 2022; Wilkinson, 2010). Some who criticize it appear to expect political perfection (Rambukkana, 2015), which is both unrealistic and rather unfair when considering that this is a way of engaging in intimate relationships first and foremost. It seems perfectly reasonable to me that some people may wish to embrace a polyamorous lifestyle simply for the sense of joy and pleasure that this may bring them. They may even believe that living this life—in contrast to a more traditional monogamous one—is a radical political act, offering a challenge to the relational status quo. To some extent, this belief is correct, even if we might question whether it really is the most radical mode of nonmonogamy. The critics too often adopt a politics of the ideal and fail to engage sufficiently with 'real politics' (Geuss, 2008), expecting too much of people trying to find pleasure in their lives rather than giving them over completely to political activism.

That said, the criticisms of polyamory stand, and community members—especially those who make a claim for the radical potential of this relationship form—might wish to attend seriously to the concerns being raised. This is a mode of nonmonogamy that may actually shut down opportunities for radical challenges to mononormativity. That is, if polyamory is the only story of nonmonogamy to be encouraged and heard within the public sphere, even if other stories are being told, then there is a risk that it serves to reinforce existing conservative values regarding acceptable and permissible relationship forms. Wilkinson (2012: 132) argues that 'we are witnessing the coexistence of de-traditionalization and re-traditionalization as ideals of traditional intimacy are reworked and, conversely, reinforced'. The ideology of *compulsory romantic love*—as opposed to just compulsory heterosexuality—now prevails, with profound implications for recognition of relationship and family diversity, perceived permissibility of lifestyle choices, and decisions about social policy (Wilkinson, 2012).

Furthermore, if community members continue to adopt and advocate through a critical story that this is a 'superior' way of relating, then polyamorous people and communities may be guilty of producing new dividing lines that further disenfranchise other more marginal communities, beyond those produced and policed through the dominance of a heterosexual monogamous norm itself. It would be ironic indeed if an avowedly (and supposedly radical) political nonmonogamous relationship form was complicit in shutting down other marginalized—for example, more overtly sexual or culturally diverse—relationship choices. Well-publicized accounts within poly communities of prejudice towards other forms of nonmonogamy (such as swinging) are worrying in this regard. The lack of diversity and rather insular nature of polyamorous communities, allied to normative narratives that are arguably grounded in potentially racist discourse (Willey, 2016), are also concerning. More positively, these problems have been identified by community members already, with some clearly seeking to transcend some extant divisions already (see, e.g., Ferrer, 2022), so we shall have to see whether that results in material change concerning cultural diversity and modification to the present normative story of ethical superiority bound exclusively to the traditional value of love and contractual communication. At present, however, the story of polyamory present within the public sphere speaks as much to traditional, almost Hollywood-style, stories of love and romance.

128 SEXUAL CITIZENSHIP AND SOCIAL CHANGE

The paradox is that this very traditional normative narrative is reproduced—in form if not content, albeit sometimes both—as if a form of radical critique.

Conclusions

The examples discussed above highlight the way that critique may act as a new ideology: in this instance as narratives of neoconservatism. What is ostensibly utopian critique is becoming indistinguishable from the ideology that it sought to overthrow. This is a pernicious transformation of critique, one that itself demands critical interrogation or we risk these neoconservative narratives becoming canonical. There are already signs of them becoming hegemonic, serving as the primary narrative in which individuals make sense of themselves and communities operationalize to claim citizenship. The risk is not simply that communities invoke ideological narratives of tradition in their citizenship claims but that these narratives fix individuals and communities within a regressive social imaginary that limits meaning-making opportunities. These neoconservative narratives also expose communities to problematic intervention from individuals and institutions that are hostile to citizenship claims. That is, stories of BDSM as therapy, while appreciated within some communities, may provide hostile others with an opportunity to pathologize. And while stories of love told of polyamorous communities may provide a valuable opportunity to articulate socially acceptable claims for citizenship, they may serve to silence other more overtly sexual stories from the public sphere and risk the production of a desexualized polyamorous identity that limits the expression of sexual diversity within the broader community that it concerns.

For Girard, mimetic desire may develop to such a degree that the person ultimately wants to become their mediator. That is, it is not the pursuit of the object per se that fuels the desire but instead a 'metaphysical desire' to become the mediator, the object being a mere token of this more fundamental desire. Such metaphysical desire leads to a rivalrous obsession that can never be satisfied, as we can never become the other. In the context of sexual citizenship this rivalry can be seen between BDSMer and psychiatry over the fight for ownership of BDSM itself, both using the language of the 'psy' sciences. It can also be seen between polyamorist and the ideal of the marital couple through the trope of love, deployed within poly to excess. Many of these rivalries were not possible until recently, with the gradual erasure of the hierarchy between medical authority and patient, sexual practice and re-production, heterosexual marriage and the family. These rivalries manifest themselves as endogenous actors or community allies adopting the stories of their oppressors, albeit through distorted versions of the original narrative of tradition. The distorted nature of the narrative—with it being refashioned as radical critique—serves as the means to rationalize and justify the obstacle addiction on show.

So, while accepting the important insights of theorists like Hammers (2014) and Cruz (2016) about the potential for people and communities to rethink—and work through—sexual and/or racial trauma, I think we may be justly concerned about the way the story of medicine, and the 'psy' professions in particular, is now increasingly the story being embraced by BDSM practitioners themselves, albeit in a slightly modified form. The very noticeable rise in the telling of a narrative of BDSM as psychologically thera-peutic appears to offer a valuable way of articulating the experience of BDSM practice for a growing number of people. It invariably involves some notion of BDSM being healing and a journey from mental illness and/or trauma to psychological health, which of course conjures up the question central to the narratives of the 'psy' professions of old about there being some underlying pathology at the heart of BDSM desire. If there were not a pathology in the first place, then why would so many need to be 'healed'?

Whilst key players from activists to academics are attempting to con-struct narratives of choice to claim rights and recognition for BDSM and polyamory, this is not entirely in their hands to determine. Stories need a receptive audience willing to listen (Plummer, 1995). A story of trauma and pathology, while personally exciting or liberating for some practitioners, is exactly the story that those beyond these communities who view them with concern or even revulsion wish to embrace. The history of pathology that is attendant to BDSM, and has caused so much pain, risks a muscular reasser-tion in the social imaginary just as the medical profession itself is backing away from this mode of thinking and practice. The O'Neill case is a good ex-ample, as is the growing public and governmental concern about an increase in sexual choking (Herbenick et al., 2022), an issue increasingly being linked back to BDSM communities. Perhaps, as Hammers (2014) and Cruz (2019) suggest, trauma-focussed play may offer something of value inside these communities, but—I would argue—these stories may be better left opaque to those who do not belong to the communities (Glissant, 1997; Sundén, 2023). There may well be times when complete transparency about sexual life is

130 SEXUAL CITIZENSHIP AND SOCIAL CHANGE

inappropriate, notably when sharing stories beyond particular communities that may put those very communities at risk.

In the case of polyamory, the story being told and heard is one in which sex no longer plays much of a role. The only story of multiple-partner sex being heard is the one that privileges love and care above all else, with any notion of sex beyond the dyadic quickly returned to the closet. There may be the odd peek in the sexual closet, a moment of titillation in a news report, but amongst activists and journalists alike there is a determined effort to construct a story of love first and foremost. Even with nascent stories, where there are critically aware activists and academics ready to narrate them apparently as they wish, the political struggle remains complicated and not within our own hands, no matter how politically aware we might believe ourselves to be. The risk is that the culturally acceptable story of polyamorous love, in a similar manner to the therapeutic story of BDSM, may become hegemonic, with alternative—more overtly sexual—forms of multiple-person sex/intimacy firmly relegated to a subordinate position on the margins, as well as polyamory itself fixed in this desexualized form within the public sphere.

And finally, it is worth stressing that the two examples discussed in this chapter are two of many possible examples that could have been examined. The argument being made in this chapter and the book more generally about the need to engage critically with critique stands beyond the specific examples given here, and beyond the specific national context too. Other ostensibly critical sexualities may be usefully subject to the same critique, not just BDSM and polyamory. There has been a wave of new sexualities framed within the normative language of identity and citizenship, claiming radical critical potential in recent years. New stories of asexual and aromantic identities, for instance, appear at times to represent another incarnation of a narrative of tradition framed as an ostensibly critical narrative of emancipation (see, e.g., Scherrer, 2008; van Anders, 2015; Guz et al., 2022; Hile, 2023, for reviews). Like polyamory and BDSM, we can see naturalized essentializing identities and normative claims for citizenship framed as stories of critique. And while individuals and communities may find this expanding array of identities personally meaningful, the choice of narratives deployed to make sense of them are as potentially problematic as the stories of BDSM and polyamory discussed in this chapter. As much as these new identities provide a sense of recognition and community, they may also reinforce dangerous old ideologies, shut down other possibilities, and divide.

Notes

1. https://www.ncsfreedom.org/
2. https://www.theatlantic.com/health/archive/2015/01/bdsm-versus-the-dsm/384138/
3. https://www.theatlantic.com/health/archive/2015/01/bdsm-versus-the-dsm/384138/
4. http://www.spiked-online.com/newsite/article/in-dystopian-britain-the-police-now-hunt-down-8216pre-rapists8217/17954#.WlIz50vLgk8

6

Spectacular critique and abject citizenship

Spectacular is of course a point of view. Some might consider all sex in this book spectacular. That said, I want to argue that there is a specific distorted and distorting form of critique that seeks out or otherwise serves to create the spectacular. The focus in this chapter is on critique from within by community members and allies that hunts out and appears to revel in the spectacular, often at the risk of harm to those it concerns. This is critique without tradition—there is no sign of Ricoeur's (1986) dialectic of tradition and critique here. This is critique without accountability. Critique is problematic in this context in a number of ways. It can be disconnected from empirical evidence—for instance, the tradition of empirical scientific practice—in large part because of a failure to question assumptions about the spectacular. It can also be problematic for the way that sexual subjects are used to advance an argument that is primarily one of concern to the academic theorist rather than the people themselves. This is a form of critique that deploys people and communities to advance a thesis that may—or may not—bear much relation to the phenomenology of the participants. The casual relationship between theory and lived experience works for these theorists because they are driven primarily by their theoretical argument. Indeed, the apotheosis of spectacular critique is the deployment of often quite arcane theory. And perhaps most worryingly of all, spectacular critique may also lead academics and activists to lose sight of important ethical limits in pursuit of what is novel, sometimes in quite disturbing ways.

I want to discuss a demonstrably damaging example first, the case of the 'down low', which involves public health researchers, and many others besides, clinging to a theory that is fundamentally flawed. The down low is a term with varying and disputed meanings (Boykin, 2005) but has usually been deployed in the context of public health to mean men who have sex with men in secret. It is a phenomenon that has been associated with the Black/African American community, with the down low used as an explanation for the high rates of HIV among Black/African American women in the United States (Boykin, 2005). This story involves a spectacular focus

Sexual Citizenship and Social Change. Darren Langdridge, Oxford University Press. © Oxford University Press 2024.
DOI: 10.1093/oso/9780199926312.003.0006

that is distinctly racist, with damaging consequences. This is something that can only have happened through a serious breakdown in the link between theory, empirical evidence, and lived experience itself. This example serves to demonstrate how a spectacular idea when taken up and deployed in ostensibly positive ways becomes self-sustaining, despite a lack of evidence. It also serves to demonstrate the very real damage that can be caused to individuals and communities when critique is not tempered by tradition, as argued for by Ricoeur (1986), and when critique becomes an end in itself rather than a means by which to gain greater understanding or effect change within oppressed communities.

My second example of spectacular critique focuses on 'barebacking', originally meaning deliberate unprotected anal sex, and involves queer theorists and others engaged in reproducing a story of spectacular sex solely in the service of advancing their theoretical positions. An honest account focused on the betterment of the lives of the men in question is very much secondary to the intellectual project of the theorist. In my analysis, I focus on Tim Dean's—albeit now quite dated—account of barebacking as a primary exemplar. This was a key early text demonstrating the phenomenon I seek to describe and has inspired a generation of scholarship since that adopts the same problematic spectacular queer trope. So, while my focus is on a text that is in many ways now—in the light of pre-exposure prophylaxis (PreP) and effective HIV medications—almost irrelevant, the problem of spectacular critique within academic culture remains and is growing fast. We continue to see studies of the spectacular, in queer scholarship in particular, following this form, from work continuing to link sex with death (see, e.g., Palm, 2019; Robinson, 2013) to recent work on 'pig sex' (Florêncio, 2020), along with the recent emergence of queer trans scholarship (Chu, 2019; Lavery, 2022).

Finally, I will discuss what has been termed 'minor-attracted persons' (MAPs) or in everyday parlance child sexual abusers or paedophiles. This is undoubtedly the most disturbing example where we see critique focussed on the 'spectacular', and with this example I move across the boundary of consensual sexual activities that I initially set for myself. I discuss this issue because it highlights how critique untethered from tradition can go dangerously wrong. Here we see a complete failure among sexuality scholars writing about this topic to recognize how the academic desire to find the latest spectacular focus for their critical sensibility has caused them to lose touch with important ethical norms. The use of the language of progressive sexual citizenship for those who seek to abuse others is particularly disturbing and yet has been reproduced and reinforced by academics who should know better. This is critique detached from wider societal values. It provides succour to all those who claimed the granting of sexual and gender minority rights was a slippery slope to a disturbing dystopia in which paedophilia, bestiality, necrophilia, and the like are the inevitable end point of this political project. And moreover, and more significantly still, it provides succour to those that find pleasure in abusing others and likely a sense of horror to all those who have been subject to such abuse.

Down low culture and the threat of Black (homo)sexualities

HIV disproportionally affects Black/African American men who have sex with men and Black/African American heterosexual women in the United States, with far greater numbers infected than amongst other groups (Centers for Disease Control and Prevention [CDC], 2018). In 2018, 42% of new HIV diagnoses were among Blacks/African Americans, who composed only 13% of the population of the United States. This was made up of 31% men and 11% women, with 80% of infections within men coming from same-sex sexual contact and 92% among women from heterosexual sexual contact (CDC, 2018). It has commonly been assumed that the cause of this statistical fact was a 'bisexual bridge' and existence of a down low culture in which Black/African American men (who are mostly not out gay or bisexual men) get together to have (invariably unprotected) sex and then also have sex with heterosexual women (Friedman et al., 2014).

There has been the reproduction of a pernicious narrative about a spectacular and dangerous subculture—the down low—despite serious concerns about the evidence base for this story of disease and, of course, individual culpability. It appears that the down low has been constructed as—or through—a potent blend of fear and exoticism in the face of same-sex sex and Black sexuality. Bisexuality has long been assumed to be a key route of HIV transmission, and the application of this idea to Black cultures is a fascinating, and quite disturbing, example in which the bisexual figures as the subject of sexual excess. When the bisexual is added to extant racist perceptions about Black men and women, along with the spectacular pornographic fantasy of down low culture, we witness the production of a toxic mess of thinking.

SPECTACULAR CRITIQUE AND ABJECT CITIZENSHIP 135

Contrary to the assumption outlined above, meta-analytic research that has focussed on HIV prevalence among bisexually behaving men in the United States provides evidence that the 'bisexual bridge' theory is very likely not responsible for the high rates of HIV infection among (Black) women (Friedman et al., 2014). It is worth quoting at length how they describe the situation based on CDC statistics and their meta-analysis of extant empirical research on the topic:

> Though our findings suggest that MSMW[1] present potential to both acquire and transmit HIV, heterosexual women appear likely to encounter an HIV-positive male sexual who acquired HIV through injection drug use (IDU) or through heterosexual sex, given CDC estimates that 110,900 heterosexual males and 131,600 heterosexual male IDU are living with HIV/AIDS. Using the same logic, an MSMO would be almost four times as likely to encounter another MSMO who was HIV positive (458,200) than an HIV-positive MSMW. In view of these comparisons, we suggest that (1) at the population level, MSMW likely present no greater risk of HIV transmission to women than exclusively heterosexual partners; (2) MSMW likely present substantially less risk of HIV transmission to men than MSMO; (3) the dizzyingly disparate HIV rate ratios reported among MSM are likely even higher if measured specifically for MSMO; and (4) the HIV/AIDS risk that MSMW themselves face from each other, from MSMO, and from their female sexual partners is currently under-researched and unmitigated by dedicated intervention development and delivery attuned to bisexually behaving men and their particular needs.

So, there is no good evidence that bisexually behaving men, whether this is an out bisexual man or a man having sex with another man in secret 'on the down low', pose any greater risk of HIV transmission to women than heterosexual men. Bisexually behaving men also pose less risk to MSMO than other MSMO. We can also note that there is a lack of accurate information about the risk to bisexually behaving men from sexual contacts with MSMO and women, presumably because hitherto the root of transmission was only conceived of in one way: from bisexual male to heterosexual female. The more likely explanation for the high numbers of HIV infections within Blacks/African Americans in the United States almost certainly

---

[1] MSMW: men who have sex with men and women; MSMO: men who have sex with men only.

136 SEXUAL CITIZENSHIP AND SOCIAL CHANGE

involves a complex blend of poverty and inequality (e.g., in access to health care), racism and its numerous associated effects, HIV stigma, LGBTQ prejudice, and a problematic masculinity within some Black/African American communities (see, e.g., Banks et al., 2020; Fields et al., 2012, 2015; Mustanski et al., 2013; Quinn et al., 2015; Saleh & Operario, 2009).

So, given there is good evidence that the bisexual bridge and down low cultures are not the primary root for HIV transmission within Black/African American communities within the United States, fully accepting they may still play some equivalent role to heterosexual and nonsexual HIV transmission, what have been the drivers behind this dominant, enduring, and sadly also damaging narrative? There appears to be a salacious interest driving the spectacular (re)production of this minority subculture, one that is inflected by both sexual prejudice and racism. 'Down low' is an endogenous term within African American communities, originally signifying keeping something secret. African American men who have sex with men (who do not identify as gay/bisexual) then appropriated the term to describe their engagement in secretive same-sex activities whilst avoiding gay or bisexual identity labels (Boykin, 2005; Saleh & Operario, 2009). So, like barebacking discussed below, the down low emerged within specific minority communities as a form of self-identification of a set of sexual practices. This may well have come about as a result of racism within White gay communities and homophobia within African American communities (Saleh & Operario, 2009), with narratives of the down low and associated identities facilitating access to desired same-sex sexual contact whilst also shoring up the men's racial/ethnic identities.

Early media reports of the down low, like that of barebacking, were sensational and driven by fear of contagion, with public health ostensibly the primary concern. In the case of the down low this was focused on HIV transmission from sexually promiscuous bisexual African American men to their unsuspecting female partners. We might first seek to question the underlying logic of the bisexual bridge deployed within this narrative for how it inevitably positions Black men as the active (sexually driven and therefore irresponsible) causal agents in transmission and (mostly Black) women as the passive (arguably naïve) victims. As Saleh and Operario (2009) point out, again just as I will note with barebacking, the exogenous use of terminology like 'down low' is problematic in multiple ways. First, it results in African American men becoming disproportionately associated with secretive same-sex behaviour in spite of the fact that this occurs across all races/ethnicities

SPECTACULAR CRITIQUE AND ABJECT CITIZENSHIP   137

(Boykin, 2005). Second, there is an assumption—now proven likely incorrect—that down low activity is associated with HIV risk. Third, there is a belief that these men are really gay but cannot be open about it, thus further reinforcing existing problematic notions about African American sexuality (Boykin, 2005). And finally, exogenous use of down low terminology serves to reinscribe a category label onto a group of men without adequate attention to the historical and cultural derivation of the term. Saleh and Operario (2009: 392) highlight how the use of this category label for a group of persons oversimplifies group differences:

> The ahistorical, asocial, and de-contextualized use of the DL label places these men as exotic sexual objects, casting them as the sexual 'other' with implicit comparisons made to 'valid' heterosexual African American men and homosexual or gay-identified men. In overlooking the social dynamics that call for new expressions and self-identifications of sexuality among these men, exogenous use of this label connotes a pathological sense of denial for men who identify themselves or their behaviour as DL [down low].

With the exogenous use of terms like the 'down low' and 'barebacking' there is a risk of creating and fixing a community in a way that fails to allow for variation or change within it, in addition to any failure to understand the way such subcultures may operate for both good and bad. This approach also serves to provide an eager media with stories that are voyeuristic and invariably spectacular, as that is what they demand, which may then further inscribe racist and homophobic discourse about particular communities. But engagement with minority subcultures such as the down low may be problematic even when ostensibly from 'within'. The spectacular, and dangerously reckless, (re)production of subcultures from allies and community members alike may cause just as much harm as exogenous use, if there is insufficient care about the accuracy of portrayal or potential for damaging effects.

The damage here is deeply troubling. The focus on the wrong aspect of public health has clearly failed to meet the needs of this community, along with the widespread promotion and reification of pernicious racist narratives. The down low demonstrates the very real danger from spectacular critique even when conducted with the best of intentions by ostensibly well-meaning folk. And this is true whether those well-meaning folk are allies or even members of the communities in question. Minority group membership does not assuage us of responsibility for others, not in the least. Indeed, we might

138 SEXUAL CITIZENSHIP AND SOCIAL CHANGE

make a case that membership should ensure we are more alert to the risks, but I fear the increasing numbers of scholars and activists focused solely on critique too often brings with it the eschewal of responsibility for each other as fellow citizens. A grounding in phenomenology—as opposed to critical theory—would help here, as a way to reconnect with people's everyday lives as lived and temper theoretical critique with empirical tradition.

Perhaps most puzzling of all is how this story has persisted despite persuasive attempts to challenge it. For instance, Boykin's (2005) trade book *Beyond the Down Low: Sex, Lies, and Denial in Black America* tackles the myths surrounding this topic head on. Ranging widely across the topic, Boykin (2005) highlights the many flaws in the logic underpinning discussion of the down low and the damaging effects this has for Black Americans. As Lynn Harris (2004) remarks in the foreword:

> Over the years, I have met too many black women and men whose lives have been dramatically affected by HIV, and I have seen how the down low discussion has drawn some of them apart. Indeed, the most visible public discussions about the down low lately have been more about finger-pointing and dividing the community than about establishing honest and open dialogue.

Boykin's (2005) honest and open account approaches the topic in a way that deliberately moves away from the spectacular such that everyday lives and sensible initiatives about sex and HIV/AIDS become his focus. He does not deny the challenges for Black communities regarding HIV/AIDS but equally he does not accept lazy assumptions or ill-informed prejudice. He encourages us all to resist divisive binaries and instead find ways to embrace each other. This is sage advice for academics and activists alike.

Barebacking and the spectacular repathologization of the subject

The notion of barebacking, the intentional act of engaging in unprotected anal intercourse, first emerged in the late 1990s and has been encouraged by a curious array of friends (and foes, of course). Much like the down low, this story grew at an astonishing rate within academic and professional health promotion circles and wider popular culture, most often in media panics about a dangerous new breed of gay men wanting to harm themselves and others or otherwise engaging in dangerously reckless behaviour. That is, like the down low, stories of barebacking serve to construct a sexual narrative identity imbued with a distinctly pathological self-loathing. This story continues today, albeit at a much lower level of interest. Much of the furore has lessened because of improved treatments and particularly in the light of PreP and treatment as prevention (TasP), but this pernicious story continues to be discussed, with many of the narrative tropes now used in the latest exercise in pathology, namely one focussed on what has been termed 'chemsex' or 'party and play'. The story of barebacking is intriguing and disturbing in equal measure for the way it brings together such an unlikely array of people in the service of constructing a pathological sexual subject.

Barebacking is a term of its time, and whilst it is still in use, along with other terms like 'raw', it carries somewhat less meaning in the contemporary context beyond categorizing a still popular porn genre. That said, the story of barebacking has been significant in the history of HIV/AIDS, not because we witnessed the emergence of a newly self-destructive homosexual menace but because of how it demonstrates the way that a variety of 'friends' may work together to coax—perhaps even coerce (Plummer, 1995), in some instances—a story of critique that repathologizes the gay/bisexual male. The story of barebacking has been produced and reproduced by a curious assemblage of the sensational right-wing media, 'concerned' health psychologists, and queer humanities scholars. The resurrection of the psychoanalytic death instinct and, arguably, the personal desire for notoriety amongst some health psychologists and queer theorists, along with sensationalist journalists, have been at the heart of this problematic reinvention of the pathological gay/bisexual male subject.

I'll begin the exploration of this narrative with an account of gay male pathology produced by an ostensibly LGBTQ-supportive health psychologist in the United Kingdom. Michelle Crossley (2004) wrote an article in a leading British social psychology journal that served up a disturbing story of gay/bisexual male pathology as part of an attempt to help gay and bisexual men to stop engaging in these damaging acts of self-harm. This work carried weight as Crossley was academically established and respected within the field, and her article ostensibly provided valuable new insight into the seemingly intractable problem of why people continue to engage in risky behaviours (in this case unprotected anal intercourse) when they know of the risk entailed (HIV infection). To this end, Crossley deviated from the more

140 SEXUAL CITIZENSHIP AND SOCIAL CHANGE

usual health psychological methodologies that she had hitherto employed to instead analyse a series of texts including gay fiction, pornography, and autobiography. These texts were cherry-picked for 'evidence', rather than systematically sourced. The thesis was also grounded in a psychoanalytic mode of thinking, in support of an argument that gay men engage in barebacking in response to public health (condom-focused) campaigns due to a gay male 'cultural psyche' infused with sexual excess, transgression, and death. Her article begins with the following quote from Freud (1958, cited in Crossley, 2004: 225): 'An organisation which was slave to the pleasure principle and neglected the reality of the external world could not maintain itself alive for the shortest time.' Paul Flowers and I (Flowers & Langdridge, 2007) sought to reply at the time to the account of gay male sexuality produced by Crossley (2004), as did—for instance—members of the (then titled) Lesbian and Gay Psychology Section of the British Psychological Society (Barker et al., 2007). This was driven in no small part by our shared fears for how this rapidly cited account may be used to limit funding to sexual health care services for gay and bisexual men, something that was already in jeopardy. Our primary concern was that there was a ready audience to hear this pathologizing story of gay male sexuality among the politicians and policymakers within the United Kingdom, especially when told by an 'ally' seeking to reduce harm within the community that she had hitherto researched quite supportively. It took some time to get our replies published in the journal as it was not something previously undertaken in that UK social psychology journal, but replies were thankfully eventually published.

The Crossley (2004) article uses a number of different strategies to construct a pathological gay male subject, which have been documented in detail by Flowers and Langdridge (2007) and Barker et al. (2007). The first issue, one also employed in the problematic accounts of this phenomenon produced by queer theorists discussed below, is the immediate conflation of unprotected anal intercourse (UAI) with barebacking, by which is meant the intentional act of engaging in UAI. UAI has been documented as a route of transmission since the early years of the AIDS pandemic, but this is not equivalent to barebacking (most UAI is not intentional). Additionally, whilst UAI was increasing at the time Crossley was writing, she failed to acknowledge that the maintenance of protected sex by the vast majority of men in the West was normative and that protected sex had become normative within such communities (see Flowers & Langdridge, 2007). Furthermore, Crossley, much like Dean below and with echoes of the way the down low

SPECTACULAR CRITIQUE AND ABJECT CITIZENSHIP   141

was conceptualized, singularly deployed 'barebacking' for UAI between men with no consideration of heterosexual anal intercourse. As Flowers and Langdridge (2007: 685) note:

> HIV/AIDS is a global epidemic primarily affecting heterosexuals (see UNAIDS). It is associated with poverty, war, societal break down (often associated with debt crises), political change (e.g. Low et al., 1993) and the crossborder movement of peoples in search of greater economic security (Van der Vliet, 1996). Yet, as a result of global health inequalities (i.e. technologies of diagnosis, monitoring and disease surveillance) and an artefact of epidemiological reporting, the association between HIV/AIDS and gay men emerged (in the West) in the early 1980s (Gottleib et al., 1981).

So, why is HIV—and critically barebacking—so clearly associated with gay men? Even if we accept that barebacking has particular meaning for gay men, as suggested by Crossley and also Dean (2009), the singular focus on the gay male, allied to the construction of a singular gay male 'community', fails to recognize the possibility that UAI may have meaning for heterosexuals as well. There is also a failure to acknowledge other practices beyond those within this sexual context, whether smoking or dangerous sports, in which there might be a similar profile of risk (Barker et al., 2007). It is only risk in the context of sex, and particularly gay sex, that requires this level of critical attention. Of course, consideration of heterosexual sex in equivalent terms— or indeed, consideration of similar but nonsexual risky practices—serves to foreclose the primary aim of providing an explanation for the death-ridden sexual 'cultural psyche' of the gay male community. In many ways, this situation is itself at least partly the result of how HIV has been constructed more generally as an epidemic of signification (Treichler, 1987), one in which the gay and bisexual male is invariably positioned as culpable, one way or another, for the continuing manifestation of this disease. And this may be due to pernicious and powerful cultural processes of 'splitting' and othering of gay men (Bech, 1997; Flowers & Langdridge, 2007) and/or a form of protective projection on the part of the general public (Flowers, 2001).

The methodological moves required to construct the Crossley case against the gay male subject are also deeply problematic, much like those of many other spectacular critiques. First, Crossley (2004: 226–227) eschews the voices of gay men themselves on the basis of her previous interview-based research through a dismissal of their accounts for how they were apparently

142 SEXUAL CITIZENSHIP AND SOCIAL CHANGE

'produced in a rather "pat" and easy manner—almost as if they were part of a cultural repertoire that people unthinkingly drew upon when asked to account for their behaviour'. So, instead, she decided to rely on her own burgeoning insight that gay men were unconsciously engaging in 'rebellion against dominant social values' (p. 227), something in need of further investigation and psychoanalytic explanation. The psychoanalytic unconscious is of course the ally of choice for the suspicious outsider (and sometimes sadly also the insider; see below) seeking to supplant or even undermine the voice of the other. To this end, Crossley decided that a better source of data than gay men themselves would be fictional and quasi-autobiographical accounts but seemingly only those that neatly fit her initial suspicion, as the choices made were distinctly limited. She also neglected to account for the literary or cultural context of the work chosen (e.g., making no distinction between fantasy and reality, fiction vs. fact), instead treating these books as sources of data that simply describe the singular gay sexual context that could then be drawn upon in the service of her narrative of choice. This is further compounded by a frequent elision in which the authorial voice deploys textual (and extratextual) material to effect some troubling rhetorical flourishes: for instance, the use of Foucault's death as a rhetorical device—'He died of AIDS in 1984' (p. 232)—to illustrate irony given that Foucault doubted the existence of AIDS was really quite disturbing (Barker et al., 2007).

Finally, whilst remaining focused on the Crossley (2004) article, I'd like to mention ethics, as this is also pertinent to the next episode that I discuss below. Psychologists—and all other social scientific researchers—have an ethical requirement to not infringe on the rights and dignity of their participants. And—of course—this is particularly important when working with marginalized and stigmatized groups. The use of hermeneutics of suspicion (Ricoeur, 1970), and particularly the imposition of a psychoanalytic reading, must be undertaken with great care and thought for the subjects of an investigation. This should include consideration for not only any subjects recruited to participate—or otherwise engaged with in a study—but also the wider community of subjects to which the topic applies. We have an obligation not only to 'the truth', best served through the use of systematic methodologies and care in the handling of data, but also to the broader political position of the subjects of our investigations, and this continues beyond the point at which we publish our 'findings'. All writing when published becomes part of the social imaginary (Ricoeur, 1986) that serves to construct the narrative identities in question, and these voices of critique can

SPECTACULAR CRITIQUE AND ABJECT CITIZENSHIP   143

be powerful narrative allies or enemies, sometimes unintentionally, to those currently engaged in political struggle to resist oppression.

Sadly, the problematic narrative of barebacking does not end with the episodic work of just one British health psychologist, even when allied to copious sensational media coverage. Queer theorists somewhat surprisingly also play an important role in constructing the pathological gay male subject within this spectacular narrative, and more generally helping to facilitate the development of an academic culture of spectacular critique. Tim Dean's (2009) book *Unlimited Intimacy* arguably represents the zenith of the spectacular reproduction of barebacking, this time through the lens of queer theory within a North American context. In what is presented as an ethnography of the barebacking subculture in San Francisco, Dean singularly eschews any attempt to engage with the subtleties of ethnographic methodology in favour of a very particular distorted presentation of this phenomenon. Through the subtle absence of care to attend to the many social and psychological factors implicated in such overdetermined activities, let alone the bare epidemiological facts, an account is produced that serves to provide the basis for a readily formulated narrative that merely creates the very thing it claims to investigate. Dean (2009), like Crossley (2004), is rather careless with his terminology and focus. He moves seamlessly from barebacking to 'bug chasing', a term describing those people (invariably gay men of course) who actively seek out infection by HIV through UAI, and then to cruising more generally.

Dean (2009) explicitly seeks to avoid pathologizing those who engage in barebacking or indeed judge the practices he describes, and to be fair, he mostly succeeds in this aim. His pathologizing move is more subtle than that seen in Crossley (2004), even if that too contained more than its fair share of disclaimers and qualifications. The problem in the account produced by Dean (2009) is that he creates the 'subculture' he claims to be studying through his narrative account, grounded in revelatory accounts of his own sexual practice and a selective analysis of pornography. Dean relies on the spectacular presentation of his own sexual activity, the appearance and content of a limited number of websites, and a random array of pornography catering to barebackers, with only an occasional reference to an academic study and even then, often in ways that misuse the findings they provide.

Notable in the account of Dean (2009) is the way that he quickly brushes over key facts or fails to even address relevant epidemiological data. For instance, he swiftly dismisses the extent to which people engage in bug chasing

144 SEXUAL CITIZENSHIP AND SOCIAL CHANGE

as almost irrelevant despite then talking extensively about bug chasing as a specific subculture (it is the entire focus of Chapter 1, 'Breeding Culture'). He uses a study of barebacking websites by Tewksbury (2003) as a key part of the setup to his argument. This study has only one important conclusion, and that is how few adverts on a website specifically dedicated to barebacking, one that actively eschews any notion of safety and is the focus of much attention from Dean, involve people who are HIV negative searching for HIV-positive sexual partners for unprotected anal intercourse (less than 1%). In other words, the study suggests there are very few people even fantasizing about engaging in bug chasing, let alone actually practicing it, which is remarkable given this is on a website dedicated to bareback sex. Instead, Dean quickly moves to suggest that 'even if' there are very few people engaging in bug chasing, then the fantasy alone is worthy of examination (p. 17). Maybe it is, but it is a very different project to deploy psychoanalytic theory to examine a minority cultural fantasy (via literary sources) than to artfully construct a subculture that sets an entire train of theoretical and empirical work in motion for many years to come, which is unfortunately what Dean ends up doing. By bringing in his own anecdotal personal experience, he repeatedly moves from fantasy back to reality and undermines the bare facts that this is—if anything at all—a very marginal activity and instead serves to narratively construct a spectacular fantasy world, of his own making. Through this and the use of a psychoanalytic theory that offers little room for the subject to speak, and especially for people other than Dean to comment or criticize, we see a gay male identity emerge once again as an agentic site of cultural deviance in need of investigation and explanation.

This careless approach to ethnography is a shame as there are some valuable reflections in the book. The final chapter includes some thoughtful comment on the closure of public sex venues and how the increasing privatization of sex reduces the possibility of encountering otherness, for instance. This entire chapter draws on cruising rather than barebacking (or bug chasing) to make the case, raising the question of why we needed the graphic accounts of Dean's sex life (real and fantasy) at all in the previous chapters. And indeed, the entire point of the work, which—I think—is about seeking to rethink relationality among gay men, is itself potentially valuable, even if missing much of the relevant sociological and psychological literature. But much as we used to witness in the *Jerry Springer Show*, whilst there is claimed to be no moralizing on the part of the author, there is instead the steady presentation of a spectacular sexual subject. And even given the desire to avoid

SPECTACULAR CRITIQUE AND ABJECT CITIZENSHIP 145

judgement, which I believe to be sincere, there remains a morality on show as some forms of sexual encounter become privileged for what they offer to the theoretical argument of the author. That said, it is mostly left to the reader—and then more problematically all those who may take only what they want from this via hearsay and second-hand reporting—to encounter the text from a moral stance.

The Dean study is methodologically problematic; it is not a formal ethnographic investigation that we might expect to see in the social sciences but rather a partial theoretically driven narrative account from an English scholar. Had Tim Dean been a social/human scientist trained in ethnography, he would have had to subject himself to a formal ethical review process. I doubt very much whether most ethical review boards would be happy with the approach taken by Dean, especially the personal accounts of bareback sex. And most notably, the review board would undoubtedly have raised some questions about safety, much to Dean's chagrin of course, and the implications of conducting and reporting upon such a study without serious reflection on the consequences for the population in question. That is, any researcher conducting a serious piece of social scientific research would have needed to properly explain and warrant their methodological choices, as well as think through the ethical implications for the population in question in advance, put in place any necessary protections, and ensure that the findings were properly produced and contextualized, with limitations acknowledged.

It is the authorial creation of a subculture that may serve to reinforce existing prejudice against sexual minorities that is the lasting legacy of this work. Even today, in a world in which living with HIV and AIDS has now become biomedically transformed through PrEP and TasP, there continues to be humanities scholarship dedicated to the phenomenon of bug chasing (see, e.g., Palm, 2019; Robinson, 2013) set in motion in large part because of the recklessly spectacular presentation of Dean (albeit note Dean, 2015). And saddest of all is that even this more recent work continues to rely on the original presentation of bug chasing provided by Dean, and a small number of other queer theorists, with no attempt at all to engage the broader empirical literature.

But this is not the only legacy, for this style of scholarship has become entrenched in the humanities, spilling out into the social sciences too. The theorization of the spectacular has become normative within contemporary queer theory and beyond, ushering in work that—while often clever—risks serving only the intellectual project of the author. Whether deliberate or not, this work is not produced in the service of the people and communities of which it speaks; they too often serve only as expedient material to draw attention to the intellectual project of the author through the re-presentation of a spectacular other. This is heavy—often tediously so—theory-driven analysis located within an academic culture in which the subject of the analysis is too often disposable. There is precious little care for the subject of this work, paradoxical given the authors invariably inhabit the worlds they represent or narratively create.

Reading some of the most recent work in this tradition, we see how the subject continues to be seemingly inconsequential for the authors. To give just one example, Florêncio's (2020) work on barebacking and 'pig sex' is an echo of Dean's (2009) work, strangely similar methodologically and theoretically, and equally apparently unconcerned for the people and communities of which it speaks. Barring one brief discussion of ethics, in which drug deaths are casually set aside, there is no attempt to move beyond the theoretical argument being made. It even draws on the same porn—a bareback porn film called *What I Can't See*—as Dean (2009), albeit reading it differently to Dean given the author's different theoretical ambition. This moment helps to demonstrate how the material is mostly irrelevant other than in service of the spectacular, with the people behind the materials having no real voice. Their voices, in the rare moments when they appear, are simply material to be read through arcane critical theory. Moreover, the theoretical argument that Florêncio (2020) seeks to make about hospitality and the other in his book could as easily be made through a reading of almost any textual source about contemporary queer life, whether sexual or not. Sadly, there is a body of esteemed (and equally reviled) recent queer trans scholarship that follows the same model of theoretical density allied to an apparent disdain for the subject of the work, even when autobiographical (see, e.g., Chu, 2019; Lavery, 2022).

Child sexual abuse and the language of sexual citizenship

The use of the politics and language of progressive sexual citizenship to describe child sexual abusers as 'minor attracted persons' (MAPs), and animal abusers as animal-attracted persons, is a particularly worrying new development in contemporary academic life and associated queer activism. In this last section I outline the emergence of a phenomenon that represents a perverse vision driven, at least in part, by a focus on spectacular critique, similar to that of the theorists described above. This is critical scholarship that is detached from the everyday, from history, and from even the most basic of ethical foundations, whether intentional or not. The recent focus on what has been termed MAPs (along with those who wish to engage positively with bestiality; see, e.g., Rudy, 2012) shows the dangers of the allure of critique and failure of the academy to provide necessary checks. To use sexual minority language like this on such topics by scholars and activists is indefensible—even if theoretically comprehensible—and a worrying sign of a serious cultural problem within contemporary sexual and gender studies. This linguistic—and conceptual—shift risks consensual sexual identities and practices being conflated with nonconsensual acts of violence, as already seen in some recent media reporting, thereby creating a renewed backlash against sexual minorities engaging in consensual adult sexual practice. More concretely, we are now witness to people who wish to sexually abuse children seeking to refer to themselves in the language of identity politics as MAPs. And, more problematically still, we have ostensibly critical academics, practitioners, and activists reinforcing the validity of such identity claims by reproducing them in their scholarship (see, e.g., Andersson, 2022; Harper et al., 2022; Lievesley et al., 2020; Lievesley & Lapworth, 2022; Sorrentino & Abramowitz, 2021; Vaerwaeter, 2022; Walker, 2021).

While this term has been used at least since 1988 (Bindall, 2023), it was publication of the book *A Long Dark Shadow: Minor Attracted People and Their Pursuit of Dignity* in 2021 by Allyn Walker, then an assistant professor in the sociology and criminal justice department at Old Dominion University in the United States, that brought the spectre of scholarship about MAPs to the attention of the wider public. The book was accompanied by an interview piece published on the website of the Prostasia Foundation, an organization that claims to be a 'new kind of child protection organization', one that provides access to a 'MAP Support Club' on its homepage. Combined, the effect was an outcry about Old Dominion University employing someone who many argued was an apologist for child sexual abusers. Walker eventually left Old Dominion University, but this new story of MAPs has only just begun.

The remarkable thing about this book and associated public engagement materials involving the author is the lack of awareness regarding public sentiment about this topic and possible harmful consequences. While the author is clear that they do not condone child sexual abuse and wish to encourage

148 SEXUAL CITIZENSHIP AND SOCIAL CHANGE

MAPs to desist from acting on their desires, they still willingly embrace the language of the abuser rather than subject it to the sustained critique that it demands. The entire book is sympathetic to would-be abusers. When asked in the Prostasia interview about their use of the term 'MAP' in the book, Walker (2021) replies:

> I use the term Minor-Attracted Person or MAP in the title and throughout the book for multiple reasons. First of all, because I think it's important to use terminology for groups that members of that group want others to use for them. MAP advocacy groups like B4UAct have advocated for use of the term, and they've advocated for it primarily because it's less stigmatizing than other terms like pedophile. A lot of people when they hear the term pedophile, they automatically assume that it means a sex offender. And that isn't true. And it leads to a lot of misconceptions about attractions toward minors.

This statement needs unpacking. The motivation for using the term 'MAP' given by Walker is because people who wish to abuse children and associated 'advocacy groups' want others to embrace this term because it is less stigmatising. In this move, Walker adopts a position that is immediately sympathetic to those with these desires and furthermore trusts that these would-be child sexual abusers are telling the truth when they say they are not currently abusing children nor will do so in the future. The linguistic move initiated by would-be child sexual abusers is thereby normalized through the cultural capital of the academic and their published work, with remarkably little thought about the consequences of such a move. In that same interview, Walker (2021) adds:

> I've definitely heard the idea that you brought up though that the use of the term minor attracted person suggests that it's okay to be attracted to children. But using a term that communicates who someone is attracted to doesn't indicate anything about the morality of that attraction. From my perspective, there is no morality or immorality attached to attraction to anyone because no one can control who they're attracted to at all. In other words, it's not who we're attracted to that's either okay or not okay. It's our behaviors and responding to that attraction that are either okay or not okay.

The focus here, which undoubtedly will offend many readers, is entirely on the author's own moral opinion about the separation of behaviour from

SPECTACULAR CRITIQUE AND ABJECT CITIZENSHIP 149

attraction and the consequent need to reduce stigma—and indeed, even increase 'dignity'—for the would-be offender. There is minimal thought or reflection about the victims of sexual abuse, the validity of these distinctions (morally or empirically), or the societal need to maintain stigma towards activities that are simply wrong. That is, Walker adopts an entirely empathic position with the subjects of their research, astonishingly detached from the everyday values of most people concerning this topic. There is an arrogance here, common to all spectacular critique, that undergirds the moral certainty on display by the author in this deeply unpleasant book. Even if it were found to be the case that destigmatization of would-be child sexual abusers helped reduce offending—and we are a very long way from this being established, even if those advocating for it worryingly seem to think differently—then this would need to be handled with great care. This would require us to treat accounts from would-be abusers with considerable scepticism given that child sexual abuse and cognitive distortions/deception are fundamentally intertwined (see, e.g., Tierney & McCabe, 2001) and involve self-deception (Wright & Schneider, 1999). And, of course, sexual interest in children is the primary risk factor for abuse (McPhail et al., 2019), something Walker seems all too willing to gloss over. Such work would also need to be incredibly mindful of the impact on victims/survivors and wider possible consequences.

To this end, for instance, there has been insufficient reflection about the possible damage that may be caused to sexual minorities who engage in consensual adult sexual behaviours being associated with would-be child sexual abusers deploying the language of sexual identities and citizenship. The idea that sexual minorities, gay men in particular, are predatory and desirous of children is an old but pernicious trope frequently deployed by those opposed to equality (Herek, 2002; Simon, 1998; Stevenson, 2000). It has taken many years of sustained effort on the part of academics and activists to demonstrate that this trope is both empirically untrue and morally shameful. And yet, despite those early claims from the conservative right that equality for lesbians and gays will inevitably lead to acceptance of similar claims from paedophiles and animal abusers, here we are in 2023 with—at best—ostensibly well-meaning, if breathtakingly naïve, academics making such a case on their behalf again. Walker (2021: 8) glibly acknowledges this link: 'If an enduring attraction to minors constitutes a sexual orientation, and if queer populations are individuals with non-normative sexual orientations, certainly MAPs apply under the large queer umbrella.' And while Walker

150 SEXUAL CITIZENSHIP AND SOCIAL CHANGE

claims to find this association uncomfortable, they still support it, with the only distinction made by them on this point founded on a distinction between desire and behaviour. This fine distinction is not one I fear most sexual minorities would wish to defend, nor should they. It is plainly wrong. MAPs are already acting on their desires through their move to find others, create 'support groups', and engage in advocacy to support their desires being framed as sexual attraction rather than sexual violence and abuse. Walker is not a lone figure, of course; there is evidence of an increasing number of sympathetic scholars blurring the boundaries between adult and childhood sexuality, consensual and nonconsensual practices and associated identities, and growing use of the language of (ostensibly progressive) sexual citizenship for child sexual abuse/paedophilia in contemporary academia and activism (see, e.g., Andersson, 2022; Breslow, 2011, 2021; Harper & Lievesley, 2022; Harper et al., 2022; Lievesley et al., 2020; Lievesley & Lapworth, 2022; Moen, 2015; Sorrentino & Abramowitz, 2021; Vaerwaeter, 2022). I should also note that much of this work has been published by leading academic presses and celebrated in reviews by other established scholars. This is a serious systemic problem for contemporary queer studies scholarship.

This movement is frighteningly like early attempts to destigmatize paedophilia, such as the UK Paedophile Information Exchange founded in 1974 and the North American Man/Boy Love Association (NAMBLA) founded in 1978, again reinforced and amplified by some academics and activists (see, e.g., Wilson & Cox, 1983). It has taken concerted efforts to remove the association between groups like these and LGBTQ folk, and yet here we are again. Those in search of the spectacular would do well to critically interrogate their own work with a little more sense of tradition—and the expectations and norms of wider society in particular—such that there might be better recognition of the potential harm they are causing. Academic practice plays a crucial role in encouraging the spectacular through the focus on individual academic novelty and achievement. Revelling in that which is perceived to be novel, especially when it is regarded as 'edgy', has become privileged within contemporary critical theory concerned with sex, sexuality, and gender and queer scholarship in general. This work has become increasingly out of touch and intellectually self-indulgent, with precious little learnt from history.

To provide a further example, there has recently been extensive media reporting about a PhD student, Karl Andersson, at the University of

Manchester, United Kingdom, who published an article in the journal *Qualitative Research* in 2022 about his autoethnographic masturbation over pornographic drawings of young boys. Like Walker (2021), Anderson has sought to defend his position through an intellectually heavy distinction between fantasy and behaviour, albeit complicated further by the fact that pornographic drawings of children are illegal in the United Kingdom, even if not in all other countries. He has also sought to draw upon the claim that early gay rights movements were intertwined with advocates of 'man/boy love' as a positive rationale for his own interests. The journal article in question, titled 'I Am Not Alone—We Are All Alone: Using Masturbation as an Ethnographic Method in Research on Shota Subculture in Japan', has now been retracted by the journal editors. The bigger question is why this student was undertaking this work in the first place and how on earth it came to be published in a legitimate social science journal. The journal editors in their statement about the retraction fail to provide sufficient explanation and remain in their post despite this appalling oversight.

The article in question is a relatively brief account by the author of his frustration about the use of interviews with fans of Shota, a Japanese genre of comics and illustrations that feature young boy characters in a sexually explicit manner (Andersson, 2022). This frustration led to him deciding to masturbate to Shota himself for 3 months as a form of autoethnography, so that he could grasp something more about the embodied experience. The outcome of this 'experiment' was utterly trivial: 'What I learned from this experiment was to attach greater meaning and value to the act of masturbation, and especially of doing it to two-dimensional material in the form of comics.' The fallout is anything but trivial, raising important questions about contemporary standards of academic scholarship, scrutiny, and ethics. Furthermore, media exposure has also raised serious concerns about the motives of Andersson himself, a mature student in his 40s from Sweden who published *Destroyer Magazine* from 2006 to 2010, with the stated purpose of bringing back 'the adolescent boy as one of the ideals of gay culture' and featuring boys as young as 13. The University of Manchester and UK police force are investigating this matter. The question most raised, however, is how academic scholarship on sex and sexuality could have become so intellectually and methodologically reduced that the masturbatory account of an individual sexually excited by images of underage boys appears to pass muster (ditto for a queer feminist sympathetic to bestiality; Rudy, 2012). I would

152 SEXUAL CITIZENSHIP AND SOCIAL CHANGE

argue that this is what happens when critique is detached from tradition, such that spectacular queer critical practice of this kind becomes normalized within academic scholarship and activism. Tradition serves to temper critique and act as a repository of older values, which are not always ideal but similarly not something to simply ignore or sweep aside. It also suggests there is something seriously wrong in contemporary academic life that is in urgent need of reform.

Let's be clear here. While there is space for fantasy in sexual life, even when deviant in nature, that is not to accept an equivalence between people who engage in consensual adult sexual practice (of whatever kind) and those who desire to engage in nonconsensual acts of violence, whether this is with minors, animals, or any other living being that is unable to consent. Equally, it is of course perfectly correct for academics to study all sorts of difficult and 'sensitive' topics. It is also important to encourage viewpoint diversity in academia and society more broadly. But that said, we should have little time for people engaged in activism or even research on these topics unless it is quite clearly about finding ways to reduce the likelihood of offending by people pathologically predisposed towards sexual relations with inappropriate sexual objects. And even when work is conducted by people ostensibly motivated by a desire to reduce acts of violence, the use of progressive language regarding sexual citizenship, language that is historically rooted in fights for sexual and racial equality, results in an appalling equivalence that is frankly objectionable. For years, LGBTQ campaigns have resisted the notion that there was any association with paedophilia, a dominant trope of the conservative right that has caused so much damage. Lesbians and bisexual women have had their children forcibly removed using this as a pretext. More widely, LGBTQ folk have been subject to false imprisonment and loss of employment, as well as vile acts of violence, on this basis. There has been a hard-fought battle to undermine the false but pernicious association between sexual minorities and paedophilia over many years, and this history must not be forgotten. To associate child sexual abusers (or animal abusers) once again with sexual minorities engaged in consensual adult sexual practice, through the indulgent use of an equivalent language of rights and responsibilities, is truly perverse. The wider sexual minority community might now seek to apply a brake to the proliferation of identities under the 'queer umbrella' that have no commonality or historical connection and that only serve to destabilize hard-fought-for rights. It is time to draw a line in the sand.

Conclusions

Critique that is in search and service of the spectacular provides us with some particularly troubling examples of the dangers of critique detached from tradition. All three illustrative cases discussed above have caused or have the potential to cause serious harm to sexual minority individuals and communities. And yet these cases all involve people who are from or allies of minority communities and who will claim, with sincerity, that they are doing this for the betterment of others. The conditions that facilitate such spectacular critique need proper interrogation as this is not simply the fault of misguided or naïve individuals, even if they do need to be held individually accountable. This problem emerges from academic scholarship and activism that has lost its way, has become fatally detached from tradition, and incentivizes academics and activists in profoundly problematic ways. Academic work on the down low, barebacking, and MAPs involves a conflagration of individuals and cultures of academic practice in pursuit of the spectacular. The down low is most anchored within traditional academic practice, which arguably makes the persistence of this distorted story of Black sexuality even more disturbing. Critics have raised concerns for many years and yet this story continues to inform public health, becoming almost canonical while shoring up pernicious racial stereotypes. Stories of barebacking have clearly had their day in the main, due almost entirely to new biomedical technologies. That said, the early theoretical focus on barebacking formed a foundation for a continuing focus on the spectacular within queer theory, with repeated attempts to reassert a link between sex and death for the sexual minority subject through an analytically detached psychoanalytic theoretical apparatus. The spectacular reasserts and amplifies existing stereotypes. We see this with the racist and homophobic stereotypes founded upon the notion of hypersexualization and internalized stigma. In a similar fashion, scholars of MAPs are helping to link LGBTQ (and other consensual) sex with that of (actual or would-be) sexual abusers. These are old tropes of oppression but clearly pernicious ones that are returning through the language of contemporary critical scholarship and associated activism.

Put simply, there are some stories that should just not be narrated through the language of sexual citizenship. This must surely be true of sexual abuse, along with other stories of violence. And yet, we see theoretical arguments and a displaced emotional empathy driving research and activism to a place of darkness, dangerously detached from academic (and humanistic)

154   SEXUAL CITIZENSHIP AND SOCIAL CHANGE

traditions of reason, ethics, or even the most basic morality. The perspective taken by the academics involved with MAPs is very far away from that of the dispassionate scientist. The work is instead a dangerous integration of theory and activism, lacking the distance required to see the bigger picture and associated risks. Just because an argument can be made does not mean it should be made, nor that it has validity or value. And when the subjects of research wish to do harm to others, then their desire to claim rights, responsibilities, and respect does not warrant the same empathy that might be afforded to oppressed others. It demands serious scrutiny instead, with questions asked about the value of such claims and the consequences of us meeting them with openness and generosity, most especially mindful of those who have been subject to violence by such people.

This all rather suggests that we need to subject contemporary academic culture and practice itself to serious critical scrutiny. We need to turn our critique upon the institutions that encourage this detached form of critical scholarship. Whilst academics and activists are free to go where they wish with their research, the reception of such activity is not entirely in their hands to determine. The abject may usefully alert us to the limits of present claims to citizenship (Lee, 2016), but that does not mean we should necessarily breach those limits or encourage the narration of all stories of citizenship in an equivalent manner. Like all stories, academic accounts enter the social imaginary of stories we collectively inhabit (Ricoeur, 1986). The relationship between story and audience is key, and all stories require a receptive audience willing to listen (Plummer, 1995). Spectacular stories, while well received within academia and some activism, may be met with an audience beyond academia that finds them dangerously out of touch with tradition. Indeed, many within academia will likely be similarly perturbed, but the disciplinary silos we inhabit may well mean the spectacular academic has only limited awareness of such critical opinion. This problem is particularly acute in disciplines employing critique where academic practice merges with advocacy, often with limited awareness of or reflection upon possible tensions therein. The problem runs particularly deep within critical academic culture, where theoretical trends and fashions reward a focus on the spectacular while simultaneously silencing dissent. More so now than ever, we need to see critical scholarship itself subject to critique and (re)grounded in a dialectical relationship with tradition (Ricoeur, 1986), with renewed recognition of the importance of anchoring critique with its necessary opposite, such that it becomes tempered and less likely to be seduced by the spectacular.

SECTION 3

SECTION 3

7
Towards a politics of hospitality

Oh tell me, who was it who first announced, who first proclaimed that man only does vile things when he does not know where his real interests lie? and that if he were enlightened, if his eyes were opened to his real, normal interests, he would at once cease doing vile things and would immediately become good and honourable, because being enlightened and understanding where his real advantage lay, he would indeed see his own personal advantage in goodness, and because it is well known that no one can knowingly act against his own personal advantage, he would find himself as it were obliged to do good. Oh, you child! You sweet innocent babe!

—Dostoevsky (1864/1991: 22)

We need to have some difficult conversations. There has undoubtedly been considerable change concerning sex, sexualities, and citizenship over the past 30 years or so, much of it positive. However, contemporary narratives of sexual citizenship continue to twist and turn, with a variety of different actors playing a role in determining how the lines of acceptability and permissibility are being drawn. In this book, I have departed somewhat from contemporary arguments on this topic, and the cultural zeitgeist within academia in particular, and made an argument that we need to recognize the importance of both tradition and critique if we are to effect long-lasting change and avoid inflaming the 'culture wars'. To that end, I have sought to show how critique can get dangerously out of hand when untethered from tradition. This is not an argument from the conservative right against critique in favour of returning to or preserving long-past tradition, not at all. I believe critique is still vital for uncovering injustice and oppression and illuminating new and exciting utopian possibilities for how we might live better together. This is instead a challenge to the progressive left—a benevolent intervention, if you will—designed to shine a light on the dangers of critique when those seeking

Sexual Citizenship and Social Change. Darren Langdridge, Oxford University Press. © Oxford University Press 2024.
DOI: 10.1093/oso/9780199926312.003.0007

158 SEXUAL CITIZENSHIP AND SOCIAL CHANGE

to deploy it have lost sight of the value of tradition. This book is not about finding scapegoats or targets for cancellation. It is, of course, critical itself but I hope not engaged in unfettered critical comment, detached from tradition or *real politik*. Instead, it is intended as a book that addresses contemporary concerns in sexual politics while attempting to avoid falling afoul of extant political hegemonies. The arguments I make seek to attend to contemporary politics with respect to inequalities regarding sex, sex/gender, sexuality, race/ethnicity, and class/poverty while resisting an ever more atomized and reified identity politics.

The ideological ground has certainly shifted a good deal in a relatively short time with respect to many sexual identities and practices, in the West at least. That said, there remains a stubborn rump of prejudice, which is particularly pernicious within public space and often driven by religious intolerance. This has resulted in an increasingly privatized sexual citizenship, one mostly centred on those who fit heterosexual definitions of acceptability, and represents much more limited progress than otherwise has been suggested. The dominant contemporary narrative suggests this war has been won, and yet, as a number of other authors have noted, there remains some way to go for the minority sexual citizen (e.g., Duberman, 2018; Mowlabocus, 2021; Signorile, 2016; Walters, 2014; Yoshino, 2007). It is all too easy to be swept away on a tide of optimism about the depth of social change occurring over the last 50 years, but upon closer inspection things are not always quite as positive as they may at first appear.

The 'enemies' of the progressive politics of sexual citizenship are not simply the same 'old guard' conservatives who want a strongly proscribed limit to what is and what is not acceptable or permissible. The situation is now more complex than this. The 'old guard' still exists, of course, but the stories they tell are picked up and promoted much less frequently and heard much less willingly than they once were, in the United Kingdom and much of continental Europe at least. The progressives have seemingly won that discursive battle, for now at least, although perhaps rather less so in nation-states like the United States, where the relationship between religion and politics is more fundamental, embedded, and public than it is in the United Kingdom. Beyond remaining instances of raw prejudice, when we see opposition to change it is often complex, involving disclaimers and distancing and not so immediately identifiable with traditional opposition. Contemporary battles concerning sexual citizenship also involve structural opposition within public institutions. This is key to understanding what enables—and

TOWARDS A POLITICS OF HOSPITALITY 159

will continue to enable—the policing of acceptability and permissibility with respect to sexual practice, despite an apparent increased acceptability and growing political awareness. The challenge regarding the liberal march of progress is more complex when we have the addition of structural resistance and less obviously antagonistic voices acting to narrate problematic narratives of sexual citizenship.

That said, for my own part herein, I have sought to argue that a new danger for contemporary sexual citizenship emerges from problems in the mode of critique. This is critique that is detached and unfettered, set loose from the usual anchor of tradition. And this is critique that emerges from within minority communities and their allies, not imposed upon them by antagonistic others. I have tried to show that even the most ostensibly well-meaning critic—and associated critique—can become problematic when the arguments are detached from tradition. As such, critique that is out of touch with tradition may provoke unnecessary conflict within communities, result in the internalization of pathology, become conservative within the context of an ersatz performative radicalism, inadvertently repathologize sexual subjects, and risk dangerous unintended consequences when using the language of progressive sexual citizenship with that which is abject. Tradition and critique—through ideological and utopian stories of citizenship—need each other, ideally within a dialectic, or risk becoming extreme or otherwise detached from everyday concerns. In the drive for change, in search of our personal utopia, it is easy to forget the value of tradition. Tradition locates us in history, grounds us in a community, and thereby provides us with a way of understanding the world (Shils, 1981). It is not fixed but ever changing, providing innovation itself. And importantly, it acts to temper critique.

I set out to show how *critique can become detached* from tradition in Chapter 4, expressed through a clash of values. The first example of religious protests mobilized against diversity education in UK schools was an example of tradition, simple old-fashioned prejudice if you will, dressed up as critique through a trope about the sexualization of children. That is problematic in its own right, but most significantly there was also a notable lack of critique of this tradition of religiously motivated sexual and gender prejudice. The teachers were left to fend for themselves. The fear of causing offence—particularly being accused of Islamophobia—appears to have resulted in a failure of the wider political community, which ostensibly supports diversity education, to come to the aid of these teachers (and their students). This example entailed a clash of values between a religious worldview and LGBTQ

160 SEXUAL CITIZENSHIP AND SOCIAL CHANGE

education in which there was a lack of critique to challenge the resurgence of old-fashioned prejudice, albeit dressed up in the language of contemporary social critique. The second example of a lack of engagement between tradition and critique concerning sex and gender politics is the contrast pole. Academic and activist claims regarding trans rights represent a radical critique of traditions concerning sexed bodies, leading to an angry clash of values with feminists and others wishing to maintain those traditions. But, like the school protest example, there has been a lack of engagement between the two warring parties, with arguments becoming ever more shrill. Both cases demonstrate the dangers of cancel culture politics in which one party attempts to silence the other. Accusations of racism or transphobia operate here to shut down much-needed engagement and the possibility of dialogue in search of recognition across the divide between tradition and critique.

In Chapter 5, I explored the way that contemporary *critique can become distorted* such that it appears almost identical to previously oppressive tradition. This is tradition dressed up in critical clothing. This latter point is important for this is not mere assimilation to the traditional norms of responsible sexual citizenship but a distinctly modern phenomenon. The first example is the growth of a therapeutic narrative within BDSM communities. It is indeed ironic—and perhaps significant—that just as we see progress in shaking off the historical association between BDSM and psychological trauma, an association that has been profoundly problematic for individuals and communities, we are witness to BDSM communities themselves making sense of their sexual practice through the very same narrative. The critical argument that this is about BDSMers taking charge of the narrative has some merit but also masks the very real dangers of such a distorted mode of critique, especially given the continued expansion of 'psy' discourse in wider culture. The second example of polyamory provides a similar but distinctly different case in which a sexual identity/practice is framed as radical critique—in this instance, of the tradition of monogamy—but then deploys a story grounded in love that is almost indistinguishable from that traditional narrative. The story of BDSM carries the very real risk of encouraging the telling of a story of pathology, even inviting the 'psy' professions back in, while the story of polyamorous love serves to reinforce the very same naturalizing discourse it sets out to critique. Furthermore, both discourses draw—whether intentionally or not—upon the seductive power imbued in the canonical narratives they mimic, such that they may rapidly become hegemonic. Such hegemonic stories of sexual citizenship expose all within these

TOWARDS A POLITICS OF HOSPITALITY   161

communities to the external authoritarian risk while also serving to silence alternative critical narratives.

And finally, in Chapter 6 I set out to highlight the dangers of spectacular critique, where *critique can become extended beyond important limits* and become dangerously out of control. This is critique without tradition or accountability, with a notable need for a Ricoeurean (1986) dialectic to temper the allure of the spectacular. This is also critique that also runs up to or even breaches the acceptable and permissible limits of sexual citizenship, a citizenship of the abject. And while the abject may play an important role in enabling us to test the validity of present limit conditions to citizenship, it may also lead to critics losing sight of important aspects of tradition. The first example I discussed of the 'down low' serves as a warning about the seductive nature of the spectacular. With this case, we see the production of a story of sexual life that was ostensibly for the good of those it concerned and that became self-sustaining despite a lack of evidence. The desire to hold on to this story of dangerously spectacular sexualities served to reinforce and continue pernicious racist stereotypes. The not unrelated story of barebacking provided my second example. This story is in many ways the natural corollary of the story of the down low, albeit a story amplified through the voices of critical social science and queer theory. An unusual array of figures has helped create a culture of critical scholarship that has grown increasingly powerful within contemporary academia. It has also become ever more detached from traditional academic and activist values. The seductive power of this mode of thinking has become undergirded by academic cultures (and activism) in which critique has become the new ideology. This is never more apparent than in the example of scholarship and activism concerning minor-attracted persons (MAPs). All the arguments made by those opposing citizenship for lesbians and gay men that this was a slippery slope have come true, with this representing a very dangerous tipping point for contemporary sexual citizenship. The attempt to expand progressive claims for citizenship concerning adult consensual sexual practices and identities to include the abject—those who wish to engage in nonconsensual acts of sexual violence—represents the end point for the project of sexual citizenship. This is a line that must never be crossed and serves as a warning that we need to urgently reassert the value of tradition and rein in this dangerously out-of-control critique.

The episodes and stories explored in these chapters have implicated a wide array of narratively constituted selves (Ricoeur, 1992), all of which serve to create a particular kind of moral subject. In the religious school protests,

162 SEXUAL CITIZENSHIP AND SOCIAL CHANGE

the prejudiced protestors recast themselves as the moral self who is worried about the sexualization of children. Trans activists and their allies cast themselves as the moral self that seeks to be inclusive (with the gender critical self being positioned as the prejudiced other). Meanwhile, the gender critical feminists seek to present themselves as the moral self who wishes to protect girls and women (and the trans self as dangerous interloper). The BDSM community that embraces a therapeutic narrative is working to refigure themselves as good people having sex for their mental well-being. By contrast, the story of the down low relied on an (im)moral male self that puts others at risk, allied to a vulnerable female self that has no agency. The story of barebacking amplifies and extends this story of an immoral male self by adding intent: this is the moral self who wishes to overthrow extant notions of morality. And finally, with the narrative of the MAP we see an attempt to recast the abject self who wishes to abuse and harm others for their own pleasure as a moral victim, struggling to control themselves in the face of unwanted and uncontrollable desires. Kaplan (2003: 91) states that 'a narrative identity is a dialectic of personal experience and impersonal circumstance'. In all instances herein, the self that has been produced through these stories brings together personal experience with impersonal circumstance to serve a moral purpose, to position the storyteller as either morally good or bad. These stories of sexual citizenship are in many ways simple old-fashioned morality tales dressed up in the language of the present era, with individuals and communities serving to narrate their experience in a manner that is of most personal and political benefit.

That said, it is important to note that the stories of sexual citizenship explored in this book should be seen as illustrative rather than definitive. They have been fixed here in this text but will inevitably change further, quite likely even before publication, with progress in some places and resistance emerging elsewhere. New sexual stories will arise, while some will be extinguished. Some will resonate in other territories, while others will not. Regardless, the argument I have made about the need to hold critique in a dialectical relationship with tradition still holds. This is a consistent narrative trope for the present age, even if the substantive content underpinning that argument may change. There is an insatiable nature to critique; it is seductive and never satisfied. Sexual citizenship involves—indeed, requires—engagement between tradition and critique, and, while the manner in which this is manifest may shift and change, sometimes in quite subtle ways, this is an enduring principle. And of course, I should note at this end point that the presentation herein is not representative of all contemporary sexual life. There are many people telling stories of sexual citizenship that may offer something more beneficial to sexual politics than those discussed in the previous chapters. The account presented here is necessarily partial but deliberately so to highlight the dangers facing contemporary sexual life.

Envisioning the future

So, having described the challenge, where now for sexual citizenship? How might we envision a more productive future sexual politics? Sexual citizenship is arguably at the vanguard of what has been termed the 'culture wars' (Hunter, 1991), with sex (and gender) once again figuring centrally in many contemporary cultural struggles. Not that much has changed since Rubin was writing in the 1960s it seems. Unlike so much contemporary critical social theory, I do not want to only deconstruct or offer critique. We need a 'real politics' (Geuss, 2008) that engages with the world as it is and starts from this foundation to think through how it could be made better. So, what do we need to do to effect political change? There is obviously much more still to do with respect to sexual citizenship, but critically, I think we must now change our (ostensibly) progressive politics and social movements. We need to move away from the rigid binary thinking and ideological blindness that pervade contemporary politics. We need to move beyond overly simplistic views of left vs. right, conservative vs. progressive, and recognize the need for both ideology and utopia, as tradition and critique within society. In other words, we need to deploy our critical faculties upon ostensibly progressive political thought and action, as much as we do with conservative opposition to change.

Human action, identity, and a politics of recognition

The focus in Ricoeur's work has been consistently on human action rather than acts, which is distinct from many contemporary moves in citizenship studies. Ricoeur maintains a strong commitment to the Kantian notion of persons as ends rather than means so that it is necessary to distinguish between persons as agents from objects. And this is an important distinction for the argument being made here about the dangers of critique. Speaking of

164 SEXUAL CITIZENSHIP AND SOCIAL CHANGE

Ricoeur's (1992) classic text *Oneself as Another*, Kaplan (2003: 83) describes his aim with the move to action as follows:

> One of the tasks of Oneself as Another is to shatter the illusion of the immediacy of the cogito that was meant to establish an ultimate foundation of knowledge. Another task is to shatter the illusion of the death of the subject and the subsequent destruction of the problem of any foundation of knowledge. The self is neither a Nietzschean-postmodern illusion, a Kantian limit, nor a Hegelian synthesis, but a narratively constituted 'analogical unity' that is a socially responsible agent, capable of speaking, understanding, initiating, and suffering actions. Ricoeur shows how we can conceive of a self that is neither an ultimate foundation nor a fragmented illusion but a 'capable person' who is able to speak, act, recount oneself, and act responsibly.

Action involves recognition of accomplishments and so—unlike a focus on will or acts—implies a necessary material relationship between individuals and the institutions and societies they inhabit. As such, we are able to hold people accountable for their actions and attribute them with responsibility for their decisions. And, of course, politics necessarily presupposes the existence of persons to whom we can attribute responsibility. Ricoeur argues that our mode of action as human beings corresponds to Heidegger's (1962) notion of 'care' as the fundamental way we inhabit the world, providing a foundation for an ethical politics.

But the politics that Ricoeur espouses is not an identity politics but rather a politics of recognition (Ricoeur, 2005). Individual identities—whether narrative or otherwise—are, of course, tied up with group identities. Our cultural, social, and political identities are constituted through the stories we tell, driven by both individual agency and social forces. Ricoeur is keen to stress that group, as much as individual, stories can be subject to ideological colonization, particularly political identities that—in themselves—require a storyteller with absolute conviction. Political (and academic) narratives are therefore always embedded within the dialectic of ideology and utopia, offering both the reproduction of tradition and critical ruptures in the status quo. They distort as well as integrate, and therefore offer unrealistic visions as well as visionary possibilities. It has hitherto been ideology where there has been thought the greatest risk to political progress, subject as it is to stories built on founding events and a linking back to particular traditions

TOWARDS A POLITICS OF HOSPITALITY   165

and particular ideological struggles. The danger is that such foundational narratives may become fixed, tied to a particular historical telling and offering no space for critique, only conviction. When political stories become 'sedimented' (Merleau-Ponty, 1945/1962) into doctrine, we can see ideology in action and the complete absence of utopian possibilities. The present age offers up a new challenge, however, the risk that critique—like tradition—may become fixed or ideologically distorted, and this has been my focus in this book.

Ricoeur's arguments (1998) about the need for a politics of recognition, rather than identity, involve a concern for how the requirement for sameness within identity politics serves to exclude others or rather 'always involves something violent with respect to others ... [whilst] ... the search for recognition implies reciprocity' (p. 60). His worry is that identity politics results in an 'ideology of difference' that means greater consolidation of group difference and less opportunities for dialogue across these differences. And it is only through dialogue that Ricoeur sees the possibility for understanding.

> The ideology of difference, by failing to differentiate among differences, destroys the critical spirit which rests on shared common rules of discussion and on the participation of communities of argumentation recruited on bases other than the historical constitution of different group affiliations. The paradox is indeed that the praise of difference ends up reinforcing the internal identities of the groups themselves. (Ricoeur, 1998: 56)

And whilst this might be overstating the case somewhat, perhaps missing some of the gains achieved through identity politics, it still resonates with the challenges outlined herein about contemporary sexual politics. His wish is for us to embrace a politics of recognition, which avoids, in Kaplan's (2003: 158) words, 'the ideology of integration that obliterates group differences ... and ... the ideology of difference that fragments and disintegrates social life beyond repair'. Ricoeur does understand why we have seen the growth of identity politics, in opposition to liberal universalism, but thinks it is vital to retain the idea of universality whilst acknowledging difference. Political action demands that at some point we stop engaging in critique and instead adopt a position of conviction where we seek recognition of and through the Other.

Ricoeur's politics of recognition is further complicated by the fact that ideology and utopia are permanent features of political life. The constitutive

166 SEXUAL CITIZENSHIP AND SOCIAL CHANGE

narratives we deploy may function as ideology or utopia, integration or disruption of the status quo. They must therefore be subject to interpretation and even contestation rather than treated as statements of truth. Furthermore, he argues that the central way to meet Otherness and enable recognition is through an 'ethics of linguistic hospitality'. In this mode we seek to share our stories, our histories, in order to learn how to experience life for the Other.

> Despite the conflictual character which renders the task of the translator dramatic, he or she will find satisfaction in what I like to call linguistic hospitality. Its predicament is that of a correspondence without complete adhesion.... Linguistic hospitality, therefore, is the act of inhabiting the word of the Other paralleled by the act of receiving the word of the Other into one's home, one's own dwelling. (Ricoeur, 2004, cited in Kearney, 2007)

Against 'either/or' politics: the importance of conviction and critique

What I want to argue, following Ricoeur, is that the fuel for battles within the 'culture wars' more often than not comes about as a result of an either/or narrative, a narrative founded on an exclusionary logic that divides. Such dividing narratives will inevitably fuel the fight, with little chance of true listening, dialogue, and recognition. This is not (necessarily) a deliberate strategic choice for division on the part of the actors involved; many involved are likely convinced they are simply fighting a just battle against oppression or holding the line against a perceived aggressor wanting to take away something precious. That said, some are clearly in this for the fight. Recognition through conversation—no matter how challenging—sublimates the otherwise angry desire to destroy the other that opposes one's worldview. It is important that we take a moment to look at the political strategies underpinning contemporary narratives of sexual citizenship and subject them to scrutiny, in the hope that we can find a pathway out of the wars towards mutual recognition and consensual progressive change, where feasible.

Much is discussed about the problems of identity politics driving—or at least centrally implicated in—a culture war between right and left or perhaps more accurately urban left progressives and more conservative political communities (Hunter, 1991). This is particularly acute in the United States but is also present and growing within Europe. In the UK context, debates have arisen around identity politics in the context of Brexit in particular but also across a range of identity categories including race, gender, and sexuality. Now, some of the 'wars' are clearly confected by those who wish to resist change at every turn and see this as an opportunity for advantage—that is to be expected. But beyond this 'traditional' opposition, which seeks only to distort, might there also be something problematic within progressive politics that itself fuels conflict?

The point I wish to make is that progressive politics too readily fails to acknowledge the need for and power of tradition. There is an understandable but all too quick rush for what is new, what is 'progressive', what appears to move us beyond the status quo towards some utopia. Sadly, this often means a rather casual abandonment of what went before, with only very limited scrutiny of any possible unintended consequences of such political change. That is, with every progressive advance there will likely be an attendant loss, material and symbolic. This may be necessary, desirable even, but that loss needs to be taken seriously both for the fact that it means someone—some community—will feel they are losing an important aspect of their tradition and because there may be value in that tradition that we rush to wish away at our peril. There is also a need to draw a line, to accept the role of boundaries regarding the acceptability and permissibility of contemporary sexual life, albeit not uncritically. Not everything is or should be acceptable or permissible. This may appear somewhat arbitrary at times, but if grounded in tradition, this 'arbitrariness' should be the product of practical wisdom and cultural consensus. If it is not, then it will likely be—and rightly be—subject to appropriate critique and pressure to change.

A successful politics—following Ricoeur—requires that we account for both tradition and critique within a dialectic, with genuine respect for both, while being attentive to power imbalance between positions (see, e.g., Langdridge, 2013). Tradition and critique will not be evenly balanced within a dialectic, nor should they be, of course. Change will only occur if there is movement between positions, with power transferring and adhering accordingly. But if one position comes to dominate—becomes hegemonic—then the opportunity for dialogue and practical wisdom, so essential to the progressive spiral of ideology and utopia, may end prematurely. As such, a progressive politics that seeks to singularly advance its cause without proper account of the positive arm of tradition inherent within ideology, as well as the potential loss that may occur with change, will never carry people with it and risks the creation of unnecessary conflict. And of course, the resolute

168 SEXUAL CITIZENSHIP AND SOCIAL CHANGE

maintenance of tradition to hold onto tradition, or even power only, simply for the sake of it is equally problematic. The present culture wars sadly are a very good example of this tension. Contemporary sexual politics is so often about 'either/or' when we need 'and': there has been a profound and consistent failure of cultural Boolean logic within contemporary discourse on sex and sexuality. I'd argue we need to learn from Ricoeur and his lifelong pursuit of a pathway through ostensibly opposed positions that is focused on recognition of the other. He always sought to learn from the good in ostensibly opposed positions, adopting an approach that brings ideas and people together rather than driving them yet further apart.

The dangers of utopian critique and the need to renew 'the period of effervescence' within ideology

Recognizing the value of tradition and critique for an effective and consensual contemporary politics is not the end, however. We also need to ensure critique is deployed thoughtfully and with care such that there is space for progressive as well as reproductive imagination (Stiver, 2019). That is, we cannot and should not rely on utopian critique alone to be the voice of progressive politics, nor should this critique go unchallenged, even when we agree with it in the main. Utopian critique alone may risk a rupture with positive ideological tradition and miss out on the opportunity for shifts within rather than total rejection of extant ideologies. When there is a narrative orthodoxy, it becomes difficult to have a conversation, to speak and be heard. The dominant voice tends to close down alternate voices, and this is as true of (progressive) utopian narratives of critique as it is for those of (conservative) narrative tradition. Hard divisions, especially where they involve silencing of the other, lead inevitably to the production of disenfranchised people. And when people feel they are not allowed to speak or cannot get their voices heard, then disengagement, frustration, and anger will inevitably follow.

When we seek to engage in critique, Ricoeur (1970) argues—following Freud—that we must first apply such suspicion to ourselves through a critique of the illusions of the subject. The danger in engaging hermeneutics to uncover meaning through critique is that we may inadvertently project our own subjectivity onto the phenomenon, simply replacing one ideology with another. This can be seen within sexual politics, of course, where conservative and progressive voices may fail to engage a critical sensibility towards their own position. With the progressives, this may lead to an unnecessarily crude critique—through what we might term an 'ideological blindness'—in which there is no attempt to understand the other, engage in a dialogue with the convictions of tradition, and explore whether there might be space for compromise towards a common cause. It may also result in the all too ready employment of narrative tropes that are themselves damaging and that—likely inadvertently—serve to produce new ideological distortions that disenfranchise others or otherwise cause harm.

Ricoeur (1970, 1981) recognizes that there is an inherent distanciation within selfhood that itself requires a hermeneutic turn. We are not completely transparent to ourselves, with our actions subject to influence by layers of consciousness outside awareness that may serve to distort. As such, we would be well served to subject ourselves to the same critical scrutiny as we do any other meaning system, and thereby bring a critique of false consciousness (Habermas, 1971) into the hermeneutic project. While Ricoeur (1970, 1981) draws upon Marxist and Freudian critique to uncover these hidden layers, I have advocated an approach where we deploy suspicious hermeneutics beyond these two alone (Langdridge, 2003, 2007). Notwithstanding the various options for critique, the underlying principle I want to advance here, however, is that we subject ourselves to the same level of critique as we do the objects of our critical imagination. Such an approach encourages a healthy sense of humility and encourages uncertainty about our position, given the introduction of doubt about personal motivation and judgement. This critical counter to the certainty that may accompany ideology and utopia allows space for serious self-reflection, as well as an openness to the worldview of the Other.

Critique must not be left only to those progressives seeking to advance a particular revolutionary utopian vision. Stiver (2019) builds on Ricoeur's (1986) arguments about ideology and utopia to advance the case for what he terms a 'period of effervescence' within ideology critique. That is, Stiver (2019) rightly recognizes that critique may occur from within ideology itself rather than only from a utopian nowhere. Not all critique need be so radical or destructive, with much that is constructive and progressive emerging from within, as a consequence of the failure of ideologies themselves. This idea is prefigured within Ricoeur's thinking but not hitherto worked through. The point being made by Stiver is that critique may come about through a renewal or reform within an ideology, particularly when there is an opportunity to appeal back to an original vision. That is, ideologies often come about from an original utopian vision before becoming distorted, buried, or forgotten: an original 'period of effervescence' that continues to provide the possibility of a stimulus for renewal (Stiver, 2019). There is an opportunity through a re-engagement with these founding moments—through a 'feeling backward' (Love, 2007), for instance—to recapture some of the originating power within an ideology that may be productive rather than simply reproductive. This aspect of ideology—of tradition—must not be forgotten in the rush to embrace the new through the revolutionary zeal of the utopian activist, for it too offers hope of change and progress. Such change may be less radical, but it will also likely be change that results in less conflict and loss.

To provide a concrete example, notwithstanding the lack of supportive empirical evidence (see, e.g., Bartos et al., 2019), there may be rhetorical value in a critical concept like 'homonationalism' (Puar, 2007). This is the argument that LGBTQ rights are deployed to assert the cultural superiority of the West as a means to justify colonialism. It usefully alerts us to the way that minority sexualities may be used for racist political purposes. That said, the way that same-sex sexualities are now deployed politically, through the use of concepts like homonationalism, may also be deeply problematic for LGBTQ people and communities themselves. Many ostensibly progressive critical theorists now use LGBTQ sexualities in weaponized form only to attack a particular version of Western cultural imperialism. This fuels the myth that LGBTQ life is now settled in the United Kingdom, North America, and other Western democracies, such that these sexual subjects come into critical focus only when they prove useful to an argument about Western cultural and political dominance within the global political sphere. The well-being of people who are LGBTQ, at least in settings other than those seen as oppressed by the West, is, as a result, mostly lost from the productive imagination of the contemporary critical theorist.

This is particularly true for the White Western gay male who occupies an almost reviled position within the contemporary academic and activist sexual hierarchy, seemingly regardless of his class, status, or actual power. The notion of privilege—and the related concept 'intersectionality' (Crenshaw, 1989), at least as presently operationalized—may be problematic in this context. What may be useful as an analytic concept within a sociological analysis—highlighting how some groups may have historical advantage or entitlement—is more often than not inappropriate when deployed at the individual level against people within particular identity groups (Downing, 2019). It is crass and exclusionary, a tool of division, deployed as if a weapon in a rhetorical power battle rather than a means of enabling reflection, such that we might find common cause with the other. It leads to an inevitable division between identity categories within some dubious moral battle for preferred victim status. We need to resist setting up false oppositions, which fuel unnecessary division within already disadvantaged communities. Progressive sexual politics should not be a zero-sum 'game' in which people are set against one another in a fight to claim an advantage on the basis of some perceived group disadvantage. There should surely be enough progressive energy to sustain more than one fight at a time such that we might attend to the experience of the person we encounter as an individual rather than as some replaceable generic representative of a group.

Translation and linguistic hospitality

Finally, I'd like to turn to how we might best meet the foreign Other, how we might seek to bridge the disturbing gap between self and Other, such that the encounter can be a productive one. Ricoeur's (2006) work on translation provides a model for how we might seek to engage with Otherness, with him putting (*linguistic*) *hospitality* at the core of the process, alert to the imperialistic danger of any desire to achieve 'a perfect *logos* of the future' (Kearney, 2019: 1). In other words, his work recognizes the tension between hostility that may result from an attempt to reduce guest and host to the same versus the hospitable acknowledgement of difference inherent in the labour of translation. There is always the possibility of 'betrayal as well as rebirth' in any encounter with foreignness (Kearney, 2019: 5), and 'one is best advised to take a middle road of "linguistic hospitality" where one honors both host and guest languages equally while resisting the take-over of one by the other. The good translator is neither master nor slave'. (Kearney, 2019: 1). Translation is not merely intellectual work for Ricoeur but also an ethical problem, such that the linguistic hospitality required of translation may serve as a model for other forms of hospitality. And this is the claim I want to make here, that we can follow the model of linguistic hospitality from Ricoeur (2006) within contemporary sexual politics as a means to work productively between positions of difference—between ideology and utopia, tradition and critique—and thereby avoid further cultural alienation.

Ricoeur (2006) distinguishes between linguistic and ontological paradigms of translation. The former concerns the translation of meaning

172 SEXUAL CITIZENSHIP AND SOCIAL CHANGE

from one language into another, that is, the common usage of the term. The latter, however, refers to 'the ontological act of speaking as a way of not only translating oneself to oneself (inner to outer, private to public, unconscious to conscious) but also, and more explicitly, of translating oneself to others' (Kearney, 2007: 150).

The encounter with the Other cannot be avoided as it is within us as well as between us in any act of speaking: there is an original plurality to humanity. Perfect translation is not possible; it is never final or complete. There is a delicate balance to be struck between hospitality towards that which is foreign and recognition that something will always be lost in translation, that some difference will always remain. Translation is—for Ricoeur—a process of *working through* (*Durcharbeitung*: Freud, 1914), an arduous task and trial of patience. This is not an easy achievement. It involves

> a process of mourning and letting go—and in particular the renunciation of the egocentric drive to reduce the alterities of the guest to one's own will for total adequation. As if, in translation, there were only one true language: my own. Our own. . . . Hospitable translation thus renounces all claim to absolute sovereignty acknowledging that we share words as we share clothes. Or to paraphrase Ricoeur, we should let our language try on the garments of strangers at the same time as we invite them to step into the fabric of our own speech. (Kearney, 2019: 2–3)

We share not only words but also worlds. These worlds contain our hopes and aspirations as individuals and communities, and it is here within our worlds that we must recognize the fragile and fallible nature of translation, a never-ending process that carries risk but also possibility. We must mourn the loss of the fantasy of shared truth—of the fusion of self and Other—and instead work through the continuing challenge of plurality. This is, however, in contrast to, for example, Derridean deconstruction, a *conditional* hospitality in which there remains an interpretive process of judgement with regard to what we seek to welcome (Kearney, 2019). This is a mode of translation that is itself translatable into a real politics (Geuss, 2008) and not simply some idealized abstraction or mystical dream, 'which goes some way to explaining Ricoeur's claim that the difference between him and Derrida is that between the terms "difficult" and "impossible"' (Kearney, 2019: 6). Being hospitable to the other, whether that other advocates a narrative of ideology or utopia, tradition or critique, is undoubtedly a 'difficult' task but not an 'impossible' one.

Ricoeur (1996) outlines five ethical functions for translation (Kearney, 2007): (a) an ethic of hospitality, (b) narrative flexibility, (c) narrative plurality, (d) transfiguring the past, and (e) an ethic of forgiveness. In essence this means the following:

- We should approach the other with generosity, starting from a position grounded in a sympathetic desire to understand their concerns. This must involve an awareness that every story can be told from different perspectives, an awareness that should also alert us to the dangers of seeking to reify events into dogma.
- We should remember that the past is not simply history—what is bygone and now of no concern to the present—but also a memory that represents the 'unfulfilled future of the past' (pp. 5–11). If we seek to bridge the gap between critique and tradition, then we must be sensitive to the promises of the past that remain unfulfilled.
- We need to engage in the painful process of forgiveness for the suffering of the past. This involves a necessary sharing of narratives of pain and suffering such that there is understanding of the hurt that has been caused, but also much more than this. There must also be a 'shattering of the debt' if we are to move forward. There needs to be a *working through* of the pain caused such that it results in mourning and letting go. This is not about forgetting or the denial of justice but about a surplus of charity.

This is a process we must undertake with sexual citizenship, a task becoming increasingly urgent and ever more difficult but arguably not impossible. We can—and must—continue to fight against oppression wherever it is found while also remaining generous in spirit—hospitable—to the Other. If we do not, then we risk ever more polarization, pointless echo-chamber politics, and ever more people becoming 'dangerously crazy about sexuality' (Rubin, 1984/1993: 3–4). At times of great social stress come risks but also opportunities, and we have an opportunity now to engage a more hopeful politics, a politics of forgiveness, hospitality, and justice: in other words, a progressive politics of tradition and critique.

APPENDIX

A dialectic of ideology and utopia

In his *Lectures on Ideology and Utopia* Ricoeur (1986) argues that ideology and utopia operate at three levels in social life: as distortion, legitimization, and integration/identity (Ricoeur, 1986). They do not simply represent the social world as it is but function in differing ways in relation to praxis. Ricoeur's analysis is unusual because he attempts to locate ideology and utopia within a common conceptual framework. Traditionally, ideology and utopia have been treated quite separately: ideology the province of the critical social theorist and utopia the province of the literary. According to Ricoeur (1986), only Mannheim (1936) has attempted to locate these two concepts within a common, albeit flawed, conceptual framework, at least in recent years. Ricoeur pays due regard to Mannheim but formulates a more positive understanding of the relationship between the two concepts. He does this through a *genetic phenomenology*, that is, an analysis of the *things in their appearing*, working backward from surface meaning/s to uncover the deeper meaning/s. The two concepts have, perhaps understandably, been treated separately because they represent very different concepts with quite different histories. Ideology has been that which others are accused of possessing, from a critical political tradition, whilst utopia is that which is claimed and wished for, most often within the literary tradition. Ricoeur focuses his attention on ideology and identifies two levels of meaning moving from the superficial to the fundamental. At the most superficial level Ricoeur recognizes the early Marxist conception of ideology as distortion. He takes this position on board and then by way of Weber's notion of legitimacy uncovers a more profound and positive role for ideology within the social imaginary: as integration/identity. In a similar move, Ricoeur highlights the two complementary aspects of utopia: as escape and as an imaginative way to shatter the present order represented in the prevailing ideology. In the sections that follow I detail Ricoeur's analysis of the Marxist notion of ideology, the vital role of power and Weber's notion of legitimacy, and finally his positive conception of ideology as integration formulated through Geertz's notion of the symbolic. I then present Ricoeur's arguments for a more nuanced understanding of utopia and the relationship of this aspect of the social imaginary with ideology.

Marxist ideology

Ricoeur (1986) begins his discussion of ideology with, perhaps not surprisingly, analysis of the Marxist critique of ideology. It is with Marx that we see the most prevalent and significant conceptualization of ideology to date. Ricoeur concentrates on the early works of Marx (the *Critique of Hegel's 'Philosophy of Right'*, the *Economic and Philosophic Manuscripts of 1844*, and *The German Ideology*), recognizing a more humanistic notion of ideology in the early works. Arguably, the foundational conceptualization of ideology in Marxist thought comes from the well-known *camera lucida* metaphor, where we see ideology represented as distortion through inversion. Ideology operates to invert real social understanding and therefore distort it. This concept of ideology stems from, and extends,

176   APPENDIX

Feuerbach's view of religion as ideology (Ricoeur, 1986). Ideology is very much a negative concept (as it has been since Napoleon) operating to obscure the processes of real life. Ricoeur argues that the opposition in the early Marxist conception of ideology is between ideology and reality, and most specifically reality as praxis, rather than between ideology and Marxist science, as it would later become. With this reading of Marx, ideology serves to invert the real and the role of a Marxist critique of ideology is to invert the inverted.

The second stage in the Marxist conception of ideology comes with *Das Capital*, where ideology is broadened to encompass all that is not Marxist science. Marxist science is the body of knowledge paradigmatically expressed in *Capital*. Ideology now includes all pre-scientific aspects of life and not just religious or idealist inversion of reality and therefore reaches out to engulf utopia. Utopia must be ideological as it is nonscientific, in the Marxist sense of the term. Ricoeur (1986) argues that the concept of ideology is continually broadened from the narrow conception in early Marxist thought through the mature Marxism of *Capital* to later Marxist and post-Marxist thought from theorists such as Althusser and Habermas. The broadening is such that, Ricoeur argues, everything becomes ideological. And since it is not likely that any person will live their life completely as a Marxist scientist, then it is very likely that everyone lives within some kind of ideology. Ricoeur (1986) does not seek to dispute the Marxist notion of ideology as distortion because it patently represents some phenomenological truth about our lived experience. However, he does seek to offer a challenge to the all-encompassing quality of ideology by seeking to identify some more positive aspects.

Mannheim's paradox

One of the consequences of the extension of the concept of ideology is what has been termed *Mannheim's paradox*. That is, if everything we think and say is distorted, then how can we have a theory of ideology itself that is not ideological? Mannheim's starting position was the Marxist notion of ideology. He argued that if the Marxist notion of ideology is true, then he himself must be engaged in ideology too, an ideology of an intellectual kind. The paradox arises because the extension of the concept of ideology is such that the theory of ideology becomes ideological itself. Mannheim's paradox is not simply a concern for Marxism, however. He reached this position through an epistemological extension of Marxism, and as such, the paradox can be restated in more general epistemological terms thus:

> What is the epistemological status of discourse about ideology if all discourse is ideological? How can this discourse escape its own exposition, its own description? If sociopolitical thought itself is entwined with the life situation of the thinker, does not the concept of ideology have to be adsorbed into its own referent? (Ricoeur, 1986: 9)

Manheim tried to resolve the paradox and escape the charge of relativism through appeal to a notion of situational *relationism*, an alternative to relativism based on an evaluation of historical processes. However, this proved most unsatisfactory as he failed to recognize the inability of the historical onlooker, required for his relationism, to stand outside relationism itself and judge what in history is in correlation. Ricoeur does not confront Mannheim's paradox head on but instead questions the premises upon which it is based. He argues that the foundational error in the paradox was the epistemological extension of

APPENDIX   177

later Marxism, with the contrast between ideology and Marxist science. Ricoeur argues that the more fundamental opposition is to be found in the earlier works of Marx, with the opposition between ideology and praxis. And furthermore, even this contrast must be reformulated such that ideology is not in opposition to praxis but is *connected* to praxis. Ricoeur (1986: 10) argues that distortion can only operate on the back of a pre-existing symbolic system:

> If social reality did not already have a social dimension, and therefore, if ideology, in less polemical or less negatively evaluative sense, were not constitutive of social existence but merely distorting and dissimulating, then the process of distortion could not start.

The result is that Ricoeur is now faced with finding a more fundamental function for ideology, one that precedes distortion. He turns to the work of Clifford Geertz (1973) for an answer to this problem. Geertz (1973) focuses on the function of ideology, something somewhat ignored by Marxists and non-Marxists alike, arguing, in line with Ricoeur, that all social action is symbolically mediated. Furthermore, it is ideology that fulfils the role of mediating social action implicated in preserving sociocultural identities. I address this further below but first turn to the second level of Ricoeur's analysis of ideology. This level acts to connect the fundamental role of ideology as integration/identity with the more superficial role of ideology as distortion.

Weber and the legitimization of power

Ricoeur turns to Weber (1986) to argue that the relationship between the ruling class and those being ruled needs to be understood in motivational rather than causal terms. Like many humanists, Ricoeur prefers the earlier work of Marx with human alienation, or more broadly human motivation, as a key criterion for historical change. Power inequalities cannot simply depend on a causal pattern of economic conditions, as described in *Capital*, but must involve human motivation. This is because systems of authority cannot rely on brute force alone. All enduring political systems, perhaps all social systems in general, require consent and not simply domination. That is, leadership needs power granted through legitimate authority.

Weber's (1986) motivational model provides the framework for understanding these power relations and the necessary role of ideology in maintaining power relations. Ideology serves to maintain power relations through *legitimization* of the ruling class. For Weber every social order involves a *claim* to power by those who rule and a *belief* among those subject to such rule in the legitimacy of the claim to rule. Ricoeur expands Weber's model through the inclusion of ideology as that which bridges the gap between the claim to rule and belief in such rule. Ideology has a necessary role in this motivational model, for there is always a gap between a claim and belief in that claim, with a need for a new theory of surplus value, not of work but of power. Weber shows that no completely rational system of legitimacy exists because, Ricoeur (1986: 13) argues, there is never complete 'equivalence of belief with claim'. A theory of the surplus value of power is needed because 'every authority asks for more than what its members offer in terms of belief or creed' (Ricoeur, 1986: 14), and it is ideology that fulfils the need for surplus value. Thus, ideology, in these terms, serves to support and provide legitimacy to authority—and

178 APPENDIX

therefore the status quo—operating as the mediating link between ideology as distortion and ideology as integration, to which I now turn.

The symbolic system of Geertz

The conception of ideology proposed by Geertz (1973) represents, for Ricoeur, the most fundamental and positive understanding of ideology. Geertz, like Ricoeur, emphasizes the symbolic nature of action and sees ideology fulfilling a symbolic mediating role between social action and meaning. Ideology is therefore concerned with the preservation of social identities, and it is only on the basis of this fundamental symbolic role that ideology, through the legitimization of authority, can become distorted.

Geertz (1973) argues that Marxist and non-Marxist sociologists of knowledge alike have failed to adequately examine the function of ideology, instead only being concerned with what causes ideology. This is perhaps not surprising given the presumption that ideology must have a negative function. Geertz (1973), however, raises the possibility of a positive role for ideology in the social imaginary. The important move is to take rhetorical devices from literary theory and examine social action in the light of these devices. By analysing social action in terms of rhetoric, Geertz is better able to appreciate the positive role of ideology in the social imaginary. What is needed to understand social action is a map of social discourse about such action. Just as biology is understood from a genetic foundation, so must social action be understood from a sociocultural foundation of meaning. These sociocultural foundations provide a pattern or map for all social action. As Dauenhauer (1998: 215) puts it:

> When one realizes that all human action is symbolically structured and organized, then he or she can see not only how the several actions of an individual person fit together as a coherent life, but also how a multiplicity of persons can be integrated into a stable community. Without some such hypothesis, one could understand neither how an individual person nor a community achieves its integration and identity. With Geertz, Ricoeur defines an ideology as a set of symbolic structures that constitutes an identifiable community. There are as many ideologies as there are sets of symbolic structures. Without some set of these structures, human community would be impossible.

Ideology understood in this way becomes a source of identity and integration for cultures, something constructive, rather than simply a source of legitimacy for authority or, even worse, a source of distortion of the social imaginary.

Dreams of utopia: Mannheim, Saint-Simon, and Fourier

The last three lectures of Ricoeur's *Lectures on Ideology and Utopia* are concerned with utopia and address both the positive and negative poles of utopia. Utopia has generally been a position advocated and identified with an individual (Moore's utopia, for instance) and treated, perhaps unfairly, as merely a vision of fantasy or escape. Ricoeur recognizes this pathological role for utopia but also wishes to rescue a more constructive understanding within his motivational framework for the social imaginary. The positive aspect

APPENDIX   179

of utopia, as rupture and challenge, provides a necessary balance for the pathological aspects of ideology, as distortion and legitimization for authority.

But what is utopia? Unlike ideology, it is not possible to discern an overarching theme to utopia. Utopias have been wide ranging with little consistency and so must be defined in terms of their function rather than their phenomenology. Ricoeur (1986) recovers the original meaning of utopia as a *nowhere*, a place to cast a critical gaze on the stagnancy of ideology. It provides a challenge to 'what is' (Ricoeur, 1986: 16), to ideology and the status quo. And like ideology, utopia is concerned with power, for utopias, in Ricoeur's terms, seek to realize themselves in very practical ways. They provide an *opposition* and thus 'create a distance between what is and what ought to be' (Ricoeur, 1986: 179).

Ricoeur (1986) goes on to explore the meaning of utopia in detail through consideration of the utopias of two figures: Saint-Simon and Fourier. Saint-Simon and Fourier both present socialist utopias that Ricoeur uses as a test for Mannheim's (1936) typology of utopias. One of the problems identified with the utopias of both Saint-Simon and Fourier is the way in which they turn their visions into *pictures*. Their dynamic visions, which seek to challenge the stagnancy of the prevailing ideology, themselves become frozen. Through a reductive desire to specify every detail, once-revolutionary visions become mere pictures of possibilities, and this is a risk for all utopias. Such utopian visions of society risk becoming dangerously authoritarian technocracies.

Ricoeur's lectures end through consideration of the way in which ideology and utopia must function within a common framework. He argues that they form a practical circle, a circle that is impossible to break out of 'for it is the unrelieved circle of the symbolic structure of action' (Taylor, 1986: xxiii). Ricoeur's social imaginary also becomes a victim of Mannheim's paradox. Whilst it may not be possible to leave the circle of the social imaginary, bounded by ideology and utopia, Ricoeur argues that 'we must try to cure the illnesses of utopias by what is wholesome in ideology—by its element of identity . . . and try to cure the rigidity, the petrification, of ideologies by the utopian element'. The circle need not be timeless, however, constantly vacillating between ideology and utopia, but can become a spiral, progressive rather than regressive, if we have the desire to make it happen.

References

Ahmad, A. (1992). *In theory: Classes, nations, literatures*. London, UK: Verso.

Alexander, M. J. (1994). Not just (any) body can be a citizen: The politics of law, sexuality and postcoloniality in Trinidad and Tobago and the Bahamas. *Feminist Review, 48,* 5–23.

American Psychiatric Association (APA). (2000). *Diagnostic and statistical manual of mental disorders* (4th ed., text rev.). Washington, DC: Author.

Anapol, D. (1997). *Polyamory: The new love without limits*. San Rafael, CA: IntiNet Resource Centre.

Anderson, E. (2009). *Inclusive masculinity: The changing nature of masculinities*. London, UK: Routledge.

Andersson, K. (2022). I am not alone—We are all alone: Using masturbation as an ethnographic method in research on Shota subculture in Japan. *Qualitative Research*. Online first [Retracted]. Advance online publication.

Anderson, E., & McCormack, M. (2016). *The changing dynamics of bisexual men's lives: Social research perspectives*. Switzerland: Springer International Publishing.

Andrews, K. (2021). *The new age of empire: How racism and colonialism still rule the world*. London, UK: Allen Lane.

Anthias, N., & Yuval-Davies, N. (1992). *Racialized boundaries: Race, nation, gender, colour and class, and the anti-racist struggle*. London, UK: Routledge.

Anti-Social Behaviour, Crime and Policing Act (2014). https://www.legislation.gov.uk/ukpga/2014/12/contents.

Appiah, K. A. (2007). *Cosmopolitanism: Ethics in a world of strangers*. New York, NY: Penguin.

Ashcroft, M. (2023). *Scottish independence, gender recognition, de facto referendum . . . My latest polling from Scotland*. Retrieved from https://lordashcroftpolls.com/2023/02/scottish-independence-gender-recognition-de-facto-referendum-my-latest-polling-from-scotland/

Attwood, F., & Smith, C. (2013). Leisure sex. More sex! Better sex! Sex is fucking brilliant! Sex, sex, sex, SEX. In T. Blackshaw (Ed.), *Routledge handbook of leisure studies* (pp. 325–336). Abingdon, UK: Routledge.

Baggaley, M. (2005). Is an interest in BDSM a pathological disorder or a normal variant of human sexual behaviour? *Lesbian and Gay Psychology Review, 6*(3), 253–254.

Banks, D. E., Hensel, D. J., & Zapolski, T. C. B. (2020). Integrating individual and contextual factors to explain disparities in HIV/STI among heterosexual African American youth: A contemporary literature review and social ecological model. *Archives of Sexual Behavior, 49,* 1939–1964.

Barker, M. (2005). This is my partner, and this is my . . . partner's partner: Constructing a polyamorous identity in a monogamous world. *Journal of Constructivist Psychology, 18*(1), 75–88.

182 REFERENCES

Barker, M. J., Gupta, C., & Iantaffi, A. (2013). The power of play: The potentials and pitfalls in healing narratives of BDSM. In D. Langdridge & M. J. Barker (Eds.), *Safe, sane, and consensual: Contemporary perspectives on sadomasochism* (pp. 203–222). London, UK: Palgrave.

Barker, M., Hagger-Johnson, G., Hegarty, P., Hutchison, C., & Riggs, D. W. (2007). Responses from the Lesbian & Gay Psychology Section to Crossley's 'Making sense of "barebacking"'. *British Journal of Social Psychology, 46*(3), 667–677.

Barker, M., Heckert, J., & Wilkinson, E. (2013). Polyamorous intimacies: From one love to many loves and back again. In T. Sanger & Y. Taylor (Eds.), *Mapping intimacies: Relations, exchanges, affects* (pp. 190–208). Basingstoke, UK: Palgrave Macmillan.

Barker, M., & Langdridge, D. (2009). Silencing accounts of silenced sexualities. In R. Ryan-Flood & R. Gill (Eds.), *Secrecy and silence in the research process: Feminist reflections* (pp. 86–98). Abingdon, UK: Routledge.

Barker, M., & Langdridge, D. (Eds.). (2010a). *Understanding non-monogamies.* New York, NY: Routledge.

Barker, M., & Langdridge, D. (2010b). Whatever happened to non-monogamies? Critical reflections on recent research and theory. *Sexualities, 13*(6), 748–772.

Barnes, H. (2023). *Time to think: The inside story of the collapse of Tavistock's gender service for children.* London, UK: Swift Press.

Bartos, S. E., Fife-Shaw, C., & Hegarty, P. (2019). Is homonationalism influencing public opinion? Experimental and survey evidence from the UK and Romania. *Psychology of Sexualities Review, 10*(1), 20–35.

Bech, H. (1997). *When men meet: Homosexuality and modernity.* Cambridge, UK: Polity Press.

Beck, U. (1999). *World risk society.* Cambridge, UK: Polity.

Becker, G. (1999). Narratives of pain in later life and conventions of storytelling. *Journal of Ageing Studies, 13*, 73–87.

Beckmann, A. (2009). *The social construction of sexuality and perversion: Deconstructing sadomasochism.* Basingstoke, UK: Palgrave Macmillan.

Beiner, R. (Ed.). (1995). *Theorizing citizenship.* Albany, NY: State University of New York Press.

Bell, D., & Binnie, J. (2000). *The sexual citizen: Queer politics and beyond.* Cambridge, UK: Polity Press.

Berlant, L. (1997). *The queen of America goes to Washington city: Essays on sex and citizenship.* Durham, NC: Duke University Press.

Berlant, L. (2011). *Cruel optimism.* London and Durham, NJ: Duke University Press.

Bersani, L. (1995). *Homos.* Cambridge, MA: Harvard University Press.

Bhabha, H. K. (1994). *The location of culture.* London, UK: Routledge.

Biggs, M. (2022). Queer theory and the transition from sex to gender in English prisons. *Journal of Controversial Ideas, 2*(1), 2. doi:10.35995/jci02010002

Biggs, M. (2023). Why does the census say there are more trans people in Newham than Brighton? *The Spectator,* 9 April 2023. Retrieved from https://www.spectator.co.uk/article/why-does-the-census-say-there-are-more-trans-people-in-newham-than-brighton/

Bindall, J. (2023). Keep child abusers off the rainbow flag. *UnHerd.* Retrieved from https://unherd.com/2023/04/keep-child-abusers-off-the-rainbow-flag/

REFERENCES 183

Blackless, M., Charuvastra, A., Derryck, A., Fausto-Sterling, A., Lauzanne, K., & Lee, E. (2000). How sexually dimorphic are we? Review and synthesis. *American Journal of Human Biology, 12,* 151–166.

Boykin, K. (2005). *Beyond the down low: Sex, lies, and denial in Black America.* New York, NY: Carroll & Graf Publishers.

Brandzel, A. (2005). Queering citizenship? Same-sex marriage and the state. *GLQ A Journal of Lesbian and Gay Studies, 11*(2), 171–204.

Brennan, T. (1997). *At home in the world: Cosmopolitanism now.* Cambridge, MA: Harvard University Press.

Brennan, T. (2001). Cosmopolitanism and internationalism. *New Left Review, 7*(January/ February). Retrieved from https://newleftreview-org.libezproxy.open.ac.uk/issues/ii7/articles/timothy-brennan-cosmopolitanism-and-internationalism

Breslow, J. (2011). *Sexual alignment: Critiquing sexual orientation, the pedophile, and the DSM V.* Brief descriptions of presentation at Pedophilia, Minor-Attracted Persons, and the DSM: Issues and Controversies, B4U-ACT Symposium, Baltimore, MD, August 17. Retrieved from https://web.archive.org/web/20211206025901/https://www.b4uact.org/wp-content/uploads/2014/09/Breslow_abstract.pdf

Breslow, J. (2021). *Ambivalent childhoods: Speculative futures and the psychic life of the child.* Minneapolis, MN: University of Minnesota Press.

Brown, A., Barker, E. D., & Rahman, Q. (2020). A systematic scoping review of the prevalence, etiological, psychological, and interpersonal factors associated with BDSM. *Journal of Sex Research, 57*(6), 781–811.

Bruner, J. (1986). *Actual minds, possible worlds.* Cambridge, MA: Harvard University Press.

Bruner, J. (1990). *Acts of meaning.* Cambridge, MA: Harvard University Press.

Bruner, J. (2002). *Making stories: Law, literature, life.* New York, NY: Farrar, Straus & Giroux.

Brunskell-Evans, H. (2020). *Transgender body politics.* North Geelong, Victoria, Australia: Spinifex Press.

Butler, J. (1990). *Gender trouble: Feminism and the subversion of identity.* New York, NY: Routledge.

Butler, J. (1993). *Bodies that matter: On the discursive limits of 'sex'.* New York, NY: Routledge.

Butt, T., & Langdridge, D. (2003). The construction of self: The public reach into the private sphere. *Sociology, 37*(3), 477–494.

Byrne, A. (2018). *Is sex binary?* Retrieved 17 August 2022, from https://medium.com/arc-digital/is-sex-binary-16bec97d161e

Byrne, A. (2020). Are women adult human females? *Philosophical Studies, 177,* 3783–3803.

Byrne, A. (2021). Gender muddle: Reply to Dembroff. *Journal of Controversial Ideas, 1*(1), 5. doi:10.35995/jci01010005.

Byrne, A. (2022). The female of the species: Reply to Heartsilver. *Journal of Controversial Ideas, 2*(1), 11. doi:10.35995/jci02010011

Byrne, A. (2023). Pronoun problems. *Journal of Controversial Ideas, 3*(1), 1–22. doi: 10.35995/jci03010005

Calhoun, C. (1994). Social theory and the politics of identity. In C. Calhoun (Ed.), *Social theory and the politics of identity* (pp. 9–36). Oxford, UK: Blackwell.

Califia, P. (1994). *Public sex: The culture of radical sex.* Pittsburgh, PA: Cleis Press.

184 REFERENCES

Cardoso, D. (2014). My Spivak is bigger than yours: (Mis-)representations of poly-amory in the Portuguese LGBT movement and mononormative rhetorics. *LES Online*, 6(1), 45–64.

Cardoso, D. (2019). The political is personal: The importance of affective narratives in the rise of poly-activism. *Sociological Research Online*, 24(4), 691–708.

Carr, D. (1986). *Time, narrative, and history*. Bloomington, IN: Indiana University Press.

Centers for Disease Control and Prevention (CDC). (2018). *HIV and African Americans*. Retrieved 12 January 2021, from https://www.cdc.gov/hiv/group/racialethnic/afric anamericans/index.html

Chibber, V. (2013). *Postcolonial theory and the specter of capital*. London, UK: Verso.

Chu, A. L. (2019). *Females*. London, UK: Verso.

Clarke, A. E., Mama, L., Fosket, J. R., Fishman, J. R., & Shim, J. K. (2010). *Biomedicalization: Technoscience, health, and illness in the U.S*. Durham, NC: Duke University Press.

Clements, B., & Field, C. D. (2014). Public opinion toward homosexuality and gay rights in Great Britain. *Public Opinion Quarterly*, 78(2), 523–547.

Cohler, B. J., & Hammack, P. L. (2007). The psychological world of the gay teenager: Social change, narrative, and 'normality'. *Journal of Youth and Adolescence*, 36(1), 47–59. https://doi.org/10.1007/s10964-006-9110-1

Collins, P. H. (1990). *Black feminist thought: Knowledge, consciousness, and the politics of empowerment*. London, UK: HarperCollins Academic.

Coontz, S. (2004). The world historical transformation of marriage. *Journal of Marriage and the Family*, 66(November), 974–979.

Cossman, B. (2002). Sexing citizenship, privatising sex. *Citizenship Studies*, 6(4), 483–506.

Coyne, J. (2018). Once again: Why sex is binary. Retrieved from: https://whyevolutionist rue.com/2018/12/11/once-again-why-sex-is-binary/.

Crenshaw, K. (1989). Demarginalizing the intersection of race and sex: A black femi-nist critique of antidiscrimination doctrine, feminist theory and antiracist politics, *University of Chicago Legal Forum*, 1989(1), article 8. Available at http://chicagounbo und.uchicago.edu/uclf/vol1989/iss1/8

Crossley, M. (2004). Making sense of 'barebacking': Gay men's narratives, unsafe sex and the 'resistance habitus'. *British Journal of Social Psychology*, 43, 225–244.

Cruz, A. (2015). Beyond black and blue: BDSM, internet pornography, and Black female sexuality. *Feminist Studies*, 41(2), 409–436.

Cruz, A. (2016a). *The color of kink: Black women, BDSM, and pornography*. New York, NY: New York University Press.

Cruz, A. (2016b). Playing with the politics of perversion: Policing BDSM, pornography, and black female sexuality. *Souls*, 18(2–4), 379–407.

Cruz, A. (2021). Not a moment too soon: A juncture of BDSM and race. *Sexualities*, 24(5–6), 819–824.

Curtice, J., Clery, E., Perry, J., Phillips M., & Rahim, N. (Eds.). (2019). *British social attitudes: The 36th report*. London, UK: National Centre for Social Research.

Dauenhauer, B. P. (1998). *Paul Ricoeur: The promise and risk of politics*. Lanham, MD: Rowman & Littlefield.

Dauenhauer, B., & Pellauer, D. (2012). Paul Ricoeur. In E. N. Zalta (Ed.), *The Stanford en-cyclopedia of philosophy* (Spring 2012 ed.). Retrieved from https://plato.stanford.edu/ entries/ricoeur/

REFERENCES 185

Davies, D., & Barker, M. J. (2015). How gender and sexually diverse-friendly is your therapy training? *The Psychotherapist, 61*, 8–10.

Davis, A. Y. (1981). *Women, race and class.* New York, NY: Random House.

de Boise, S. (2015). I'm not homophobic, 'I've got gay friends': Evaluating the validity of inclusive masculinity. *Men and Masculinities, 18*(3), 318–339.

Dean, J. (1996). *Solidarity of strangers: Feminism after identity politics.* Berkeley, CA: University of California Press.

Dean, T. (2009). *Unlimited intimacy: Reflections on the subculture of barebacking.* Chicago, IL: University of Chicago Press.

Dean, T. (2015). Mediated intimacies: Raw sex, Truvada, and the biopolitics of chemoprophylaxis. *Sexualities, 18*(1/2), 224–246.

Dembroff, R. (2020). Escaping the natural attitude. *Philosophical Studies, 178*(3), 983–1003.

Deweer, D. (2013). Ricoeur on citizenship: A picture of a personalist republicanism. In G. S. Johnson & D. R. Stiver (Eds.), *Paul Ricoeur and the task of political philosophy* (pp. 35–50). Lanham, MD: Lexington Books.

DiAngelo, R. (2018). *White fragility: Why it's so hard for white people to talk about racism.* Boston, MA: Beacon Press.

Dostoevsky, F. (1991). *Notes from the underground* (J. Kentish, Trans.). Oxford, UK: Oxford World Classics. (Original work published 1864)

Downing, L. (2007). Beyond safety: Erotic asphyxiation and the limits of SM discourse. In D. Langridge & M. Barker (Eds.), *Safe, sane and consensual: Contemporary perspectives on sadomasochism* (pp. 119–132). Basingstoke: Palgrave Macmillan.

Downing, L. (2013). Safewording!: Kinkphobia and gender normativity in Fifty Shades of Grey. *Psychology & Sexuality, 4*(1), 92–102.

Downing, L. (2019). *Selfish women.* Abingdon, UK: Routledge.

Doyal, L., Naidoo, J., & Wilton, T. (Eds.). (1994). *Aids: Setting a feminist agenda.* London, UK: Taylor & Francis.

Duberman, M. (2018). *Has the gay movement failed?* Oakland, CA: University of California Press.

Easton, D., & Liszt, C. A. (1997). *The ethical slut: A guide to infinite sexual possibilities.* San Francisco, CA: Greenery Press.

Edelman, L. (2004). *No future: Queer theory and the death drive.* Durham, NC: Duke University Press.

Ellison, N. (1997). Towards a new social politics: Citizenship and reflexivity in late modernity. *Sociology, 31*(4), 697–717.

Elsbree, L. (1982). *The rituals of life: Patterns in narrative.* Port Washington, NY: Kennikat Press.

Embery, P. (2021). *Despised: Why the modern left loathes the working class.* Cambridge, UK: Polity.

Equality Act. (2010). London, UK: HMSO.

Evans, D. (1993). *Sexual citizenship: The material construction of sexualities.* London, UK: Routledge.

Fausto-Sterling, A. (2000). *Sexing the body: Gender politics and the construction of sexuality.* New York, NY: Basic Books.

Faye, S. (2021). *The transgender issue: An argument for justice.* London, UK: Allen Lane.

Ferguson, J. (2006). *Global shadows: Africa in the neoliberal world order.* Durham, NC: Duke University Press.

186 REFERENCES

Ferrer, J. N. (2022). *Love and freedom: Transcending monogamy and polyamory*. London, UK: Rowman & Littlefield.

Fields, E. L., Bogart, L. M., Smith, K. C., Malebranche, D. J., Ellen, J., & Schuster, M. A. (2012). HIV risk and perceptions of masculinity among young black men who have sex with men. *Journal of Adolescent Health, 50*(3), 296–303.

Fields, E. L., Bogart, L. M., Smith, K. C., Malebranche, D. J., Ellen, J., & Schuster, M. A. (2015). 'I always felt I had to prove my manhood': Homosexuality, masculinity, gender role strain, and HIV risk among young black men who have sex with men. *American Journal of Public Health, 105*(1), 122–131.

Florêncio, J. (2020). *Bareback porn, porous masculinities, queer futures: The ethics of becoming-pig*. London, UK: Routledge.

Flowers, P. (2001). Gay men and HIV/AIDS risk management. *Health, 5*, 50–75.

Flowers, P., & Langdridge, D. (2007). Offending the other: Deconstructing narratives of deviance and pathology. *British Journal of Social Psychology, 46*(3), 679–690.

Foucault, M. (1977–1978). *The history of sexuality* (R. Hurley, Trans.). New York, NY: Pantheon.

Foucault, M. (1978). *The history of sexuality* (Vol. 1): *An introduction*. New York, NY: Vintage.

Foucault, M. (1979). *The history of sexuality, volume 1: An introduction*. Harmondsworth: Penguin.

Fraser, N. (2001). Recognition without ethics? *Theory, Culture & Society, 18*(2–3), 21–42.

Freud, S. (1914). Errinern, Wiederholen und Durcharbeiten (Weitere Ratschläge zur Technik der Psychoanalyse, II). *Internationale Zeitschrift für ärtztliche Psychoanalyse, 2*, 485–491; Remembering, repeating and working-through. SE, 12, 147–156.

Friedman, M. R., Wei, C., Klem, M. L., Silvestre, A. J., Markovic, N., & Stall, R. (2014). HIV infection and sexual risk among men who have sex with men and women (MDMW): A systematic review and meta-analysis. *PloS ONE, 9*(1), e87139.

Fukuyama, F. (1992). *The end of history and the last man*. New York, NY: Free Press.

Furedi, F. (2004). *Therapy culture: Cultivating vulnerability in an uncertain age*. London, UK: Routledge.

Fuss, D. (Ed.). (1991). *Inside/out: Lesbian theories, gay theories*. New York, NY: Routledge.

Gadamer, H-G. (1989). *Truth and method* (2nd rev. ed., J. Weinsheimer & D. G. Marshall, Trans.). New York, NY: Crossroad.

Gamson, J. (1995). Must identity movements self-destruct? A queer dilemma. *Social Problems, 42*(3), 390–407.

Geertz, C. (1973). *The interpretation of cultures*. New York, NY: Basic Books.

Gergen, K. J. (1973). Social psychology as history. *Journal of Personality and Social Psychology, 26*, 309–320.

Gergen, K. J., & Gergen, M. (1986). Narrative form and the construction of psychological science. In T. Sarbin (Ed.), *Narrative psychology: The storied nature of human conduct* (pp. 22–44). New York, NY: Praeger.

Geuss, R. (2008). *Philosophy and real politics*. Princeton, NJ: Princeton University Press.

Ghaziani, A. (2014). *There goes the gayborhood?* Princeton, NJ: Princeton University Press.

Giddens, A. (1991). *Modernity and self-identity*. Cambridge, UK: Polity Press.

Giddens, A. (1992). *The transformation of intimacy: Sexuality, love and eroticism in modern societies*. Cambridge, UK: Polity Press.

Girard, R. (1966). *Deceit, desire and the novel: Self and other in literary structure* (Y. Freccero, Trans.). Baltimore, MD: Johns Hopkins University Press.

REFERENCES 187

Girard, R. (1986). *The scapegoat* (Y. Freccero, Trans.). Baltimore, MD: Johns Hopkins University Press.

Glissant, É. (1997). *Poetics of relation* (B. Wing, Trans.). Ann Arbor, MI: University of Michigan Press.

Goffman, E. (1963). *Stigma: Notes on the management of spoiled identity*. London, UK: Penguin.

Goodwin, M. (2023). *Values, voice and virtue*. London, UK: Penguin.

Gottlieb, M., Schroff, R., Schanker, H. M., Weisman, J. D., Fan, P. T., Wolf, R. A., et al. (1981). Pneumocystis carinii pneumonia and mucosal candidiasis in previously healthy homosexual men: evidence of a newly acquired cellular immunodeficiency. *New England Journal of Medicine, 305*, 1425–1431.

Goymann, W., Brumm, H., & Kappeler, P. M. (2023). Biological sex is binary, even though there is a rainbow of sex roles. *BioEssays, 45*, e2200173. https://doi.org/10.1002/bies.202200173

Gribble, K. D., Bewley, S., Bartick, M. C., Mathisen, R., Walker, S., Gamble, J., Bergman, N. J., Gupta, A., Hocking, J. J., & Dahlen, H. G. (2022). Effective communication about pregnancy, birth, lactation, breastfeeding and newborn care: The importance of sexed language. *Frontiers in Global Womens Health, 3*(818856). doi:10.3389/fgwh.2022.818856

Grosz, E. (1995). *Space, time, and perversion*. London, UK: Routledge.

Guha, R., & Spivak, G. C. (Eds.). (1988). *Selected subaltern studies*. New York, NY: Oxford University Press.

Guz, S., Hecht, H. K., Kattari, S. K., Gross, E. B., & Ross, E. (2022). A scoping review of empirical asexuality research in social science literature. *Archives of Sexual Behavior, 51*, 2135–2145. https://doi.org/10.1007/s10508-022-02307-6

Habermas, J. (1971). *Knowledge and human interests* (J. J. Shapiro, Trans.). Boston, MA: Beacon.

Habermas, J. (1989). *The structural transformation of the public sphere* (T. Burger & F. Lawrence, Trans.). Cambridge, UK: Polity Press. (Original work published 1962)

Hall, D. E. (2009). *Reading sexualities: Hermeneutic theory and the future of queer studies*. Abingdon, UK: Routledge.

Hall, S. (1996). Who needs 'identity'? In S. Hall & P. Du Gay (Eds.), *Questions of cultural identity* (pp. 1–17). London, UK: Sage.

Hammack, P. (2005). The life course development of human sexual orientation: An integrative paradigm. *Human Development, 48*, 267–297.

Hammack, P. L., & Cohler, B. J. (Eds.). (2009). *The story of sexual identity: Narrative perspectives on the gay and lesbian life course*. New York, NY: Oxford University Press.

Hammers, C. (2014). Corporeality, sadomasochism and sexual trauma. *Body & Society, 20*(2), 68–90.

Hardy, J. W., & Easton, D. (2017). *The ethical slut* (3rd ed.). New York, NY: Ten Speed Press.

Haritaworn, J., Lin, C., & Klesse, C. (2006). Poly/logue: A critical introduction to polyamory. *Sexualities, 9*(5), 515–529.

Harper, C., & Lievesley, R. (2022). Exploring the ownership of child-like sex dolls. *Archives of Sexual Behavior*. Advance online publication. https://doi.org/10.1007/s10508-022-02422-4

Harper, C., Lievesley, R., Blagden, N. J., & Hocken, K. (2022). Humanizing pedophilia as stigma reduction: A large-scale intervention study. *Archives of Sexual Behavior, 51*, 945–960.

188 REFERENCES

Harris, L. (2005). Foreword. In K. Boykin (Ed.), *Beyond the down low: Sex, lies, and denial in Black America* (pp. vii–viii). New York: Carroll & Graf Publishers.

Haslam, N. (2016). Concept creep: Psychology's expanding concepts of harm and pathology. *Psychological Inquiry, 27*(1), 1–17. https://doi.org/10.1080/10478 40X.2016.1082418

Heartsilver, M. (pseudonym). (2021). Deflating Byrne's 'Are Women Adult Human Females?' *Journal of Controversial Ideas, 1*(1), 9. Doi:10.35995/jci01010009

Heidegger, M. (1962). *Being and time* (J. Macquarrie & E. Robinson, Trans.). Oxford, UK: Blackwell.

Hemmings, C. (2020). Unnatural feelings: The affective life of 'anti-gender' mobilisations. *Radical Philosophy, 2*(9), 27–39.

Herbenick, D., Fu, T-c., Eastman-Mueller, H., et al. (2022). Frequency, method, intensity, and health sequelae of sexual choking among U.S. undergraduate and graduate students. *Archives of Sexual Behavior, 51*, 3121–3139. https://doi.org/10.1007/s10 508-022-02347-y

Herek, G. M. (2002). Gender gaps in public opinion about lesbians and gay men. *Public Opinion Quarterly, 60*, 40–66.

Hile, J. J. (2023). Beyond sex: A review of recent literature on asexuality. *Current Opinion in Psychology, 49*, 101516. https://doi.org/10.1016/j.copsyc.2022.101516

Hines, S. (2009). (Trans)forming gender: Social change and transgender citizenship. In E. Oleksy (Ed.), *Intimate citizenships: Gender, sexualities, politics* (pp. 1930–2439). New York, NY: Routledge.

Hobson, B., & Lister, R. (2002). Citizenship. In B. Hobson, J. Lewis, & B. Sim (Eds.), *Contested concepts in gender and social politics* (pp. 23–54). Cheltenham, UK: Edward Elgar.

Hoffman, J. (2004). *Citizenship beyond the state*. London, UK: Sage.

Honohan, I. (2002). *Civic republicanism*. London, UK: Routledge.

hooks, b. (1981). *Ain't I a woman? Black women and feminism*. Boston, MA: South End Press.

hooks, b. (1984). *Feminist theory: From margin to center*. Boston, MA: South End Press.

hooks, b. (1989). *Talking back: Thinking feminist, thinking black*. Boston, MA: South End Press.

Hull, C. L., & Fausto-Sterling, A. (2003). How sexually dimorphic are we? Review and synthesis. *American Journal of Human Biology 15*: 112–116.

Hunt, L. (2002). Against presentism. *Perspectives on History*, Magazine of the American Historical Association. Retrieved from https://www.historians.org/publications-and-directories/perspectives-on-history/may-2002/against-presentism

Hunter, J. D. (1991). *Culture wars, the struggle to define America. Making sense of the battles over the family, art, education, law, and politics*. New York, NY: Basic Books.

Ingram, N., & Waller, R. (2014). Degrees of masculinity: Working and middle-class undergraduate students' constructions of masculine identities. In S. Roberts (Ed.), *Debating modern masculinities: Change, continuity, crisis?* (pp. 35–51). Palgrave Macmillan UK.

Isin, E. F. (2008). Theorizing acts of citizenship. In E. F. Isin & G. M. Nielsen (Eds.), *Acts of citizenship* (pp. 15–43). London, UK: Zed Books.

Isin, E. F. (2009). Citizenship in flux: The figure of the activist citizen. *Subjectivity, 29*, 367–388.

Isin, E. F., & Nielsen, G. M. (Eds.). (2008). *Acts of citizenship*. London, UK: Zed Books.

Isin, E. F., & Turner, B. S. (Eds.). (2002). *Handbook of citizenship studies*. London, UK: Sage.

REFERENCES 189

Isin, E. F., & Wood, P. K. (1999). *Citizenship and identity*. London, UK: Sage.

Jarvis, E. (2022). 'Men' and 'women' in everyday English. *Journal of Controversial Ideas*, *2*(1), 5. Doi:10.35995/jci02010005

Jaspal, R. (2012). 'I never faced up to being gay': Sexual, religious and ethnic identities among British Indian and British Pakistani gay men. *Culture, Health & Sexuality*, *14*(7), 767–780. https://doi-org.libezproxy.open.ac.uk/10.1080/13691058.2012.693626

Jaspal, R., & Siraj, A. (2011). Perceptions of 'coming out' among British Muslim gay men. *Psychology & Sexuality*, *2*(3), 183–197. doi:10.1080/19419899.2010.526627

Jay, A. (2014). *Independent inquiry into child sexual exploitation in Rotherham 1997–2013*. London, UK: Home Office.

Jeannin, L. (2021). Was the 'Sexual Revolution' a myth? *Queen Mary History Journal*. Retrieved from https://qmhistoryjournal.wixsite.com/qmhj/post/was-the-sexual-revolution-a-myth

Joyce, H. (2021). *Trans: When ideology meets reality*. London, UK: Oneworld.

Kaplan, D. M. (2003). *Ricoeur's critical theory*. Albany, NY: State University of New York Press.

Kearney, R. (2007). Paul Ricoeur and the hermeneutics of translation. *Research in Phenomenology*, *37*, 147–159.

Kearney, R. (2019). Linguistic hospitality—the risk of translation. *Research in Phenomenology*, *49*, 1–8.

Kendi, I. X. (2019). *How to be an antiracist*. London, UK: Random House.

Kermode, F. (1967). *The sense of an ending*. Oxford, UK: Oxford University Press.

Kleinplatz, P., & Moser, C. (2004). Towards clinical guidelines for working with BDSM clients. *Contemporary Sexuality*, *38*(6), 1–4.

Kleinplatz, P., & Moser, C. (2005). Is SM pathological? *Lesbian & Gay Psychology Review*, *6*(3), 255–260.

Kleinplatz, P., & Moser, C. (Eds.). (2006). *SM: Powerful pleasures*. Binghamton, NY: Haworth Press.

Klesse, C. (2007). *The spectre of promiscuity: Gay male and bisexual monogamies and polyamories*. London, UK: Routledge.

Klesse, C. (2014). Polyamory: Intimate practice, identity or sexual orientation? *Sexualities*, *17*(1/2), 81–99.

Kosofsky Sedgewick, E. (1990). *Epistemology of the closet*. Berkeley, CA: UCLA Press.

Kosofsky Sedgewick, E. (1992). *Between men: English literature and male homosocial desire*. New York, NY: Columbia University Press.

Laclau, E., & Mouffe, C. (1985). *Hegemony and socialist strategy*. London, UK: Verso.

Langdridge, D. (2003). Hermeneutic phenomenology: Arguments for a new social psychology. *History and Philosophy of Psychology*, *5*(1), 30–45.

Langdridge, D. (2006). Voices from the margins: SM and sexual citizenship. *Citizenship Studies*, *10*(4), 373–389.

Langdridge, D. (2007). *Phenomenological psychology: Theory, research and method*. Harlow, UK: Pearson Education.

Langdridge, D. (2008). Phenomenology and critical social psychology: Directions and debates in theory and research. *Social and Personality Psychology Compass*, *2*(3), 1126–1142. doi:10.1111/j.1751-9004.2008.00114.x

Langdridge, D. (2013). Gay fathers, gay citizenship: On the power of futurism and assimilation. *Citizenship Studies*, *17*(6–7), 713–726.

190 REFERENCES

Langdridge, D. (2016). Benevolent heterosexism and the 'less-than-queer' citizen subject. In P. Hammack (Ed.), *Oxford handbook of social psychology and social justice*. New York, NY: Oxford University Press. Advance online publication. doi:10.1093/oxfordhb/9780199938735.013.21

Langdridge, D. (2022). Citizenship studies: On the need for tradition and critique. *Citizenship Studies*, 25th Anniversary Special Issue. Advance online publication. https://doi.org/10.1080/13621025.2022.2091238

Langdridge, D., & Barker, M. (2013). Sadomasochism: Past, present, future. In D. Langdridge & M. Barker (Eds.), *Safe, sane and consensual: Contemporary perspectives on sadomasochism* (pp. 3–15). Basingstoke, UK: Palgrave Macmillan.

Langdridge, D., & Butt, T. (2004). A hermeneutic phenomenological investigation of the construction of sadomasochistic identities. *Sexualities, 7*(1), 31–53.

Langdridge, D., & Parchev, O. (2018). Transgression versus (sexual) citizenship: Political resistance and the struggle for self-determination within BDSM communities. *Citizenship Studies, 22*(7), 667–684.

Lasch, C. (1979). *The culture of narcissism: American life in an age of diminishing expectations.* New York, NY: W. W. Norton.

Lavery, G. (2022). *Please miss: A heartbreaking work of staggering penis.* London, UK: Daunt Books Originals.

Lazarus, N. (2011). What postcolonial theory doesn't say. *Race & Class, 53*(1), 3–27.

Lazarus, N. (2014). Vivek Chibber and the spectre of postcolonial theory. *Race & Class, 57*(3), 88–106.

Lee, C. T. (2016). *Ingenious citizenship: Recrafting democracy for social change.* Durham, NC: Duke University Press.

Ley, D. J. (2012). *The myth of sex addiction.* Lanham, MD: Rowan & Littlefield.

Li, G., Katz-Wise, S. L., & Calzo, J. P. (2014). The unjustified doubt of Add Health Studies on the health disparities of nonheterosexual adolescents: Comment on Savin-Williams and Joyner (2014). *Archives of Sexual Behavior, 43*, 1023– 1026.

Lievesley, R., Harper, C. A., & Elliott, H. (2020). The internalization of social stigma among minor-attracted persons: Implications for treatment. *Archives of Sexual Behavior, 49*, 1291–1304.

Lievesley, R., & Lapworth, R. (2022). 'We do exist': The experiences of women living with a sexual interest in minors. *Archives of Sexual Behavior, 51*, 879–896.

Lindeman, D. (2011). BDSM as therapy? *Sexualities, 14*(2), 151–172.

Lister, R. (1990). Women, economic dependency and citizenship. *Journal of Social Policy, 19*(4), 445–468.

Lister, R. (1997). *Citizenship: Feminist perspectives.* Basingstoke: Macmillan.

Lister, R. (2002). Sexual citizenship. In E. F. Isin & B. S. Turner (Eds.), *Handbook of citizenship studies* (pp. 191–208). London, UK: Sage.

Lister, R. (2003). *Citizenship: Feminist perspectives* (2nd ed.). Basingstoke, UK: Macmillan.

Lister, R. (2008). Inclusive citizenship: Realizing the potential. In E. F. Isin, P. Nyers, & B. S. Turner (Eds.), *Citizenship between past and future* (pp. 48–59). Abingdon, UK: Routledge.

Love, H. (2007). *Feeling backward: Loss and the politics of queer history.* Cambridge, MA: Harvard University Press.

Low, N., Egger, M., Gorter, A., Sandiford, P., Gonzalez, A., Pauw, J., et al. (1993). AIDS in Nicaragua: Epidemiological, political and sociocultural perspectives. *International Journal of Public Health Services, 23*, 685–702.

REFERENCES 191

Mackay, F. (2021). *Female masculinities and the gender wars*. London, UK: I. B. Tauris.

Mannheim, K. (1936). *Ideology and utopia*. London, UK: Routledge.

Marshall, T. H. (1950). *Citizenship and social class and other essays*. Cambridge, MA: Cambridge University Press.

Mauvais-Jarvis, F., Bairey Merz, N., Barnes, P. J., Brinton, R. D., Carrero, J-J., DeMeo, D. L., De Vries, G. J., Epperson, C. N., Govindan, R., Klein, S. L., Lonardo, A., Maki, P. M., McCullough, L. D., Regitz-Zagrosek, V., Regensteiner, J. G., Rubin, J. B., Sandberg, K., & Suzuki, A. (2020). Sex and gender: Modifiers of health, disease, and medicine. *The Lancet, 396*, 565–582.

Marx, K., & Engels, F. (1970). *The German ideology* (C. J. Arthur, Ed.). London, UK: Lawrence & Wishart.

McCormack, M. (2012). *The declining significance of homophobia: How teenage boys are redefining masculinity and homosexuality*. New York, NY: Oxford University Press.

McIntosh, M. (1981). The homosexual role. In K. Plummer (Ed.), *The making of the modern homosexual* (pp. 30–49). London, UK: Hutchinson. (Original work published 1968)

McPhail, I. V., Hermann, C. A., Fernane, S., Fernandez, Y. M., Nunes, K. L., & Cantor, J. M. (2019). Validity in phallometric testing for sexual interests in children: A meta-analytic review. *Assessment, 26*(3), 535–551.

McWhorter, J. (2021). *Woke racism: How a new religion has betrayed Black America*. New York, NY: Penguin Random House.

Merleau-Ponty, M. (1962). *Phenomenology of perception* (C. Smith, Trans.). London, UK: Routledge. (Original work published 1945)

Meyer, I. H. (2010). The right comparisons in testing the minority stress hypothesis: Comment on Savin-Williams, Cohen, Joyner, and Rieger (2010). *Archives of Sexual Behavior, 39*, 1217–1219.

Miller, D. (2002). Cosmopolitanism: A critique. *Critical Review of International Social and Political Philosophy, 5*(3), 80–85. doi:10.1080/13698230410001702662

Moen, O. M. (2015). The ethics of pedophilia. *Nordic Journal of Applied Ethics, 1*(1), 111–124. doi:10.5324/eip.v9i1.1718

Monro, S. (2005). *Gender politics: Citizenship, activism and sexual diversity*. London, UK: Pluto Press.

Moosa-Mitha, M. (2005). A difference-centred alternative to theorization of children's citizenship rights. *Citizenship Studies, 9*(4), 369–388.

Morgan, H., Lamprinakou, C., Fuller, E., & Albakri, M. (2020). *Attitudes towards transgender people* (Equality and Human Rights Commission Research Report Series). Retrieved 11 August 2022, from https://www.equalityhumanrights.com/sites/default/files/attitudes_to_transgender_people.pdf

Morson, G. S., & Schapiro, M. (2021). *Minds wide shut: How the new fundamentalisms divide us*. Princeton, NJ: Princeton University Press.

Moser, C. (2016). DSM-5 and the paraphilic disorders: Conceptual issues. *Archives of Sexual Behavior, 45*, 2181–2186.

Moser, C., & Kleinplatz, P. (2005a). DSM-IV-TR and the paraphilias: An argument for removal. *Journal of Psychology and Human Sexuality, 17*(3/4), 91–109.

Moser, C., & Kleinplatz, P. (2005b). Does heterosexuality belong in the DSM? *Lesbian and Gay Psychology Review, 6*, 261–267.

Moser, C., & Kleinplatz, P. J. (2006). Introduction: The state of our knowledge on SM. *Journal of Homosexuality, 50*(2/3), 1–15.

192 REFERENCES

Moser, C., & Kleinplatz, P. J. (2020). Conceptualisation, history, and future of the paraphilias. *Annual Review of Clinical Psychology*, 16, 379–399.

Moser, C., & Madeson, J. J. (1996). *Bound to be free: The SM experience*. New York, NY: Continuum.

Mouffe, C. (1992). Feminism, citizenship and radical democratic politics. In J. Butler & J. W. Scott (Eds.), *Feminists theorize the political* (pp. 369–384). New York, NY: Routledge.

Mouffe, C. (1993). *The return of the political*. London, UK: Verso.

Mouffe, C. (2005). *On the political*. London, UK: Verso.

Mowlabocus, S. (2021). *Interrogating homonormativity: Gay men, identity and everyday life*. Cham, Switzerland: Palgrave Macmillan.

Mustanski, B., Byck, G. R., Newcomb, M. E., Henry, D., Bolland, J., & Dick, D. (2013). HIV Information and behavioral skills moderate the effects of relationship type and substance use on HIV risk behaviors among African American Youth. *AIDS Patient Care and STDs*, 27(6) (June), 342–351. http://doi.org/10.1089/apc.2012.0468

Newmahr, S. (2010). Rethinking kink: Sadomasochism as serious leisure. *Qualitative Sociology*, 33(3), 313–331.

Newmahr, S. (2011). *Playing on the edge: Sadomasochism, risk and intimacy*. Bloomington, IN: Indiana University Press.

Nguyen, V., Bajos, N., Dubois-Arber, F., O'Malley, J., & Pirkle, C. (2011). Remedicalizing an epidemic: From HIV treatment as prevention to HIV treatment is prevention. *AIDS*, 25(3), 291–293.

Neiman, S. (2023). *Left is not woke*. Cambridge, UK: Polity.

Nussbaum, M. (1999). The professor of parody. The hip defeatism of Judith Butler. *New Republic*, February 22. Retrieved from https://newrepublic.com/article/150687/professor-parody

Nussbaum, M. (2006). *Frontiers of justice: Disability, nationality, species, membership*. Cambridge, MA: Harvard University Press.

Nyers, P. (2008). Introduction: Why citizenship studies? In E. F. Isin, P. Nyers, & B. S. Turner (Eds.), *Citizenship between past and future* (pp. 1–4). Abingdon, UK: Routledge.

O'Neill, R. (2014). Whither critical masculinity studies? Notes on inclusive masculinity theory, postfeminism, and sexual politics. *Men and Masculinities*, 18(1), 100–120. doi:10.1177/1097184X14553056

Özkirimli, U. (2023). *Cancelled: The left way back from woke*. Cambridge, UK: Polity.

Pabst, A. (2021). *Postliberal politics*. Cambridge, UK: Polity.

Paglia, C. (1991). Junk bonds and corporate raiders: Academe in the hour of the wolf. *Arion*, 1(2). Retrieved from https://www.bu.edu/arion/files/2017/09/Arion-Camille-Paglia-Junkbonds-Corporate-Raiders.pdf

Palm, F. (2019). Viral desires: Enjoyment and death in the contemporary discourse on barebacking. In T. Holmberg, A. Jonsson, & F. Palm (Eds.), *Death matters: Cultural sociology of mortal life* (pp. 129–150). New York, NY: Palgrave Macmillan.

Parfit, D. (1984). *Reason and persons*. Oxford, UK: Oxford University Press.

Parry, B. (2004). *Postcolonial studies: A materialist critique*. London, UK: Routledge.

Pepper, S. (1942). *World hypotheses*. Berkeley, CA: University of California Press.

Phelan, S. (2001). *Sexual strangers: Gays, lesbians, and dilemmas of citizenship*. Philadelphia, PA: Temple University Press.

Philips, A. (1991). Citizenship and feminist theory. In G. Andrews (Ed.), *Citizenship* (pp. 76–88). London, UK: Lawrence & Wishart.

REFERENCES 193

Pieper, M., & Bauer, R. (2005). Polyamory und mono-normativatät: ergebnisse einer empirischen studie über nicht-monogame lebensformen. In L. Méritt (Ed.), *Mehr al seine liebe: polyamouröse beziehungen* (pp. 59–69). Berlin, Germany: Orlanda.

Piketty, T. (2020). *Capital and ideology*. Cambridge, MA: Harvard University Press.

Plummer, K. (1995). *Telling sexual stories: Power, change and social worlds*. London, UK: Routledge.

Plummer, K. (1996). Intimate citizenship and the culture of sexual story telling. In J. Weeks (Ed.), *Sexual cultures* (pp. 34–52). Basingstoke, UK: Palgrave Macmillan.

Plummer, K. (2001). The square of intimate citizenship: Some preliminary proposals. *Citizenship Studies, 5*(3), 237–253.

Plummer, K. (2003). *Intimate citizenship: Private decisions and public dialogues*. Seattle, WA: University of Washington Press.

Plummer, K. (2015). *Cosmopolitan sexualities*. Cambridge, UK: Polity.

Plummer, K. (2019). *Narrative power*. Cambridge, UK: Polity.

Polkinghorne, D. E. (1988). *Narrative knowing and the human sciences*. Albany, NY: State University of New York Press.

Propp, V. I. (1969). *Morphology of the folk tale* (L. A. Wagner, Ed.). Austin, TX: University of Texas Press.

Puar, J. K. (2007). *Terrorist assemblages: Homonationalism in queer times*. Durham, NC: Duke University Press.

Putnam, R. D. (1995). Bowling alone: America's declining social capital. *Journal of Democracy, 6*(1), 65–78.

Putnam, R. D. (2000). *Bowling alone: The collapse and revival of American community*. New Nork, NY: Simon & Shuster.

Quinn, K., Dickson-Gomez, J., DiFranceisco, W., Kelly, J. A., St. Lawrence, J. S., Amirkhanian, Y. A., & Broaddus, M. (2015). Correlates of internalized homonegativity among black men who have sex with men. *AIDS Education and Prevention, 27*(3), 212–226. doi:10.1521/aeap.2015.27.3.212

Rahmen, M. (2014). *Homosexualities, Muslim cultures and modernity*. Basingstoke, UK: Palgrave Macmillan.

Rambukkana, N. (2015). *Fraught intimacies: Non/monogamy in the public sphere*. Vancouver, Canada: UBC Press.

Rawls, J. (1971). *A theory of justice*. Cambridge, MA: Harvard University Press.

Reay, B., Attwood, N., & Gooder, C. (2015). *Sex addiction: A critical history*. Cambridge, UK: Polity.

Rich, D. (2016). *The Left's Jewish problem: Jeremy Corbyn, Israel and anti-Semitism*. London, UK: Biteback Publishing.

Richardson, D. (1998). Sexuality and citizenship. *Sociology, 32*(1), 83–100.

Richardson, D. (2000a). Constructing sexual citizenship: Theorizing sexual rights. *Critical Social Policy, 20*(1), 105–135.

Richardson, D. (2000b). Claiming citizenship? Sexuality, citizenship and lesbian/feminist theory. *Sexualities, 3*(2), 255–272.

Richardson, D. (2000c). *Rethinking sexuality*. London, UK: Sage.

Richardson, D. (2004). Locating sexualities: From here to normality. *Sexualities, 7*(4), 391–411.

Richardson, D. (2017). Rethinking sexual citizenship. *Sociology, 51*(2), 208–224.

Richardson, D. (2018). Sexuality and citizenship. *Sexualities, 21*(8), 1256–1260.

194 REFERENCES

Richardson, E. H., & Turner, B. S. (2001). Sexual, intimate or reproductive citizenship? *Citizenship Studies, 5*(3), 329–338.

Ricoeur, P. (1970). *Freud and philosophy: an essay on interpretation* (D. Savage, Trans.). New Haven, CT: Yale University Press.

Ricoeur, P. (1977). *The rule of metaphor: Multi-disciplinary studies of the creation of meaning in language* (R. Czerny, K. McLaughlin, & J. Costello, Trans.). Toronto, Canada: University of Toronto Press.

Ricoeur, P. (1981). *Hermeneutics and the human sciences* (J. B. Thompson, Trans.). Paris, France: Edition de la Maison des Sciences de l'Homme/Cambridge, UK: Cambridge University Press.

Ricoeur, P. (1984). *Time and narrative* (Vol. 1; K. McLaughlin & D. Pellauer, Trans.). Chicago, IL: University of Chicago Press.

Ricoeur, P. (1991). The creativity of language: Interview with Richard Kearney. In M. J. Valdes (Ed.), *A Ricoeur reader: Reflection and imagination* (pp. 463–481). Toronto, Canada: University of Toronto Press. (Original work published 1984)

Ricoeur, P. (1985). *Time and narrative* (Vol. 2; K. McLaughlin & D. Pellauer, Trans.). Chicago, IL: University of Chicago Press.

Ricoeur, P. (1986). *Lectures on ideology and utopia* (G. H. Taylor, Ed.]. New York, NY: Columbia University Press.

Ricoeur, P. (1988). *Time and narrative* (Vol. 3; K. McLaughlin & D. Pellauer, Trans.). Chicago, IL: University of Chicago Press.

Ricoeur, P. (1992). *Oneself as another* (K. Blamey, Trans.). Chicago, IL: University of Chicago Press.

Ricoeur, P. (1996). Reflections on a new ethos for Europe (E. Brennan, Trans.). In R. Kearney (Ed.), *Paul Ricoeur: The hermeneutics of action* (pp. 3–13). London, UK: Sage.

Ricoeur, P. (1998). *Critique and conviction: Conversations with François Azouvi and Marc de Launay* (K. Blamey, Trans.). New York, NY: Columbia University Press.

Ricoeur, P. (2005). *The course of recognition* (D. Pellauer, Trans.). Cambridge, MA: Harvard University Press.

Ricoeur P. (2006). *On translation* (E. Brennan, Trans.). London, UK: Routledge.

Rieff, P. (1959). *Freud: The mind of the moralist.* Chicago, IL: University of Chicago Press.

Robinson, B. A. (2013). The queer potentiality of barebacking: Charging, whoring, and breeding as utopian practices. In A. Jones (Ed.), *A critical inquiry into queer utopias* (pp. 101–128). New York, NY: Palgrave Macmillan.

Roseneil, S. (Ed.). (2013). *Beyond citizenship? Feminism and the transformation of belonging.* Basingstoke, UK: Palgrave Macmillan.

Rubin, G. (1993). Thinking sex: Notes for a radical theory of the politics of sexuality. In C. Vance (Ed.), *Pleasure and danger* (pp. 143–178). London, UK: Routledge & Kegan Paul. (Original work published 1984)

Rudy, K. (2012). LGBTQ . . . Z? *Hypatia, 27*(3), 601–615.

Sabsay, L. (2012). The emergence of the other sexual citizen: Orientalism and the modernisation of sexuality. *Citizenship Studies, 16*(5–6), 605–623. doi:10.1080/13621025.2012.698484

Sabsay, L. (2016). *The political imaginary of sexual freedom: Subjectivity and power in the new sexual democratic turn.* London, UK: Palgrave Macmillan.

Said, E. W. (1979). *Orientalism.* New York, NY: Vintage Books.

Said, E. W. (1993). *Culture and imperialism.* New York, NY: Vintage Books.

Saleh, L. D., & Operario, D. (2009). Moving beyond 'the Down Low': A critical analysis of terminology guiding HIV prevention efforts for African American men who have secretive sex with men. *Social Science & Medicine, 68*, 390–395.

Sarbin, T. (Ed.). (1986). *Narrative psychology: The storied nature of human conduct.* New York, NY: Praeger.

Savin-Williams, R. C. (2005). *The new gay teenager.* Cambridge, MA: Harvard University Press.

Savin-Williams, R. C. (2011). Identity development among sexual-minority youth. In S. J. Schwartz, K. Luyckx, & V. Vignoles (Eds.), *Handbook of identity theory and research* (pp. 671– 689). New York, NY: Springer.

Sax, L. (2002). How common is intersex? A reply to Anne Fausto-Sterling. *Journal of Sex Research, 39*(3), 174–178.

Scherrer, K. S. (2008). Coming to an asexual identity: Negotiating identity, negotiating desire. *Sexualities, 11*(5), 621–641. doi:10.1177/1363460708094269

Scoats, R., & Campbell, C. (2022). What do we know about consensual non-monogamy? *Current Opinion in Psychology, 48*, 101468. https://doi.org/10.1016/j.copsyc.2022.101468

Sedgwick, E. K. (1990). *Epistemology of the closet.* Berkeley, CA: University of California Press.

Seidman, S. (Ed.). (1996). *Queer theory/sociology.* Oxford, UK: Blackwell.

Seidman, S. (2002). *Beyond the closet: The transformation of gay and lesbian life.* New York, NY: Routledge.

Shafer, R. (1980). Narration in the psychoanalytic dialogue. *Critical Inquiry, 7*(1), 29–53.

Sheff, E. (2014). *The polyamorists next door: Inside multiple-partner relationships and families.* Lanham, MD: Rowman & Littlefield.

Sheff, E., & Hammers, C. (2011). The privilege of perversities: Race, class and education among polyamorists and kinksters. *Psychology & Sexuality, 2*(3), 198–223. doi:10.1080/19419899.2010.537674

Shils, E. (1981). *Tradition.* Chicago, IL: University of Chicago Press.

Signorile, M. (2016). *It's not over. Getting beyond tolerance, defeating homophobia, & winning true equality.* New York, NY: Mariner Books.

Simon, A. (1998). The relationship between stereotypes of and attitudes toward lesbians and gays. In G. M. Herek (Ed.), *Psychological perspectives on lesbian and gay issues: Stigma & sexual orientation: Understanding prejudice against lesbians, gay men, and bisexuals* (Vol. 4, pp. 62–81). Thousand Oaks, CA: Sage.

Simula, B. L. (2019). Pleasure, power, and pain: A review of the literature on the experiences of BDSM participants. *Sociology Compass, 13*(3), e12668.

Siraj, A. (2012). 'I don't want to taint the name of Islam': The influence of religion on the lives of Muslim lesbians. *Journal of Lesbian Studies, 16*(4), 449–467. doi:10.1080/10894160.2012.681268

Sky News (2016). https://news.sky.com/story/more-than-50-sexual-risk-orders-imposed-on-men-by-police-forces-10588142.

Soh, D. (2020). *The end of gender: Debunking the myths about sex and identity in our society.* New York, NY: Threshold Editions.

Sorrentino, R., & Abramowitz, J. (2021). Minor-attracted persons: A neglected population. *Current Psychiatry, 20*(7), 21–27. doi:10.12788/cp.0149

Spade, D. (2015). *Normal life: Administrative violence, critical trans politics and the limits of law.* Durham, NC: Duke University Press.

196 REFERENCES

Spivak, G. C. (1984/1985). Criticism, feminism and the institution. *Thesis Eleven*, 10(11), 175–189.

Spivak, G. C. (1999). *A critique of postcolonial reason: Toward a history of the vanishing present*. Cambridge, MA: Harvard University Press.

Stanley, T. (2021). *Whatever happened to tradition? History, belonging and the future of the West*. London, UK: Bloomsbury Continuum.

Stevenson, M. R. (2000). Public policy, homosexuality, and the sexual coercion of children. *Journal of Psychology & Human Sexuality*, 12, 1–19.

Stiver, D. R. (2019). Renewing the 'period of effervescence': Utopia as ideology critique. In S. A. Arel & D. R. Stiver (Eds.), *Ideology and utopia in the twenty-first century: The surplus of meaning in Ricoeur's dialectical concept* (pp. 53–72). Lanham, MD: Lexington Books.

Stock, K. (2021). *Material girls: Why reality matters for feminism*. London, UK: Fleet.

Stonewall. (2022). List of LGBTQ+ terms. Retrieved 19 August 2022, from https://www.stonewall.org.uk/help-advice/faqs-and-glossary/list-lgbtq-terms

Stychin, C. F. (2001). Sexual citizenship in the European Union. *Citizenship Studies*, 5(3), 285–301.

Suissa, J., & Sullivan, A. (2021). The gender wars, academic freedom and education. *Journal of Philosophy of Education*, 55(1), 55–82.

Sullivan, A. (2020). Sex and the census: Why surveys should not conflate sex and gender identity. *International Journal of Social Research Methodology*, 23(5), 517–524. doi:10.1080/13645579.2020.1768346

Sullivan, A. (2021). Sex and the Office for National Statistics: A case study in policy capture. *Political Quarterly*, 92(4), 638–651.

Sundén, J. (2023). Digital kink obscurity: A sexual politics beyond visibility and comprehension. *Sexualities*, Advance online publication. https://doi.org/10.1177/1363460722 1124401.

Swift, D. (2022). *The identity myth: Why we need to embrace our differences to beat inequality*. London, UK: Constable.

Taguieff, P.-A. (2001). *The force of prejudice: On racism and its doubles* (H. Melehy, Trans.). Minneapolis, MN: University of Minnesota Press.

Taguieff, P.-A. (2020a). Hucksters of the 'Postcolonial Business' in search of academic respectability: Reflections on contemporary pseudo anti-racism in France. *Telos Paul Piccone Institute Occasional Papers*, no. 2. Retrieved from http://journal.telospress.com/content/2020/193/13.short

Taguieff, P.-A. (2020b). Behind the globalized 'New Anti-Racism': A trivialized anti-white racism. *Telos Paul Piccone Institute Occasional Papers*, no. 3. Retrieved from http://journal.telospress.com/content/2020/193/36.extract

Taylor, G. H. (1986). Editor's introduction. In P. Ricoeur (Ed.), *Lectures on ideology and utopia* (pp. ix–xxxvi). New York, NY: Columbia University Press.

Tewksbury, R. (2003). Bareback sex and the quest for HIV: Assessing the relationship in internet personal advertisements of men who have sex with men. *Deviant Behavior*, 24(5), 467–482.

Tierney, D. W., & McCabe, M. P. (2001). The assessment of denial, cognitive distortions, and victim empathy among pedophilic sex offenders: An evaluation of the utility of self-report measures. *Trauma, Violence, & Abuse*, 2(3), 259–270.

REFERENCES 197

Thaler, M. (2010). The illusion of purity: Chantal Mouffe's realist critique of cosmopolitanism. *Philosophy and Social Criticism, 36*(7), 785–800. https://doi.org/10.1177/01914 53710372064

Thomas, W. I., & Znaniecki, F. (1927). *The Polish peasant in Europe and America.* New York, NY: Alfred A. Knopf. (Originally 5 volumes, 1918–1920)

Treichler, P. A. (1987). AIDS, homophobia, and biomedical discourse: An epidemic of signification. *Cultural Studies, 1*(3), 263–305. doi: 10.1080/09502388700490221

Tweedy, A. E. (2011). Polyamory as sexual orientation. *University of Cincinnati Law Review, 79*(4), 1461–1515.

Ungar-Sargon, B. (2021). *Bad news: How woke media is undermining democracy.* New York, NY: Encounter Books.

Vaerwaeter, B. (pseudonym). (2022). The pedophile as a human being: An autoethnography for the recognition of a marginalized sexual orientation. *Journal of Controversial Ideas, 2*(1), 3. doi:10.35995/jci02010003

van Anders, S. M. (2015). Beyond sexual orientation: Integrating gender/sex and diverse sexualities via sexual configurations theory. *Archives of Sexual Behavior, 44*, 1177–1213. doi:10.1007/s10508-015-0490-8

Van der Vliet, V. (1996). *The politics of AIDS.* London: Bowerdean.

Venugopal, R. (2015). Neoliberalism as concept. *Economy and Society, 44*(2), 165–187. doi:10.1080/03085147.2015.1013356

Vogel, U. (1988). Under permanent guardianship: Women's condition under modern civil law. In K. B. Jones & A. G. Jónasdóttir (Eds.), *The political interests of gender* (pp. 135–160). London, UK: Sage.

Vogel, U. (1994). Marriage and the boundaries of citizenship. In B. van Steenbergen (Ed.), *The condition of citizenship* (pp. 76–89). London, UK: Sage.

Walby, S. (1994). Is citizenship gendered? *Sociology, 28*(2), 379–395.

Walker, A. (2021). *A long dark shadow: Minor attracted people and their pursuit of dignity.* Oakland, CA: University of California Press.

Walters, S. D. (2014). *The tolerance trap: How God, genes, and good intentions are sabotaging gay equality.* New York, NY: New York University Press.

Warner, M. (Ed.). (1993). *Fear of a queer planet: Queer politics and social theory.* Minneapolis, MA: University of Minnesota Press.

Warner, M. (2000). *The trouble with normal: Sex, politics, and the ethics of queer life.* Cambridge, MA: Harvard University Press.

Watt, L., & Elliot, M. (2019). Homonegativity in Britain: Changing attitudes towards same-sex relationships. *Journal of Sex Research, 56*(9), 1101–1114. https://doi.org/ 10.1080/00224499.2019.1623160

Weber, M. (1986). *Economy and society* (G. Roth & C. Wittich, Eds.). Berkeley: University of California Press.

Weeks, J. (1995). *Invented moralities: Sexual values in an age of uncertainty.* Cambridge, UK: Polity Press.

Weeks, J. (1977). *Coming out: Homosexual politics in Britain from the nineteenth century to the present day.* London: Quartet.

Weeks, J. (1998). The sexual citizen. *Theory, Culture & Society, 15*(3–4), 35–52.

Weeks, J. (2007). *The world we have won.* Abingdon, Oxon, UK: Routledge.

Weiss, M. (2006). Mainstreaming kink: The politics of BDSM representation in US popular media. *Journal of Homosexuality, 50*(2–3), 103–132.

198 REFERENCES

Weiss, M. (2011). *Techniques of pleasure: BDSM and the circuits of sexuality*. Durham, NC: Duke University Press.

Wetherell, M. (2010). The field of identity studies. In M. Wetherell & C. Talpade (Eds.), *The Sage handbook of identities* (pp. 3–26). London, UK: Sage.

White, H. (1973). *Metahistory*. Baltimore, MD: Johns Hopkins University Press.

White, M. (2008). Can an act of citizenship be creative? In E. F. Isin & G. M. Nielsen (Eds.), *Acts of citizenship* (pp. 44–56). London, UK: Zed Books.

Wilkinson, E. (2009). Perverting visual pleasure: Representing sadomasochism. *Sexualities*, *12*(2), 181–198.

Wilkinson, E. (2010). What's queer about non-monogamy now? In M. Barker & D. Langdridge (Eds.), *Understanding non-monogamies* (pp. 243–254). New York, NY: Routledge.

Wilkinson, E. (2012). The romantic imaginary: Compulsory coupledom and single existence. In S. Hines & Y. Taylor (Eds.), *Sexualities: past reflections, future directions* (Genders and Sexualities in the Social Sciences; pp. 130–145). Basingstoke, UK: Palgrave Macmillan.

Willey, A. (2016). *Undoing monogamy: The politics of science and the possibilities of biology*. Durham, NC: Duke University Press.

Wilson, G. D., & Cox, D. N. (1983). *The child-lovers: A study of paedophiles in society*. London, UK: Peter Owen.

Wilton, T. (1997). *Engendering AIDS: Deconstructing sex, text and epidemic*. London, UK: Sage.

Wright, C. (2021). Sex is not a spectrum. *Reality's Last Stand*. Retrieved from https://www.realityslaststand.com/p/sex-is-not-a-spectrum

Wright, C. (2023). Debunking pseudoscience: 'Multimodal models of animal sex'. *Reality's Last Stand*. Retrieved from https://www.realityslaststand.com/p/debunking-pseudoscience-multimodal

Wright, R. C., & Schneider, S. L. (1999). Motivated self-deception in child molesters. *Journal of Child Sexual Abuse*, *8*(1), 89–111. doi:10.1300/J070v08n01_06

Yeatman, A. (1993). Voice and representation in the politics of difference. In S. Gunew & A. Yeatman (Eds.), *Feminism and the politics of difference*. Australia: Allen and Unwin.

Yoshino, K. (2007). *Covering: The hidden assault on our civil rights*. New York, NY: Random House.

Young, I. M. (1989). Polity and group difference: A critique of the ideal of universal citizenship. *Ethics*, *99*, 250–274.

Young, I. M. (1990). The ideal of community and the politics of difference. In L. J. Nicholson (Ed.), *Feminism/postmodernism* (pp. 300–323). New York, NY: Routledge.

Young, I. M. (2000). *Inclusion and democracy*. Oxford, UK: Oxford University Press.

Yuval-Davies, N. (1997). *Gender and nation*. London, UK: Sage.

Yuval-Davies, N., & Werbner, P. (1999). *Women, citizenship and difference*. London, UK: Zed Books.

Index

For the benefit of digital users, indexed terms that span two pages (e.g., 52–53) may, on occasion, appear on only one of those pages.

acts of citizenship, 34–37, 38, 39
Adichie, Chimamanda Ngozi, 14–15
Ahmad, Aijaz, 18–19
American Psychiatric Association (APA), 112
Andersson, Karl, 150–51
antiracism, 20
anti-Semitism, 89–90
anxiety, 3, 42, 100
articulating-vocalizing-announcing in storytelling, 72–73

barebacking, 133, 138–46
BDSM community
  medicalization and pathology, 112–14
  narrative therapy within, 12, 28, 109–20, 160–61
  sexual citizenship and, 128–30
benign sexual variation, 6–7
Beyond the Down Low: Sex, Lies, and Denial in Black America (Boykin), 138
binary logic of citizenship, 51–52
bisexuality. *See also* LGBTQ people
  emancipatory legislative change, 51–52
  HIV transmission and, 12, 134–37
  identity and, 36, 40, 73, 74–75
  queer theory and, 76
  racism and, 134
  rights-based claims of, 48, 49
  tensions among movements, 52–53
  trans politics and, 92–93
Black/African American community, 132–33, 134–38
Black women's experiences, 14–16, 116–17, 135, 136–37, 138
British Psychological Society, 139–40

bug chasing, 143–44, 145
Bruner, Jerome, 27–28, 59, 68–69, 70–71, 74–75
Butler, Judith, 5–6, 77, 85–86

cancel culture, 19, 84–86, 93, 94–95, 101–2, 107–8, 159–60
canonical narratives, 68–69, 88–89, 109–11, 115–16, 119, 160–61
Carr, David, 66
Chibber, Vivek, 18–19
Chicago School of Sociology, 66
child sexual abusers. *See* minor-attracted persons
citizenship
  acts of, 34–37, 38, 39
  alternative model of, 55
  binary logic of, 51–52
  feminist citizenship, 42–48
  identity and, 40–42
  ingenious citizenship, 37–39
  intimate citizenship and, 47–48, 49, 73–74
  liberal citizenship, 57
  theories of, 31–39
Citizenship and Social Class (Marshall), 31
civic republicanism, 31–33, 43–44
clash of rights
  diversity education, 28, 83–84, 86–92, 159–60
  gender wars, 92–104, 106–7
  introduction to, 83–86
  religious intolerance, 86–92
  sex *vs.* gender identity, 95–101
communitarianism, 30–33, 45–46
compulsory romantic love, 127
concept creep, 17–18

INDEX

consensual, sex, 25, 115–16, 121–22, 125, 133–34, 146–47, 149–50, 152–53, 161, 166, 168
contemporary sexuality
  acceptability and permissibility of, 5–10, 86–87, 91, 167, 171
  introduction to, 4–5, 6–7, 8, 9, 22–23, 26
  polyamory community and, 125–26
  positive approach to, 38–39
  problems with, 146–47, 159, 161–63, 165, 167–68
  understanding nature of, 58
cosmic time, 60–61
cosmopolitanism, 53, 57
cotton ceiling, 99
creating a culture of public problems in storytelling, 72, 73
Crenshaw, Kimberlé, 14
critical citizenship theory, 10–11
critical theory, 12–13, 18, 21, 39, 50, 60, 64, 78, 100, 137–38, 146, 150
Crossley, Michelle, 139–43
culture wars, 4–5, 57, 103, 157–58, 163, 166–68

Dean, Tim, 133, 143–46
decolonization, 16–20
discrimination, 14, 32–33, 84–85, 87–88, 99, 112–13, 117, 125
diversity
  gender diversity, 10, 16, 65–66, 83–88, 89–90, 91, 99–100, 105–6, 113–14
  neoliberalism impact on, 10
  polyamory, lack of, 125–26, 127–28
  sexual diversity, 30, 53, 77–78, 88–90, 105
diversity education, 28, 83–84, 86–92, 159–60
domino theory of sexual peril, 6–7
down low, 132–33, 134–38
Downing, Lisa, 13–16, 22
Dubrowski, Jodi, 3–4

either/or politics, 166–68
emancipation, 9, 73–74, 130
Equality and Human Rights Commission (EHRC), 101–3

eroticism, 3, 6–7, 50–51
essentialism, 5–7, 44–46
Evans, David, 26–27

fascism, 93–94
feminism
  gender critical feminists, 28, 84–85, 94–95, 98, 103, 106–7, 161–62
  intersectional, 13–17, 19
  neoliberalism and, 22
  third-wave, 15–16
feminist citizenship, 42–48
fetishism, 6–7
Foucault, Michel, 5–6, 71–72, 141–42

Gay Liberation Front, 9
gay persons
  African Americans, 136–37
  barebacking, 133, 138–46
  child sexual abuse trope and, 149–50, 151–52
  defined by Stonewall, 98–99
  emancipatory legislative changes, 51–52
  equality, 12
  heterosexuality and, 55
  homonormativity and, 9, 109
  identity and, 26–27, 34, 36, 40, 41–42, 73, 74–75, 125
  postgay culture, 3
  queer theory and, 76
  rights-based claims, 48
  sexual citizenship and, 46–47, 49, 161
  tensions among movements, 52–53
  trans politics and, 92–93
  whiteness and, 90–91, 136, 170–71
gay rights movement, 150–51
Geertz, Clifford, 178
gender-based, 106–7
gender-blind, 46–47
gender critical feminists, 28, 84–85, 94–95, 98, 103, 106–7, 161–62
gender identity, 90–91, 95–101, 103
gender politics, 9, 36–37, 159–60
Gender Recognition Reform Bill, 103
gender wars, 92–104, 106–7
Girard, Rene, 110–11
Global Alliance of National Human Rights Institutions, 103

Grosz, Elizabeth, 51–52

Harris, Lynn, 138
heteronormativity, 49, 55, 120–21
heterosexuality
    barebacking and, 140–41
    in bifurcated terms, 90–91
    down low culture and, 134–37
    homosexual–heterosexual binary, 76
    identity of, 34
    normative, 6–7
    patriarchal principles, 48–49
    polyamory and, 128–29
    sexual citizenship and, 55
    trans persons and, 84–85, 86–87
hierarchy of sex, 6–7, 8
historical time, 60–62
The History of Sexuality (Foucault), 5–6
HIV transmission
    barebacking, 138–46
    bisexuality and, 134–37
    bug chasing, 143–44, 145
    down low, 132–33, 134–38
    down low culture and, 132–33
    unprotected anal intercourse, 140–41, 143
homonationalism, 106, 170
homonormativity, 9, 109
homophobia, 3–4, 86–87, 99, 103–4, 136,
    137, 153
homosexual–heterosexual binary, 76
human time, 60–61, 62
Hunt, Lynn, 15–16

idem-identity, 63–65
identity
    bisexuality and, 36, 40, 73, 74–75
    citizenship and, 40–42
    gender identity, 90–91, 95–101, 103
    of heterosexuality, 34
    idem-identity, 63–65
    inventing identities-becoming
        storytellers, 72, 73
    ipse-identity, 63, 64–65
    narrative basis of sexual life and, 62–66
    in new sexualities, 130
    polyamory as, 125
    sexual identity, 74–75, 77–78, 87–88,
        90–91, 99, 136, 160–61

within social imaginary, 10–11
identity politics, 15–16, 22–23, 26–27,
    45–46, 51–53, 77, 99–100, 146–47,
    157–58, 164–65, 166–67
ideological formations in sexual thought,
    6–7, 69–71
imagining-visualizing-empathizing in
    storytelling, 72–73
inclusion, 24–25, 40, 47, 73–74, 87, 88–89
ingenious citizenship, 37–39
intersectional feminism, 13–17, 19
intersectional politics, 15, 22–23
intimate citizenship, 47–48, 49, 73–74
inventing identities-becoming
    storytellers, 72, 73
ipse-identity, 63, 64–65
Isin, Engin, 11, 26, 34–35
Islamophobia, 83–84, 89–90, 159–60

Lectures on Ideology and Utopia (Ricoeur),
    70, 175, 178–79
Lee, Charles, 26, 37–38
Lesbian and Gay Psychology Section of the
    British Psychological Society, 139–40
lesbians
    defined by Stonewall, 98–99
    emancipatory legislative changes, 51–52
    heterosexuality and, 55
    identity and, 36, 40, 41–42, 73, 74–
        75, 125
    queer theory and, 76
    rights-based claims, 48
    sexual citizenship and, 49, 161
    tensions among movements, 52–53
    trans politics and, 92–93
LGBTQ people. *See also* bisexuality; gay
        persons; trans persons
    homonationalism and, 106, 170
    homonormativity and, 9, 109
    homophobia against, 3–4, 86–87, 99,
        103–4, 136, 137, 153
    Muslims, 86–92
    negativity against, 8–9
    same-sex activity, 4, 8–9, 68–69, 72–73,
        74–75, 87–88, 90–91, 98–99, 122,
        134, 136, 170
liberal citizenship, 57
liberalism, 30–33, 43–44, 56

202 INDEX

life politics, 73–74
linguistic hospitality, 171–73
Lister, Ruth, 26
A Long Dark Shadow: Minor Attracted People and Their Pursuit of Dignity (Walker), 147–50

Mannheim's paradox, 176–77
marginalization, 15, 30, 31, 41–42, 46–47, 56, 105–6, 117–18, 127–28, 142–43
Marshall, T. H., 31
Marxism, 9, 18–19, 20–21, 175–76
masturbation, 150–52
Metahistory (White), 66
metaphor, 27, 59–61, 67–69
metaphysics, 67, 128–29
mimetic desire, 110–11, 128–29
minor-attracted persons (MAPs), 25, 28, 133–34, 146–54, 161
momentum concept, 8, 26, 30–31, 40–41
monogamy, 6–7, 109–10, 120–28, 160–61
moral self, 65–66, 161–62
multiple-partner relationships. *See* polyamory
Muslim LGBTQ people, 86–92

narrative basis of sexual life
    canonical narratives, 68–69, 88–89, 109–11, 115–16, 119, 160–61
    identity and, 62–66
    introduction to, 58–59
    metaphor, 27, 59–61, 67–69
    queer theory and, 76–79
    Ricoeur, Paul and, 60–62, 66
    sexual stories, 71–76
    social imaginary, 69–71
    in social sciences, 66–71
neoliberalism
    capitalism and, 10
    competition model and, 15
    critique of, 13–14, 21–22, 38–39, 122–23
    dangers of, 99–100
    feminism and, 22
    humanism and, 58
    overview of, 21–23
    polyamory and, 120–21
    sexual citizenship and, 55

nonconsensual, sex, 25, 146–47, 149–50, 152, 161
nonmonogamy, 120–25, 126–28. *See also* polyamory
No Outsiders program, 87, 88–89
Nussbaum, Martha, 53

Oneself as Another (Ricoeur), 163–64
otherness, 171–73

Paedophile Information Exchange (UK), 150
paedophiles. *See* minor-attracted persons
particularism, 31–32
patriarchal principles, 44–45, 48–50, 98
performative radicalism, 4–5, 12, 109, 159
persons of color (POCs), 16–20
Phelan, Shane, 11
phenomenological time, 60–61
Plummer, Ken, 27–28, 49, 53–54, 71–74
politics of recognition, 37–38, 125, 163–66
polyamory
    contemporary sexuality and, 125–26
    denial of sexual desire, 121–28
    lack of diversity in, 125–26, 127–28
    as love, 120–28
    performative radicalism and, 4–5, 12, 109, 159
    sexual citizenship and, 128–30
postcolonial theory
    decolonization and, 16–20
    normativity of, 13–14
    overview of, 16–21
pre-exposure prophylaxis (PreP), 133, 138–39
presentism, 15–16
pro-dommes, 115–16
progressive change, 4–5, 106–8, 123, 166
progressive sexual citizenship, 4–5, 12, 133–34, 146–47, 149–50, 159
progressive sexuality, 4–5, 12, 25, 133–34, 146–47, 149–50, 159, 170–71
Propp, Vladimir, 58–59

Qualitative Research journal, 150–51
Queer Nation, 56
queer theory
    foundation of, 5–6

intersectional feminism and, 13–14
overview of, 76–79
pathological gay male subject in, 143
sexual citizenship and, 50–53

race play, 116–17
racism
in bisexual bridge theory, 12, 135–36
bisexuality and, 134
cancel culture, 160–61
down low culture and, 28, 132–33, 137–38, 161
hypersexualization and, 153
impact of accusations, 159–60
Islamophobia, 83–84, 89–90, 159–60
minority sexualities and, 170
polyamory and, 127–28
postcolonial theory and, 16–21
race play and, 116–17
radical gender movements, 36–37, 56
rape play, 116–17
Rawls, John, 32
Reading Sexualities (Hall), 77–78
real politics, 28–29, 126–27, 163, 172
religious intolerance, 86–92
reproductive futurism, 56
reproductive sexuality, 6–7
Ricoeur, Paul
on Geertz, 178
hermeneutic philosophy of, 36–37
human action, 163–66
idem-identity, 63–65
ideology and utopia, 79, 175–76
introduction to, 10–11, 27, 28–29
ipse-identity, 63, 64–65
Mannheim's paradox, 176–77
narrative basis of sexual life, 60–62, 66
politics of recognition, 37–38, 163–66
sexual citizenship and, 36–37, 39, 42–48
translation and, 171–73
utopian critique and, 168–70
on Weber, 177–78
rights. *See* clash of rights
root metaphor, 67
Rowling, J. K., 14–15
Rubin, Gayle, 3–4, 6–7

sadomasochism, 6–7, 34, 51–52, 111–12

same-sex activity, 4, 8–9, 68–69, 72–73, 74–75, 87–88, 90–91, 98–99, 122, 134, 136, 170
Sedgwick, Eve Kosofsky, 5–6
self-constancy, 64–65
sex-based rights, 106–7
sex negativity, 6–7, 123–24
sex research field, 5–6
sexual abuse/abuser, 12, 133–34, 146–52, 153–54
sexual desire, 72–73, 74–76, 99, 109, 111–12, 117–18, 121–28
sexual diversity, 30, 53, 77–78, 88–90, 128
sexual identity, 74–75, 77–78, 87–88, 90–91, 99, 136, 160–61
sexual/intimate citizen, 48–50
sexualization of children, 65–66, 87–89, 91, 105–6, 159–60, 161–62
sexual minorities, 8, 9, 30, 101, 109, 145, 146–47, 149–50, 152–53. *See also* LGBTQ people
sexual movements, 25, 56
sexual orientation, 8, 98, 125, 149–50
sexual peril, 6–7
sexual politics, 5, 9, 28–29, 38–39, 77, 126, 157–58, 159–60, 162–63, 165, 167–69, 170–71
sexual preferences, 7–8, 113
sexual relations, 8–9, 25, 99, 115–16, 117, 122, 152
sexual stories, 71–76
sexual value/values, 3, 6–7
sexual violence, 25, 116, 149–50, 161
sex workers, 6–7, 115–16
Shafer, Roy, 66
social imaginary
identity within, 10–11
ideology and, 52–53, 54, 69, 128, 175, 178
ingenious citizenship, 38–39
Mannheim's paradox and, 179
motivational framework for, 178–79
narrative basis of sexual life, 69–71
of political discourse, 26–27
political role for, 70
of sexual citizenship, 54, 111–12
of stories, 27–28, 63, 71, 120, 129–30, 142–43, 154

204 INDEX

social justice, 11–12, 14–15, 30, 105–6
social psychology, 66, 67–68, 139–40
social sciences in narrative basis of sexual
life, 66–71
social scientific research, 5–6, 59, 142–
43, 145
social stress, 3, 173
spectacular critique
barebacking, 133, 138–46
dangers of, 161–62
defined, 132
down low, 132–33, 134–38
minor-attracted persons, 25, 28, 133–
34, 146–54, 161
state-centric models of citizenship,
11, 30, 47
Stonewall (advocacy organization), 84–85,
93, 97–98, 101–4
Stychin, Carl, 51–52

Taguieff, Pierre-André, 16, 20–21
A Theory of Justice (Rawls), 32
third-wave feminism, 15–16
tolerance trap, 105–6
totalitarianism, 13, 18, 22, 57, 93, 106–7
trans exclusionary radical feminist
(TERF), 93–94
translation and otherness, 171–73
trans persons. See also LGBTQ people
bisexuality and politics, 92–93

defined by Stonewall, 93–94
heterosexuality and, 84–85, 86–87
rights, 25, 85–86, 92–93, 94–95, 97–98,
101–2, 159–60
transphobia, 86–87, 92–93, 103–4, 105–
6, 159–60
transsexual, 6–7, 93–94
transvestism, 6–7, 93–94
treatment as prevention (TasP), 138–39

universalism, 31–32, 44–45, 46, 62–63,
124, 165
universal values, 22–23
Unlimited Intimacy (Dean), 143
unprotected anal intercourse (UAI), 140–
41, 143
utopian critique, 12–13, 53–57, 79, 106–7,
128, 168–71

victory blindness, 9

Walker, Allyn, 147–50
Weber, Max, 177–78
Weeks, Jeffrey, 48–49, 50–51, 52–
53, 55–56
White, Hayden, 66
Whiteness, 20–21, 23–24, 25, 44–45, 90–
91, 116–17, 125–26, 136, 170–71

Young, Iris Marion, 45–46